FREEDOM'S ORPHANS

RAISING YOUTH IN A CHANGING WORLD

JULIA MARGO AND MIKE DIXON
WITH NICK PEARCE AND HOWARD REED

ippr

Our trustees

CONTENTS

Acknowledgements

Freedom's Orphans could not have been written without assistance from many people and organisations. ippr would particularly like to thank Lord Gavron and the Calouste Gulbenkian Foundation for their generous financial support.

We would also like to thank the external experts who have commented on drafts of the different chapters and/or provided original analysis for our work. Thanks particularly for the time generously given by Jo Blanden, John Bynner and Kathryn Duckworth at the Institute for Education; James Heckman at the University of Chigaco; Rob Wilson at the Institute for Employment Research; and Jonathan Bradshaw at the University of York.

We have benefited from conversations with many people outside ippr. Particular thanks are due to Leon Feinstein, Kate Gavron, David Voas, Michelle Jackson and Loek Halman.

And we are very grateful for the advice and guidance supplied by our colleagues at ippr. Particular thanks are due to Richard Darlington, Georgina Kyriacou and Matt Jackson in our external affairs department. Thanks are also due to Jennifer Simms, Benjamin Leibowitz, Natalie Raaber, Holly Andrew and Daniel Golding, who provided research support. However, the views expressed in this report are solely those of the authors.

This report incorporates original data analysis using the British Crime Survey, the British Cohort Study, the British Social Attitudes Survey and the Family Expenditure Survey. All these data sets were kindly supplied by the UK Data Archive and are Crown Copyright. It also incorporates original analysis of the OECD PISA 2000 dataset. This can be freely downloaded from the OECD.

We are grateful to the UK Data Archive for the provision of the British Cohort Study data.

About the authors

Mike Dixon, *former Research Fellow, ippr.* Mike worked at ippr until September 2006, and was involved in research into socio-economic trends, youth transitions, demography, labour markets, political economy and crime. His publications for ippr included *Population Politics* (2006), *CrimeShare: The unequal impact of crime* (2006) and several chapters in *Social Justice: Building a Fairer Britain* (2005). Before joining ippr Mike worked at Ogilvy and Mather, on communications strategy. He has also recently worked for the Department for Education and Skills on the independent Teaching and Learning in 2020 Review. In September 2006, Mike took up the post of Special Adviser to the Secretary of State at the Department for International Development. He graduated from St. John's College Cambridge with a first class BA in Philosophy.

Julia Margo, *Senior Research Fellow, ippr.* Before joining ippr Julia spent three years at the *Sunday Times* as the assistant editor of the News Review. Prior to this she worked as a researcher at the *New Statesman* and at Demos, and as a parliamentary assistant to Paddy Ashdown and Simon Hughes. Julia's research interests include demographic change and fertility, youth transitions, political ideologies, and the role of the media in democratic societies. Her publications for ippr include *Population Politics* (2006). Julia graduated from the University of Bristol in 2001 with a first class BSc in Politics.

Nick Pearce, *Director, ippr.* Nick has been Director of ippr since 2004. He has written on education, social justice, immigration and citizenship, the future of the welfare state, and South American politics. He was formerly a Special Adviser to David Blunkett at the Home Office (2001-2003), where he led work on migration, asylum and citizenship, and at the Department for Education and Employment (1999-2001), where he worked on further and higher education, skills policy, and asset based welfare, including the original ideas for the Child Trust Fund. Between 1997 and 1999 Nick worked on education policy at ippr and as an adviser in the Cabinet Office and Social Exclusion Unit. During this period he helped develop the initial plans for learndirect and worked on government policies for disadvantaged teenagers. Nick studied at Manchester University and Oxford University.

Howard Reed, *Research Director, ippr.* Howard has been Research Director of ippr since 2004. Prior to this he was Director of the Work and Income Research programme at the Institute for Fiscal Studies. Howard is an economist by training with a range of publications in leading journals including the *American Economic Review* and the *Economic Journal*. His research interests include the labour market, tax, benefit and tax credit policy, pensions, education and training policy, and disability and ill health. Howard was educated at Keble College, Oxford, and University College London.

Executive summary

The 'state of youth' has become an increasingly popular subject of debate in academic, policy and media circles. Commentators fear that British youth are on the verge of mental breakdown, at risk from antisocial behaviour, self-harm, drug and alcohol abuse. These concerns are, to an extent, borne out in ippr's findings and other research, presented in this report.

Teenage social immobility

Worryingly, a disproportionate number of those committing antisocial acts, becoming teenage parents and consuming drugs and alcohol hail from lower socio-economic groups. Social mobility appears to have stalled: today British young people's futures are more strongly determined by their backgrounds and upbringing than was the case for previous generations. Efforts to encourage young people to stay on in post-16 education seem only to benefit those who would already have been in some form of training or apprenticeship, and do not seem to affect outcomes for the most disadvantaged.

Until now analysis has largely failed to grasp how the experience of youth in Britain has changed and why this has fuelled public disquiet.

The emerging importance of personal and social skills

Social class remains the most powerful explanation of behaviour and outcomes. But young people make and remake their lives within social structures. ippr's research shows that as society has changed radically over the past 30 years, the current conception of what young people need in order to succeed in life (exercising their own 'agency') and the role of the state in supporting them is increasingly anachronistic.

From the post-war period to the mid-1970s, the pathways young people followed from compulsory education to work were relatively straightforward and homogenous. For most, leaving school was swiftly followed by getting a job. Relatively few continued on to higher education – just three per cent in 1950 – but for those that did, relatively stable employment soon followed. But by the end of the 1970s, youth labour markets were collapsing under the pressures of rapid deindustrialisation, it became increasingly difficult to move directly into work, and rising unemployment set school-leavers in direct competition with more experienced workers in the hunt for jobs. Young people were decreasingly able to rely on formal organisational structures, and more dependent on their own agency and motivation. And once they were in an increasingly service-orientated economy, their personal and social skills became ever more important in determining their success.

Parallel shifts were taking place in the public sector: the education system shrugged off its deterministic view of children's development and began to emphasise choice and personalised learning, and public services – under the banner of New Public Management – became more aligned to responding to 'customer' demands. Across the board, those with good personal and social skills – 'softer' skills – began to outdo their contemporaries.

ippr's research

Our research used two large surveys that followed young people born in 1958 and 1970, and shows that in just over a decade, personal and social skills became 33 times more important in determining relative life chances. At the same time, young people from less affluent backgrounds became less likely than their more fortunate peers to develop these skills. For those born in 1958, the connection between family background, personal and social skills, and success later in life was barely discernible. But for a significant proportion of those born in 1970, social immobility – the passing on of disadvantage through families – was clearly due to the connection between family background and personal and social skills.

Why the disadvantaged in particular have been negatively affected in this way is largely down to socio-economic trends of the past 30 years and their impact on the way young people are socialised in contemporary Britain.

The socialisation gap

Rising income over the past 30 years has created a set of richer parents that are increasingly able to purchase activities and access to institutions that can enhance children's personal and social development. Those in poorer groups are unable to provide similar benefits for their offspring, meaning these children will lose out in relative developmental terms. Better-off children are much more likely to attend constructive, organised or educational activities, which research shows are associated with greater personal and social development, while poorer children are more likely to spend time 'hanging out' with friends or watching TV – activities associated with poorer personal and social development.

Just as important is the growing immersion in consumerism: research now reveals that our teenagers are more immersed and are more brand-aware than those in the US, which has problematic implications for their personal and social development. Their access to advertising is unprecedented, with many children now owning their own televisions, computers and mobile phones.

Seven- to eleven-year-olds are now worth nearly £20 million a year as consumers and have become an increasingly lucrative target audience for unscrupulous advertisers eager to harness their 'pester power'. Children are also taking greater control over spending decisions, a trend that is encouraged by advertisers and corporations but viewed as unwelcome by many parents.

One persuasive strand of thinking explains the impact of childhood consumerism in terms of its impact on children's perceptions of their identity. The central idea is that children are becoming more dependent on brands to give them a sense of what aspirations, values and possessions are important and acceptable. Brands are beginning to dictate social hierarchies in a way formerly done by communities and parents.

Furthermore, the negative impact of growing childhood consumerism is disproportionately experienced by young people from disadvantaged backgrounds. Recent research shows that children from the poorest social groups are the most interested in consumer and materialist concerns.

Children's ever earlier engagement with consumerism is reflected across their lives, as adolescence extends increasingly further into childhood. Contemporary youth live accelerated lives, as physical, emotional and social milestones are passed at younger ages. For example, over the past 50 years, the average age of first sexual intercourse fell from 20 for men and 21 for women in the 1950s to 16 for both by the mid-1990s. Pundits point to the proliferation of sex tips for teenagers in youth magazines and health and beauty spas for young girls as evidence that children are exposed to, and expected to navigate, adult concerns at ever younger ages.

This unmediated interaction with consumerism is likely to play out in other areas too – especially in terms of interaction with peers – as the socialising capacity of many parents and communities has waned.

Changes to families

Research suggests that changes to families, such as more parents working, and rising rates of divorce and single parenthood, have undermined the ability of families to effectively socialise young people.

The research indicates that British children spend more time in the company of peers, and less time with adults and parents, than young people in culturally similar countries. Recent MORI polls have shown children's concerns to include parents not always being there when needed, and not making them feel loved and cared for. Changes to family structures are significant here.

Much recent US research reports a consistent overarching finding that children who grow up in an 'intact, two-parent family' with both biological parents do better on a wide range of outcomes than children who grow up in a single-parent family. While this research may be instinctively difficult for those on the Left to accept, the British evidence seems to support it.

For example, research shows that, compared to children from 'intact, two-parent families', those living with a single parent at age 16 were by age 30 more likely to, for example, smoke, be a single parent, be in social housing, receive benefits, and be in a workless household.

Evaluations have also suggested that certain relationship support interventions, particularly those involving couple therapy, have led to better school performance and sustained increased involvement by fathers. Further, recent research in the UK using the Millennium Cohort Study has shown that children of cohabiting couples do worse than those of married couples. In response, Cameron's Conservatives are investigating the potential of marriage promotion as part of their Social Justice Policy Review.

But there are problems with this response. For example, the rates of divorce, cohabitation and single-parenthood are trends that are unlikely to reverse. And focusing support on traditional family types, regardless of need, skews resources away from single-parent families, who tend to be most in need of financial support, and is unnecessarily morally prescriptive.

Research using the Millennium Cohort Study also found that marital status matters much less than many other factors in determining whether couples stay together. But ippr's key finding is that children growing up in non-traditional family forms can succeed if warmth, stability and consistent parenting are present. Therefore, rather than penalise single parenthood or cohabitation or attempt unrealistic policies, we should consider how best to support those parents – through the traditional routes of better childcare and more flexible working arrangements as well as increased investment in parenting education, relationship education and support.

Changes to communities

In 2005, low levels of collective efficacy – the ability and willingness of local residents to intervene in youth violence and antisocial behaviour – were strongly related to disadvantage, with people in the most affluent areas more likely to intervene than those in the most deprived areas if they saw children spray-painting graffiti, for example. If this pattern has held over the last few decades, children from more advantaged communities would have experienced greater levels of intervention from their neighbours and other adults than those from more disadvantaged communities. As the impact of communities became more important, this would have meant a growing divide between the socialisation experiences of the best and worst off.

The demographic make-up of communities is also significant. In 2005, people from minority ethnic groups were much less likely to intervene if a child was rude to an adult or if children were spray-painting graffiti, than those from a white background. This highlights the importance of engaging all communities in local issues, particularly given that younger generations in the UK are much more likely to be from an ethnic minority background than older cohorts.

Overall, the research shows that compared to adults in other countries, adults in Britain are less likely to intervene in youth violence and behaviour and more likely to blame young people for their behaviour.

Rethinking youth policy

Currently, young people who do not have access to the factors that develop their non-cognitive abilities (many of whom come from disadvantaged backgrounds), who have less engaged parents, a less orderly and secure local environment and spend more time with deviant peers or under the unmediated influence of the media, are increasingly vulnerable to failure, while their better socialised peers will increasingly succeed. In response, youth policy needs to be rethought, not simply through focusing education policy on non-cognitive development, but rather with a more fundamental shift in our thinking, as shown in the recommendations below.

Key recommendations

These recommendations complement existing ippr recommendations in the area of childcare provision, parental leave, relationship support and strategies to better engage fathers.

Preventing childhood consumerism through regulating media and marketing

- Commercial television and print media advertising designed to capture the attention of children of primary school age should be proscribed.
- Commercial advertising through mobile phone and 3G platforms to handsets registered to children of primary school age should be similarly proscribed. Parents should have the option of registering phone numbers to ensure this happens.
- Commercial advertising in primary schools and other educational institutions for the primary age group should be monitored by Ofsted.

Reducing teen pregnancy

- Teenagers should be offered a full choice of contraception, including long-lasting forms. Condoms should be widely available at low or no cost, to young people in places used by and accessible to them.
- Personal, Social and Health Education (PSHE) including sex and relationship education should become a statutory subject in all primary and secondary schools in England and Wales.
- Parents should be supported to develop skills to discuss sex and relationships with their children. Services for parents, including information on parenting and childcare and access to parenting groups, should

be provided through the Extended Schools parenting support core offer.
- Access to support and information for teenage mothers and teenagers who have had abortions should be improved, to tackle the number of teenagers experiencing second pregnancies.

Ensuring fair opportunities to participate in extra-curricular activities
- Youth clubs should be vetted to ensure they offer structure and activity within secure environments. Funding should be directed towards long-running activity programmes and regular attendance promoted.
- An element of compulsion should be introduced to young people's participation in structured, positive extra-curricular activities offered as part of the Extended Schools agenda, but within a framework that promotes choice. The proposed activities should be vetted to ensure the activities on offer will benefit the participants.
- Our preferred model would be for young people aged 11 to 14 to participate in a long-term extra-curricular activity, one day a week after school, choosing from options outlined in the *Youth Matters* Green Paper. This would be mandated through an extension of the school day, creating a legal requirement for parents to ensure participation.
- The current Children and Young People's Plans should ensure that every child has the genuine opportunity to participate in a choice of structured, positive activities. This should be done by identifying barriers to participation – such as issues to do with availability, timing and transport – and proposing solutions.

Promoting positive activities through the voluntary sector
- Funding streams should be conditional on activities such as sport, drama, cadets and some forms of vocational activity being structured, regular, and constructive with a clear end goal and clearly defined, hierarchical (though malleable) roles.
- Innovation and start-up funding streams should be made available to develop the facilities and provision of positive activities in areas in which they are not available. In order to achieve this, the Department for Communities and Local Government (DCLG) in partnership with the Department for Culture, Media and Sport (DCMS), Department for Education and Skills (DfES) and the National Council of Voluntary Organisations (NCVO) should map the provision of local services provided through the voluntary sector, to identify gaps in provision.

Extending asset-based welfare, particularly for children in care
- Looked after children, such as those in care, should have their own asset account. This is a complement to ippr's previous recommendation that local authorities should make annual deposits of £50 into the Child Trust Funds of all children in care.

- The account should consist of an initial lump-sum deposit of £200; monthly deposits of £20 plus interest; and a further lump sum of £500 at age 16 to assist with the transition to independent living.
- A proportion each year should be available to be spent on 'treats', with a 'gatekeeper' worker to countersign all withdrawals.
- Larger amounts should be available for expenditure around age 16, to ensure that the asset supports the transition to independent living. The remaining lump sum should be transferred to a young person's Child Trust Fund at age 18, at which point the full amount may be spent in full, without restriction.
- Larger monthly deposits should be used to support out-of-school-hours structured activities.
- Savings made by the young person into the account could be matched in order to further develop self-efficacy and a propensity to plan.

Improving teaching and learning

- Initial teacher training should be reformed to incorporate specialist teaching strands, to enable teachers to respond better to individual pupil needs.
- One of these strands should be pedagogic techniques that improve personal and social skills development and behaviour management, such as the use of group work and peer learning.
- Another specialist strand could build on conflict resolution work currently undertaken by voluntary sector organisations such as Leap. Its in-school programme provides training for staff and young people to develop a peer mediation/education approach to building young people's responsibility and capacity to take action on conflicts that they are involved in.
- Initial teacher training and ongoing professional development for teachers should be reformed to improve skills in a range of pedagogical techniques.
- The curriculum at Key Stage 3 should be made increasingly flexible to allow teachers to personalise learning.
- Ofsted's inspection criteria should be broadened to include criteria related to the teaching of personal and social skills.

Harnessing and shaping peer effects within schools

- Ofsted inspection criteria should be broadened to include assessment of the provision of constructive activities.
- House systems should be introduced or expanded in state schools to encourage students to work collectively towards achievable goals and to break up traditional peer groups and hierarchies within schools.

- DfES should provide an annual report for head teachers of best voluntary sector practice in each area.
- DfES should map the provision of local services provided through the voluntary sector, which would also enable policymakers to identify gaps in provision.
- A National Innovation Start-up Fund should be set up to support the development of charities that work to develop young people's personal and social skills as well as those that intervene in schools to set up conflict resolution schemes.
- DfES should offer to match funding for schools that have employed intervention schemes that have been evaluated to set criteria.

Supporting communities in developing collective efficacy

A further key challenge remains in supporting communities to develop collective efficacy. Research consistently shows that the role of the wider community and other adults in socialising young people remains vital. The main focus here should be on strategies to promote collective efficacy, rather than on merely increasing trust and social capital.

The recommendations outlined above draw on a wide evidence base. More can and should be done in each of these areas – we hope that others will build on our ideas in the light of our analysis.

Introduction

Tracing 150 years of 'moral panics', Geoffrey Pearson's book *Hooligan* (Pearson 1983) showed how each generation tends to believe that the violence and disorder of its time contrasts with more peaceful golden years, classically 20 years before. At the heart of what he calls these 'respectable fears' often lies a concern about the actions of young people: whether this is the teenage mother or the youthful hooligan of his title.

More than two decades after Pearson's classic was published, there is a growing belief in the UK that we are facing a crisis of youth. Recently, a panel of experts including politicians, authors, psychologists and youth policy specialists, penned a letter to the *Daily Telegraph* warning of the catastrophic state of modern childhood, pointing to children's increased exposure to electronic media, marketing and junk food, as well as the growing pressures of modern schooling (Greenfield *et al* 2006). The group claimed that both politicians and public fail to understand what young people need in order to develop into able adults and as a result they are expected to cope with a range of inappropriate pressures. This letter, which incited responses across the press and media, represents a growing obsession with the state of childhood and youth that typifies the attitudes of modern Britain.

Newspapers contain stories of youth antisocial behaviour and troubled teenagers on a daily basis. Chapter 1 shows that the number of articles in the national press about 'antisocial behaviour' increased more than sevenfold between 2000 and 2005 – during this period there was an average of 57 articles on this theme each day. British commentators and politicians simultaneously both fret and rejoice about A-level and GCSE exam results. And we now comfortably debate children's eating habits, exercise, clothing and sexual development alongside such topics as war, politics and death in the comment pages of broadsheets. Parenting pages, once relegated to the specialist press, have sprung up seemingly overnight in flagship sections of leading newspapers and magazines.

But what lies behind these escalating concerns? Are young people in the UK facing a genuine crisis? Or is this merely another bout of largely unfounded concerns regarding delinquency, rebellion and immorality?

This report argues that contemporary analysis has largely failed to grasp how the experience of youth in Britain has changed and why this has fuelled public disquiet. We examine the real developments underpinning public concerns, explaining why they matter and what government should do in response.

The best years?

In many ways there has never been a better time to be young. In chapter 2, we provide an audit of contemporary youth. It shows that more British teenagers leave school with good qualifications and go to university than ever before. Youth unemployment (for 18- to 24-year-olds) has fallen dramatically from its peak in the 1980s, although it has remained broadly static since 2000. Today's parents are richer than their forebears, have fewer children and have access to more advice on how to raise them. But this is not the full story.

There is accumulating evidence of increasing incidences of mental health and physical disorders among young people. According to surveys, one in ten teenage girls has self harmed. Child obesity is increasing. Antisocial behaviour and teenage pregnancy rates, though lower than in recent years, are high in comparison to other European countries. British adolescents drink more, and from an earlier age, than their European counterparts. They are also more immersed in consumerism than those in the United States – indicated by their brand awareness and the amount of importance they attach to consumer goods and possessions. They spend more time in the company of peers, and less time with adults and parents than most other young people around the world.

The spectre of social class also still casts a long shadow over childhood and adolescence. A disproportionate number of those committing antisocial acts, becoming parents in their teenage years and consuming drugs and alcohol, hail from lower socio-economic groups. Perhaps most worryingly, social mobility appears to have stalled: the life chances of young people in Britain are now more strongly determined by their backgrounds and upbringing than for previous generations. What accounts for this social immobility?

The incapable generation

The roots of social immobility lie undeniably in structural causes: social class remains the most powerful explanation of behaviour and outcomes. But young people are not passive recipients of social forces beyond their control. They make and remake their lives within these structures. Our research suggests that as our society has changed radically over the past 30 years – under the influence of a range of demographic, socio-economic and cultural developments that have affected all capitalist democracies – the current conception of what young people need in order to meaningfully exercise agency (their capacity to choose and realise decisions), and the role of the state in supporting them, is increasingly anachronistic. In addition, the way young people are socialised by society has fundamentally changed. As a result, many young people today are left simply incapable of succeeding in the current socio-economic climate.

Research reported in this study finds that as opportunities opened up for Britons reaching adolescence between 1960 and 2000, young people's agency became more important in determining their outcomes throughout life, in education, in work and in their communities. This is partly because socio-economic and cultural change meant that many aspects of the life course became increasingly preference-based from the 1950s onwards. These developments affected the disadvantaged in particular. Life course events that were once normatively structured by 'traditional' institutions (early marriage, established gender roles, religious beliefs and clear, if oppressive, career paths), were increasingly left to individuals to decide on their own, leaving them to take on new responsibilities for living with the consequences of their actions. For those with the capacity to take advantage of these changes, typically the affluent, expanding opportunities led to improved outcomes. But for those without, events left them further behind than ever.

This is an intuitive yet controversial narrative: formerly it was almost unanimously accepted that the key to success in adulthood was down to the acquisition of formal qualifications. Such 'hard' skills, signalled by qualifications, remain vitally important to life chances. But our research shows that in just over a decade, personal and social skills or 'capabilities' became 33 times more important in determining relative life chances. At the same time, young people from less affluent backgrounds became less likely than their more fortunate peers to develop these skills. For those born in 1958, the connection between family background, personal and social capabilities, and success later in life was barely discernible. But for those born just 12 years later in 1970, these links had become much more decisive. By then, 22 per cent of the social immobility – the passing on of disadvantage through families – was due to the connection between family background and personal and social capabilities. And there are compelling indications that the trajectory of trends that started in the 1950s has continued and that as a result agency has continued to become increasingly important in young people's success.

The importance of social and emotional intelligence to modern youth outcomes has not gone unnoticed by the Government, which is now piloting cognitive behavioural therapy techniques borrowed from the USA, aiming to help children to build up self-esteem and positive thinking, in British schools. But ippr's research suggests this will form only part of the solution to combating social immobility.

Personality attributes such as agency, self-esteem, locus of control (the degree to which events are perceived as being within their control) and motivation are, in part, inherited. But as we show in chapter 5, the environment in which young people find themselves also has a key role in socialising these attributes and capabilities.

Specifically, spending time in secure and nurturing environments, with parents or other adults, is vital to youth outcomes. And this is proven by evidence from the behavioural sciences that finds that the major environmental factor influencing serotonin secretion patterns in the brain (which partly determines the level of self-control an individual can exert) is social instability (Robinson 2004). Other research supports the importance of spending time with parents, showing that peer-raised monkeys have lower concentrations of serotonin than those raised by parents (Bennett *et al* 2002, Kreamer *et al* 1998). And the neurogeneticist Professor Liz Gould has shown, using marmoset monkeys, that poverty, disorder and instability can damage the brain by stunting the growth of neurons, as the brain diverts energy towards survival rather than creating new cells and connections (Lehrer 2006).

The above findings are supported by new evidence that we report in chapter 6 that spending time with peers in insecure, unstructured environments (online or offline) can negatively affect youth outcomes; that young people who claim not to spend time with their parents tend to exhibit more antisocial behaviour; that young people from stable, secure families have better social and emotional outcomes than those who experience trauma and change; and that young people living in orderly, secure communities have better personal skills than those living in disorder and poverty.

This is convincing evidence of the need to rethink our policy approach to youth. Currently, young people who do not have access to the factors that develop their personal and social capabilities, who often come from disadvantaged backgrounds, have less engaged parents, a less orderly and secure local environment and spend more time with more deviant peers or under the unmediated influence of the media, are increasingly vulnerable to failure, while their better socialised peers are more likely to succeed. The solution here is not simply to focus education policy on personal and social development but to engineer a more fundamental shift in our thinking.

Against a background of rising concerns about childhood and youth this report analyses thirty years of socio-economic, demographic and cultural change, presenting new data and evidence, in order to provide a better analysis of the problems facing today's society and youth and to engender a more pervasive and effective policy response.

References

Note: web references correct at September 2006

Bennett A, Lesch K, Heills A, Long J, Lorenz J, Shoaf S, Champoux M, Suomi S, Linnoila M and Higley J (2002) 'Early experience and serotonin transporter gene variation interact to influence primate CNS functioning' *Molecular Psychiatry* 7:118-122

Greenfield *et al* (2006) letter to the *Daily Telegraph*, 12 September

Kreamer G, Ebert M, Schmidt D, and McKinney W (1998) 'A longitudinal study of the effect of different social rearing conditions on cerebrospinal fluid norepinephrine and biogenic amine metabolites in rhesus monkeys' *Neuropsychopharmacology* 2:175-189

Lehrer J (2006) 'The Reinvention of the Self: A mind-altering idea reveals how life affects the brain', *Seed Magazine*, 23 February, available at: www.seedmagazine.com/news/2006/02/the_reinvention_of_the_self.php?page =all&p=y

Morgan P (2006) *Family Policy, Family Changes* London: Civitas

Murray C (1990) *The Emerging British Underclass Choice in Welfare Series No 2* London: IEA Health and Welfare Unit

Pearson (1983) *Hooligan: A History of Respectable Fears* London: Macmillan

Robinson (2004) *Why Crime? An Integrated Systems Theory of Antisocial Behaviour* Upper Saddle River, NJ: Prentice Hall

1. A crisis of the civic order?

There is a growing belief in Britain today that the civic order is in crisis. Last year, more than 26 million people in England and Wales thought crime had increased in the previous two years and more than 10 million of these thought it had risen 'a lot' (Nicholas *et al* 2005, GAD 2005). Similar trends can be seen in relation to levels of antisocial behaviour. In fact, looking back over the last two decades, it is clear that concerns about crime, law and order, violence and vandalism are increasingly prevalent: from 1982 to 1984, just over ten per cent of Britons saw these as the most important issues facing the country. Concerns peaked in the early '90s, as crime rates spiralled, and then fell. But as Figure 1.1 shows, concerns about civic order have been rising for decades and more than 30 per cent of Britons now see these issues as the most important facing the country.

As well as being worrying in themselves, these specific concerns are also indicators of a deeper malaise. Britons are increasingly likely to say the country is less caring than they were a decade previously and more prone to point to moral and spiritual decline. In 1999, 56 per cent of people

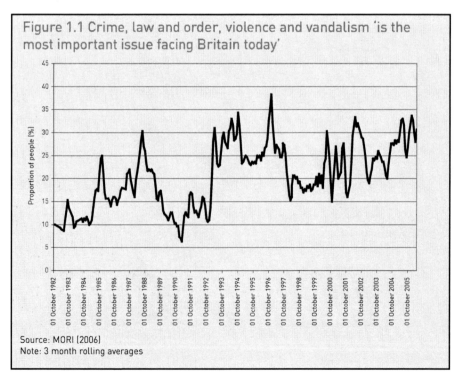

Figure 1.1 Crime, law and order, violence and vandalism 'is the most important issue facing Britain today'

Source: MORI (2006)
Note: 3 month rolling averages

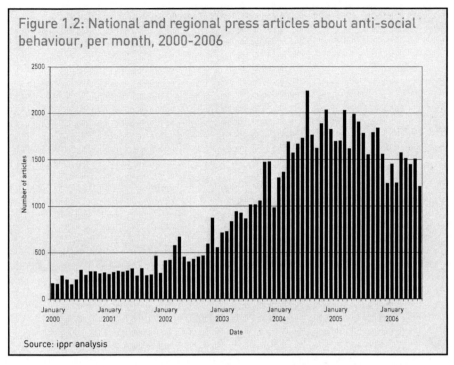

Figure 1.2: National and regional press articles about anti-social behaviour, per month, 2000-2006

Source: ippr analysis

thought there had been a decline in moral values – nearly five million more than two decades previously (MORI 1999, GAD 2005). And other research published in 2000 found that 87 per cent of Britons pointed to a decline in respect for authority as the most negative development in contemporary society (Haste 2000).

The public mood has been quick to feed through into academia, politics and the media, where there is growing interest in the state of civic order – prompting a plethora of theories and explanations about the underlying causes of civic decline. As Figure 1.2 shows, the number of articles in the national press specifically mentioning 'antisocial behaviour' increased by more than 700 per cent between 2000 and 2005, when there was an average of 57 articles on this theme each day.

Those on the right of the political spectrum have often blamed the events of the 1950s and 1960s, and the way these have played out in modern youth culture, as the root of current social ills. In popular literature and the media, this narrative has become a favoured lens through which to examine anything from crime rates to truancy (Bailey 2005), unemployment, teenage pregnancy (Morgan 2006), changes in our conduct (Truss 2005), spoken language and deference to authority (Humphrys 2004, Truss 2004). Even the Prime Minister has written lamenting the decline of respect and responsibilities, which he attributes to the long-term effects of social changes of the 1960s:

Britain, by 1997, had undergone rapid cultural and social change in recent decades ... Some social change had damaging and unforeseen consequences. Family ties were weakened. Communities were more fractured ... Civil institutions such as the church declined in importance. At the start of the 20th century, communities shared a strong moral code. By the end of the century this was no longer as true ...

(Blair 2005)

But is this narrative an accurate reflection of what has happened to British society over the past decades? In the rest of this chapter we take a rigorous, empirically grounded look at what has actually happened to civic order, to separate misconceptions from reality.

The state of civic order

Before the 1950s, recorded crime rates were low and relatively stable, as shown in Figure 1.3. But then recorded crime rates spiralled upwards for 40 years: in 1981 police-recorded crime figures were more than five-and-a-half

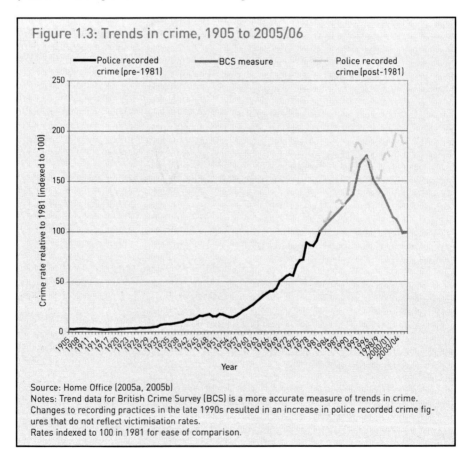

Figure 1.3: Trends in crime, 1905 to 2005/06

Source: Home Office (2005a, 2005b)
Notes: Trend data for British Crime Survey (BCS) is a more accurate measure of trends in crime.
Changes to recording practices in the late 1990s resulted in an increase in police recorded crime figures that do not reflect victimisation rates.
Rates indexed to 100 in 1981 for ease of comparison.

times cent higher than they had been in 1951, and by 1995 they had risen by a further 75 per cent.[1] Across the developed world, it seemed that the civic order was fragmenting and that crime would continue to rise inexorably.

Yet from the mid 1990s, crime rates began to fall across the world, initially in the US but soon spreading to the UK and other countries (Dixon *et al* 2006). According to the British Crime Survey – the most accurate measure of actual crime rates – by 2004/05, crime in Britain had fallen by 44 per cent from its peak and the risk of being a victim was 23 per cent – lower than at any time since 1981 (Walker *et al* 2006). This sits at odds with public perceptions, which, in placing the risk higher, now appear more than ten years out of date.

Media coverage, although an easy scapegoat, is undoubtedly partly responsible for this misperception of risk. Last year, tabloid readers were around twice as likely as broadsheet readers to think the national crime rate had increased 'a lot' in the previous two years. This is partly because reports often fail to discriminate adequately between two measures of crime. As Figure 1.3 shows, there has been a growing discrepancy between police-recorded crime figures, which show rising crime levels, and the British Crime Survey, which shows falling crime rates. Although the latter is widely regarded as more accurate by academics and policymakers alike, media coverage often presents rises in police-recorded figures as reflecting the true picture of crime; increases are in reality often merely due to improved police recording practice. Sixty-eight per cent of reported violent crime was recorded by the police in 2005, compared to just 36 per cent in 1999 (Walker *et al* 2006).[2] Although violent crime has remained stable between 2004/05 and 2005/06 according to the British Crime Survey, most newspapers reported the recent two per cent increases in recorded violent crime as significant. The *Observer*'s coverage was typical:

> John Reid's efforts to turn around the embattled Home Office will be dealt a major blow this week by figures revealing a surge in muggings and other robberies over the last year, suggesting police forces are struggling to control street crime.

(Doward *et al* 2006)

Yet looking at other indicators of civic order, such as people's assessment of community spirit in their neighbourhoods, suggests that people's day-to-day experiences are, increasingly, positive. ippr's analysis of the British Crime Survey data shows that between 1984 and 1996, community spirit

---

1. Although changes to policing and recording practices explain much of this rise, there is wide consensus that crime rates escalated dramatically over this period.
2. The last few years have seen considerable improvements in police recording of crime.

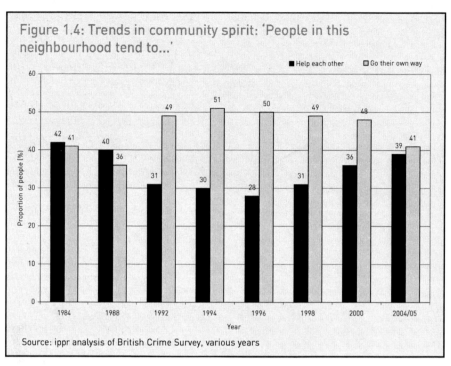

Figure 1.4: Trends in community spirit: 'People in this neighbourhood tend to...'

■ Help each other   □ Go their own way

Source: ippr analysis of British Crime Survey, various years

did appear to decline: Britons became much more likely to say that most people in their local area tend to 'go their own way' rather than 'help each other'. But after a nadir in the mid 1990s the trends reversed – at almost exactly the same time as crime rates started falling. In 1996 just 28 per cent of people thought that most other people in their area helped each other; by 2004/05 this had risen to 39 per cent, as shown by Figure 1.4.

Looking at broader measures of trust gives similar cause for caution in inferring civic decline. Although some surveys record substantial declines since the 1950s (Hall 1999), more recent measures show that people's trust in professions, ordinary people, and even politicians has remained broadly stable since at least the early 1980s, as shown in Figure 1.5. This would suggest that concerns about civic decline may be misplaced. But rather than simply dismiss public perceptions, we should consider whether these traditional measures of the state of civic order are failing to adequately capture peoples' concerns.

What underpins concerns about the civic order?

A wealth of research suggests that some crimes and disorders (such as serious domestic violence) may pass almost unnoticed by the general public, while other incidents are widely perceived to present a potential threat to the civic order. People tend to see various local disorders, such as persistent graffiti or young people hanging around in a particular place, as being actually more threatening to local safety than some more serious crimes like residential burglary (Dixon *et al* 2006).

What this and other research suggests is that disorders are distressing because they represent an apparent breakdown of previously accepted conventions of respect and responsibility to others in public places, a breakdown of acceptable local social order and of norms of personal responsibility.

The significance of this is fairly straightforward: property crime has been declining since the mid 1990s, but what indicators we have of trends in *incivilities* suggest that these began to decline only recently; violence and antisocial behaviour in public shows a similar pattern (Walker *et al* 2006). This provides some explanation for the public mood. But can our analysis go deeper?

At the heart of many of the analyses of civic decline is the growing belief that young people have changed. The growing reports of incidents of antisocial behaviour are almost always associated with youth antisocial behaviour. Concerns about local disorders and disrespect are also consistently associated with young people. Reports of rising truancy rates, drug use and youth violence resonate widely, while news of high numbers of young people not in education, employment or training (NEET) comes as little surprise to a public that seems increasingly to focus on young people's per-

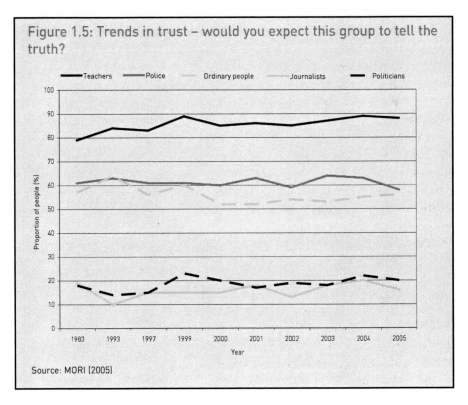

Figure 1.5: Trends in trust – would you expect this group to tell the truth?

Source: MORI (2005)

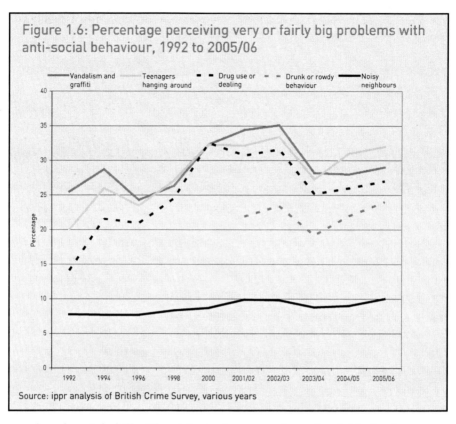

Figure 1.6: Percentage perceiving very or fairly big problems with anti-social behaviour, 1992 to 2005/06

Source: ippr analysis of British Crime Survey, various years

sonal and social skills. The debate about youth antisocial behaviour provides the most compelling evidence of this.

As Figure 1.6 shows, levels of perceived antisocial behaviour rose substantially between 1996 and 2002/03 – just as crime rates were falling. There was a 44 per cent rise in the proportion of people perceiving very or fairly big problems with vandalism and graffiti in their local area over this period and a 42 per cent rise in the complaints about 'teenagers hanging around', while the overall level of crime fell by 36 per cent (Nicholas *et al* 2005, Wood 2005). And there are worrying signs that perceptions of rates of antisocial behaviour are increasing once more: last year showed increases in all measures.

In 1992, Britons were 1.75 times more likely to cite young people hanging around as a problem than they were to complain about noisy neighbours, but last year they were more than three times more likely (Walker *et al* 2006). And there are signs that 'young people hanging around' has more of an impact on people's quality of life – and is a more common problem – than other measures of antisocial behaviour.

Our analysis of the British Crime Survey shows that more than seven million people in England and Wales felt this was a problem more or less all the time in their area in 2004/05 and more than two million felt this had a significant impact on their quality of life. And there is evidence that perceptions of antisocial behaviour as a growing problem are also encouraging a growing fear of youth.

Fear of young people

Our analysis of the British Crime Survey reveals that in 2004/05 more than 1.5 million Britons had thought about moving away from their local area due to young people hanging around and 1.7 million avoided going out after dark as a direct result. These figures add weight to the idea that public perceptions of moral decline and civic disorder are actually rooted in perceived changes to young people. There is also evidence that fear of young people has made members of the public less willing to intervene and monitor young people than in the past. Figure 1.7 examines the willingness of individuals to intervene in youth antisocial behaviour in the community.

Only in the case of harassment of an elderly person in their street was

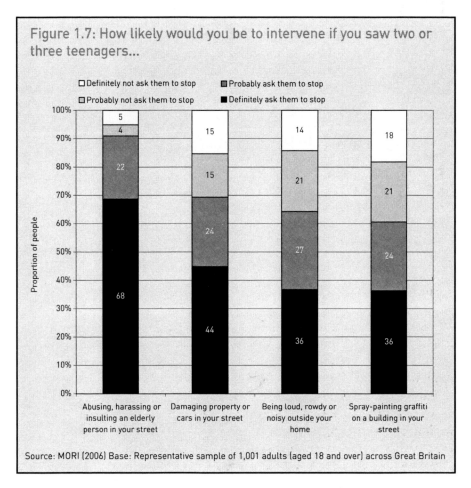

Figure 1.7: How likely would you be to intervene if you saw two or three teenagers...

□ Definitely not ask them to stop   ■ Probably ask them to stop
□ Probably not ask them to stop   ■ Definitely ask them to stop

Source: MORI (2006) Base: Representative sample of 1,001 adults (aged 18 and over) across Great Britain

there a clear majority of those willing to intervene. And if we put these questions in an international context the figures appear even less impressive. Last year Britons were less likely than citizens of most other European countries to intervene in youth violence (ADT Europe 2006). For example, 65 per cent of Germans, 52 per cent of Spanish and 50 per cent of Italians would be willing to intervene if they saw a group of 14-year-old boys vandalising a bus shelter, compared to just 34 per cent of Britons.

It is worth examining in more detail people's reasons for not intervening. Thirty-nine per cent of Britons unwilling to get involved claimed they feared being physically attacked by young people, 14 per cent were scared of later reprisals and 12 per cent feared being verbally abused. This is again indicative of an apparent growing public fear of young people. But it is not just fear of youth violence that should concern us: there is also evidence of a widespread resentment of young people.

Growing resentment of youth

There is a growing belief in academia that attitudes to young people in contemporary Britain are increasingly negative and stereotyped. Media coverage of young people has been found to be profoundly stereotypical, tending to portray them as either causing or having problems, or as simply criminal (Devlin 2006). Favoured media shorthand for youth crime such as 'ASBO youth' 'hoodies' or 'yobs' seems to capture a mood in broader public discourse that says that today's young people are problematic. The popular story told is of young people less civil and less willing to uphold social norms and values than they were in the past and less willing to take responsibility for their behaviour. This view is increasingly evident in public opinion research (Mori 1999, 2000, 2005) and features strongly in rightwing narratives of social decline (Murray 1990, Morgan 2006).

In 2004, nearly 80 per cent of Britons – and 99 per cent of those over 55 – thought that 'young people today have too much freedom and not enough discipline' (Page and Wallace 2004). Looking overseas shows this to be a particularly British worry. Although it is a concern elsewhere, Britons are more likely than other Europeans to say that young people are predominantly responsible for antisocial behaviour, and they are also more likely to cite 'lack of discipline' as the root cause: 79 per cent of Britons thought this underpinned antisocial behaviour, compared to 69 per cent of Spaniards, 62 per cent of Italians and 58 per cent of French people (ADT Europe 2006).

Looking back over time confirms the picture of a gradually increasing divide between youth and mainstream culture, shown by the small but steady rise since 1994 in the proportion of people thinking that 'young people today don't have enough respect for traditional British values', as shown by Figure 1.8.

Academics such as Murray (1990) have argued that young people repre-

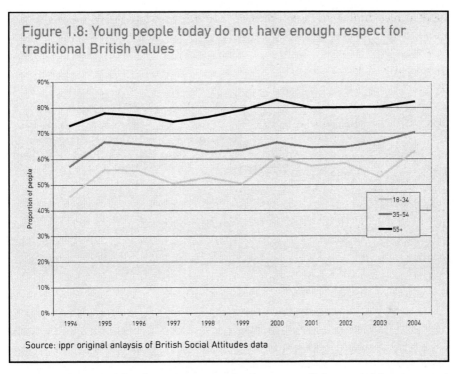

Figure 1.8: Young people today do not have enough respect for traditional British values

Source: ippr original anlaysis of British Social Attitudes data

sent a new 'underclass' – a group at the bottom of the social heap, structurally and culturally distinct from traditional patterns of 'decent' working-class life. Anti-work, antisocial, and welfare-dependent, this class of dangerous youth, Murray argues, threatens mainstream society. He is concerned not just with youth violence, but their attitudes to work and education and their seeming inability to live within our social norms and adhere to our conventions on behaviour and lifestyle. Political rhetoric is often profoundly anti-youth. Ministers have, for example, trumpeted the success of their 'anti-yob' policies in rescuing communities from teen gangs and youth crime while the recent Respect agenda is full of references to moral and civil decline and the need to restore order in society (Home Office 2006). Key ministers including the Prime Minister have personally written or spoken about 'problem youth' and moral decline (Doward *et al* 2005).

Critics such as Pitts (2001) and Muncie (2002) have argued that the Government's treatment of young people has become increasingly punitive. Antisocial behaviour legislation has been accused of criminalising children and young people by holding them morally responsible for their actions at a very young age. Committing antisocial behaviour is not in itself a criminal act, but breaching an antisocial behaviour order (ASBO) is treated as criminal. Stories of ten-year ASBOs given to ten-year-olds and the increasingly litigious behaviour of parents faced with difficult teenagers (Goodchild 2006) have attracted criticism from those believing the Respect action plan and other antisocial behaviour legislation comes more from frustration and a need to respond to public antipathy than a genuine desire to treat the causes of problem behaviour.

Others point to changes in the law that have forced young people to take moral responsibility for their actions at earlier ages. For example, until 1998, children aged ten to fourteen who were charged with a criminal offence were presumed, in any court hearing, to be *doli incapax* ('incapable of evil'). Children in this age group were thus afforded some procedural protection from the full weight of the criminal law. But the presumption of *doli incapax* was abolished by the Crime and Disorder Act 1998, resulting, in the words of one commentator, 'in an untrammelled age of criminal responsibility in England and Wales' (Bandalli 2000: 81).

Why do we resent young people?

So, negative perceptions of young people seem to centre on their decision-making and lack of respect for the norms of society and this is most apparent in the coverage of youth antisocial behaviour. Figure 1.6 clearly shows growing public concern about alcohol consumption and rowdy behaviour. But these negative perceptions play out in other debates too. Public concern seems to focus on areas where personal responsibility and young people's agency are paramount, such as teenage pregnancy, obesity and post-16 participation:

> Just one of a generation of youngsters who see underage sex as the norm, Tania was sleeping with boys at 14, fell pregnant at 15 and gave birth a year later. And – just like thousands of other teenage mums – she is entirely supported by YOUR taxes.
>
> *The People*, 23 October 2005

> Young couch potatoes risk illness: 20 per cent of day spent staring at TVs and computer screens: Dieticians urge children to become more active.
>
> *Guardian* headline (Butt 2006)

> …instead of opening up to a world full of opportunity by forging out and making a mark, young people are preferring stagnation in their own pond, supported by a bewildering and often unjustified array of benefits.
>
> *Sunday Times*, 19 February 2006

The overriding message from these newspaper quotes is one of young people's failure to live up to societal expectations and norms, particularly in areas where personal and social skills are paramount – and of a failure of society to effectively socialise them. So have young people changed – are they worse than ever before? The next chapter starts to unpick this complicated story with an audit of the state of youth in a range of areas.

References

Note: web references correct at September 2006

ADT Europe (2006) *Anti-social behaviour across Europe* London: ADT, available at http://adt.co.uk/cc4471AD-Great-Britain.pdf

Bailey S (2005) *No Man's Land: How Britain's inner city young are being failed* London: Centre for Young Policy Studies

Bandalli S (2000) 'Children, Responsibility and the New Youth Justice', in Goldson B (ed.) *The New Youth Justice* Lyme Regis: Russell House Publishing

Blair T (2005) 'Comment: Our citizens should not live in fear: Those who criticise the new criminal justice measures, such as ASBOs, fail to understand that the most important freedom is that of harm from others' *Observer*, 11 December 2005

Butt R (2006) 'Young couch potatoes risk illness', Guardian, 1 June

Devlin M (2006) *Inequality and the Stereotyping of Young People* Dublin: The Equality Authority

Dixon M, Rogers B, Reed H and Stone L (2006) *CrimeShare: The unequal impact of crime* London: Institute for Public Policy Research (ippr), available at www.ippr.org.uk/members/download.asp?f=%2Fecomm%2Ffiles%2FCrimeSh are%2Epdf

Doward J, Hinsliff G, Beach A and Temko N (2006) 'Fresh blow to Reid as violent crime rises' *Observer*, 16 July

GAD (2005) *Current national projections (2004-based)* London: TSO

Goodchild S (2006) 'Demonised: We lock them up. We give them Asbos. But is our fear of kids making them worse?' *Independent on Sunday*, 23 April

Hall P (1999) 'Social capital in Britain' *British Journal of Political Science* 29: 417-461

Haste H (2000) *Mapping Britain's Moral Values* London: Nestlé Family Monitor/MORI

Home Office (2005a) *Summary of recorded crime data from 1898 to 2004/05* London: TSO

Home Office (2005b) *British Crime Survey*, various years London: NATCEN

Home Office (2006) *The Respect Action Plan* London: TSO

Humphrys J (2004) *Lost for Words: The Mangling and Manipulating of the English Language* London: Hodder and Stoughton

MacDonald R (1997) *Youth, the 'Underclass' and Social Exclusion* London: Taylor Francis

Millie A, Jacobson J, McDonald E and Hough M (2005) *Anti-social behaviour strategies* Bristol: The Policy Press

Morgan P (2006) *Family Policy, Family Change* London: Civitas

MORI (2000) *Politics & Citizenship? Young People Don't Want To Play* London: MORI

MORI (1999) *Britain Today – Is Kindness In Decline?* London: MORI

MORI (2004) *Media Image of Young People* London: MORI

MORI (2005) *Opinion of Professions* London: MORI

MORI (2006) *MORI Political Monitor: Long Term Trends* London: MORI

Muncie J (2002) *Policy Transfers and 'What Works': Some reflections on Comparative Youth Justice* London: Youth Justice

Murray C (1990) *The Emerging British Underclass* London: Institute of Economic Affairs

NATCEN (2006) *British Social Attitudes* London: NATCEN

Nicholas S, Povey D, Walker A and Kershaw C (2005) *Crime in England and Wales 2004/2005* London: TSO

Page B and Wallace E (2004) *Families, Children and Young People – Key Issues* London: Mori

People, The (2005) 'The Shameless Generation', *The People*, 23 October

Pitts J (2001) *The New Politics of Youth Crime* Basingstoke: Palgrave

Sunday Times (2006) 'Our teens need lessons in life, not handouts', *Sunday Times*, 19 February

Truss L (2004) *Talk to the Hand: The utter bloody rudeness of everyday life* London: Profile Books

Walker A, Kershaw C and Nicholas S (2006) *Crime in England and Wales 2005/06.* HOBS 12/06 London: TSO

Wood M (2005) *Perceptions and experience of antisocial behaviour: findings from the 2003/2004 British Crime Survey.* Home Office Online Report 49/04, London: TSO

2. Auditing the state of youth

> Young people today have more opportunities than previous genera-
> tions. Most teenagers take advantage of this and make the transition
> to independent adulthood successfully... Yet in other areas there is
> little improvement or even poorer outcomes.
>
> *Youth Matters* (DfES 2005e)

It is 55 years since the word 'teenager' was first coined (Burchfield 1998).
This marked a profound shift in society's conception of youth, one that
acknowledged the increasingly distinctive role, behaviour, aspirations and
identity of young people. Over subsequent decades the experience of growing up in Britain has undergone deep changes: at the most basic level, material living standards have doubled since 1975 (ONS 2006a) and most
young people now have access to holidays, luxuries and conveniences that
were formerly the exclusive preserve of the extremely affluent just a few
decades ago (Babb *et al* 2006). But despite this progress, as chapter 1
showed, there is widespread and growing concern that contemporary youth
is in crisis.

To get to the root of this concern, this chapter provides an audit of the
state of youth across a range of the most salient indicators, charting the state
of contemporary youth in Britain against historical trends, wider indicators
of societal progress and European comparators. The focus is purposefully
on areas of concern and, as such, is meant to inform our later analysis
rather than to provide a full account of the state of modern youth.

Relevant outcomes? The current policy approach

In thinking about what we want British youth to achieve by the time they
reach adulthood, it is important not to view young people as a single,
coherent group. 'Youth' is of course a distinctive life stage but first and fore-
most young people are individuals with different hopes, plans, needs,
weaknesses and experiences. We should not predetermine what we want all
young people to be like but this does not preclude identifying the broad
attributes we would like all young people to enjoy.

In its flagship *Every Child Matters* White Paper (DfES 2004b), for example, the Government set out a framework of outcomes to which every child
should be entitled. This gave a practical commitment to the idea that whatever their background or circumstances, every child should have the support they need to 'enjoy and achieve', 'make a positive contribution',

'achieve economic well-being', 'be healthy' and 'stay safe'.

These goals are deliberately abstract, setting out generic outcomes without immediately prescribing specific indicators. This allows considerable flexibility in both assessment and targets within the overall framework: under each of these headings there is scope to change general aims and the details of particular targets without losing sight of the overall outcomes. To the Government's credit, there is wide consensus around the centrality of these goals in shaping priorities towards young people and despite considerable gaps in our ability to measure progress against these outcomes, we now have a relatively good basis on which to track many of the most important indicators of youth outcomes going forward (DfES 2005a). However, retrospectively assessing progress towards these goals over the past few decades is considerably more difficult and hampered by a lack of robust data.

In order to meet the Every Child Matters aims, the Government currently spends an estimated £4.6 billion on programmes and services for young people. Of this, £1.9 billion is earmarked for children's social services. Another £485 million is spent on the Connexions service, which provides personal advisers for the 13-19 age group, while £363 million goes to local authority youth services, which focus on the personal and social development of young people (DfES 2006d).

Notable initiatives include the Respect Action Plan (Home Office 2005), which details how the Government will encourage respect in communities, including combating youth antisocial behaviour; Transitions (ODPM 2006), which calls for more holistic services for young adults with complex needs, and the *Youth Matters* Green Paper (DfES 2005f), which addresses key issues relating to how to support and challenge teenagers, particularly in terms of providing 'somewhere to go and something to do'.

These strategies are supplemented by a wide range of voluntary sector organisations and targeted support programmes aimed at those most at risk, including Positive Activities for Young People, Positive Futures, and the Teenage Pregnancy Strategy. A range of additional targeted measures have been introduced aiming to tackle directly antisocial and 'problem' behaviour by young people. These programmes offer both punitive and palliative responses to offending, including Youth Offending Teams (YOTs), Acceptable Behaviour Contracts (ABCs), Antisocial Behaviour Orders (ASBOs) and Parenting Orders.

A further policy strand has aimed to encourage disadvantaged young people to stay in education or training and provide better routes into the labour market. The New Deal for Young People and the Educational Maintenance Allowance are flagship initiatives in this area. Recent influential reports and consultation papers in 2005 and 2006 have ensured this agenda has remained in the media spotlight.

The appointment of Children's Commissioners and the creation of

Children's Trusts are encouraging signs that the Government is firmly committed to prioritising youth problems. So too are Gordon Brown's announcement earlier this year of a UK youth volunteering programme, the announcement of proposals to direct unclaimed assets in bank accounts towards youth services, and recent plans to invest £17 million in voluntary organisations working with children, young people and families. And the Government has recently turned its attention to the emotional and social development of young people too, piloting educational programmes based on cognitive behavioural techniques borrowed from the US, which aim to teach self-esteem and behaviour management to school-age children (of which more later).

Such prioritisation should suggest commensurate improvements in youth outcomes. Yet the state of modern youth remains of key concern, as across many indicators improvements in youth outcomes have flat-lined, failed to keep pace with foreign successes, or declined altogether – particularly those charting the outcomes of the most disadvantaged.

Below we examine the state of youth in some detail, broadly following the Every Child Matters themes. We start by considering young people's health and safety, before looking at their engagement in society, in terms of civic and community participation, and personal and social skills – including looking beyond the Every Child Matters outcomes to consider changes in young people's attitudes, values and morality. We then assess their educational and economic achievement, drawing out challenges for policy. Where relevant, we place trends in international context and consider future prospects. But before doing so, we consider recent trends in child poverty and disadvantage.

Child poverty and disadvantage

In 1999 the Prime Minister famously stated that 'our historic aim [is] that ours is the first generation to end child poverty forever. It's a twenty year mission but I believe it can be done' (Blair 1999). Since then, extensive redistribution through the tax credits system and increases in employment rates, particularly for lone parents, have contributed to a 16 per cent fall measured before housing costs (BHC) and a 21 per cent fall after housing costs (AHC) (DWP 2005), as shown in Figure 2.1.

Despite this progress, child poverty rates in Britain remain high by historic standards: in 1968 just ten per cent of children lived in poverty and in 1979 just 12 per cent did so (Dixon and Paxton 2005). And the latest analyses show that while the Government looks likely to miss its target of halving child poverty by 2010, meeting the 2020 target of ending child poverty appears even less possible: to get poverty below a five per cent target would require doubling key tax credits and benefits in real terms

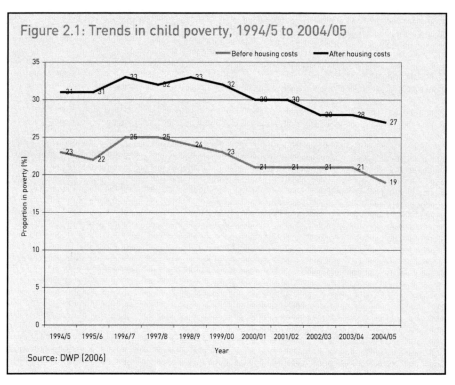

Figure 2.1: Trends in child poverty, 1994/5 to 2004/05

Source: DWP (2006)

between 2010 and 2020 at a cost of £28 billion (Hirsch 2006).

Looking internationally also gives cause for concern. Although Britain is now close to the European average – instead of bottom – and has made the biggest improvement of any EU country (DWP 2006), British child poverty rates were more than six times higher than in Denmark, nearly four times higher than Sweden and more than double those of France in 2005 (UNICEF 2006).

Income remains a useful measure of material deprivation. But it does less to capture the reality of poverty than many other indicators (Fabian Society 2006). The British public tends to be more concerned about child poverty when it is presented in less abstract terms, such as 'one in 50 children not having a warm coat in winter' or 'one in 25 missing out on a birthday celebration'.

Looking at such indicators helps demonstrate what child poverty actually means for young people's lives. Another good example is the number of books in children's homes, which is well known to be important in shaping young people's attitudes to learning. As Figure 2.2 shows, children in Britain were less likely to have at least ten books in their home in 2003 than in many other countries: nine per cent of British 15-year-olds lived in households with fewer than ten books, compared to four per cent in Spain, five per cent in Sweden and seven per cent in Germany.

These measures of income and material well-being should remain cen-

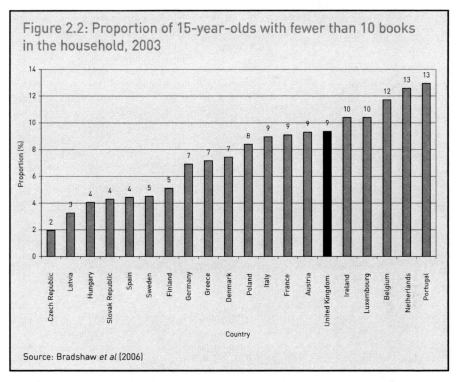

Figure 2.2: Proportion of 15-year-olds with fewer than 10 books in the household, 2003

Source: Bradshaw *et al* (2006)

tral to any discussion of young people's circumstances. But as *Every Child Matters* rightly argues (DfES 2004a), we need to look beyond these indices to gain an informed understanding of the contemporary experience of young people in Britain.

Being healthy

There is much to celebrate. For the last twenty years, life expectancy at birth has been rising by 16 minutes every hour for boys and 11 minutes an hour for girls (Dixon and Margo 2006). Boys born this year can expect to live until 2092 on average, and girls can expect to live until 2096 (GAD 2005). Much of this is due to greater technological and medical progress and improved immunization practice. Congenital abnormalities at birth halved between 1986 and 1998, Sudden Infant Death Syndrome has become much less prevalent (ONS 2000), and even over the last ten years there has been a sharp decline in levels of measles and rubella as vaccinations have become more widespread. However, the UK still lags behind many European countries in terms of universal immunization: just 80 per cent of British children had been immunized against measles in 2003, compared to 92 per cent in Germany and 94 per cent in Sweden (Bradshaw *et al* 2006).

Most young people say that they feel physically well: year on year more than nine out of ten say they are in 'good' or 'very good health' (DoH 2006c). But looking beneath the surface of these encouraging figures reveals considerable cause for concern, as many other indicators of adolescent physical and mental health are heading in the wrong direction and remain strongly skewed by social class. One international survey (using a different data source to the Department of Health figures) shows that young people in Britain are also more likely to say they are in fair or poor – rather than good – health than those in almost all other countries in Europe, as shown in Figure 2.3. Only Latvia and Lithuania have higher rates.

Childhood obesity

One reason behind this concerning picture may be Britain's high level of childhood obesity relative to other European countries. In 2001, 15.8 per cent of British 13- to 15-year-olds were overweight, compared to 10.4 per cent in Sweden and 11.2 per cent in France (Bradshaw *et al* 2006). As Figure 2.4 shows, the last decade has seen a rapid rise in childhood weight problems in the UK: in 2004, more than 25 per cent of girls aged 11 to 15 and a similar proportion of boys were clinically obese, compared to around 15 per cent nine years before. As with many indicators of childhood problems, the evidence suggests that children from more disadvantaged households are more likely to be obese: in 2001/02, children aged two to ten living in households in the lowest two quintile groups had considerably higher rates of obesity (16 per cent) than children from households in the top two income quintile groups (13 per cent) (DoH 2006c).

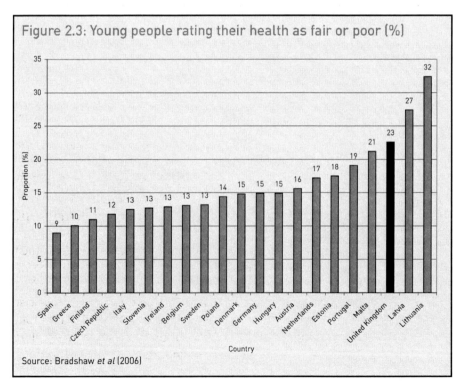

Figure 2.3: Young people rating their health as fair or poor (%)

Source: Bradshaw *et al* (2006)

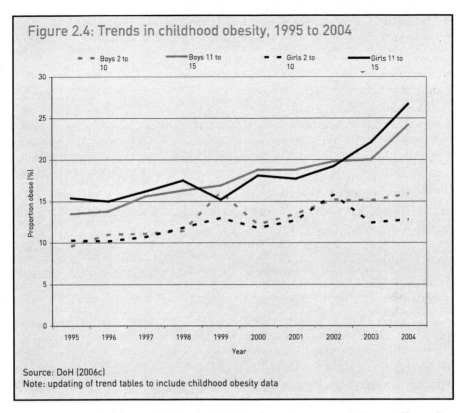

Figure 2.4: Trends in childhood obesity, 1995 to 2004

Source: DoH (2006c)
Note: updating of trend tables to include childhood obesity data

These trends have prompted continued concern in opinion polls, political speeches and the pages of newspapers and magazines about the physical health of young people. But despite widespread public acknowledgement of the problem, such as calls for a 'Tsar to tackle our obese kids' (Marsh 2006, *Yorkshire Evening Post*) or 'personal trainers to get ... children into shape' (Taylor 2006, *Guardian*), many parents are reluctant to acknowledge that their children may be overweight. One recent study found that just 25 per cent of adults with overweight children recognised the problem and as many as 33 per cent of mothers and 57 per cent of fathers described obese children as normal (Jeffery and Voss 2004). This may be partly because Britain has higher levels of adult obesity than almost all other OECD countries, suggesting parents may be more likely to see obesity as normal (OECD 2006).

British children tend to eat more unhealthily than many of their European counterparts: in 2001, just 27 per cent of British children ate fruit every day, compared to 42 per cent in Germany, 38 per cent in Italy and 34 per cent in France. And there are signs that despite efforts to promote exercise in schools, some forms of physical activity may be in decline. For example, young people are increasingly likely to take a bus or car to school rather than walk: in 1992, 61 per cent of primary school children walked to school but in 2004 just 50 per cent did so, while 41 per cent were driven, compared to 30 per cent in 1992. And for secondary school pupils the proportion going by car rose from 16 to 22 per cent over the same time period (DfT 2005).

The appropriate role of government in responding to obesity has become particularly salient in the UK in recent years, partly due to rising levels of the condition. But the relevance of this debate also reflects wider concerns about the role of government in changing public behaviour, as policymakers increasingly realise that many of the most intractable problems in Britain are proving particularly resistant to traditional policy approaches and rely on people taking action for themselves – which requires good personal and behavioural management skills, such as self-control and self-efficacy (Dixon 2006). This seems particularly true for issues, such as teenage pregnancy and sexual health, related to young people.

Teenage pregnancy and sexual health

Teenage pregnancy in Britain is a serious problem. International comparisons show that in 2003 the UK had the highest rate of live births to teenagers in the EU-25, with an average of 26 live births per 1,000 women aged 15 to 19 – nearly a fifth higher than Latvia, the country with the next highest rate, and more than four times the rate of Cyprus, Slovenia, Sweden and Denmark (Babb *et al* 2006). Despite a concerted policy effort focused on halving teenage pregnancy rates between 1999 and 2010, progress remains frustratingly slow: there were 41.4 conceptions per thousand women under the age of 18 in 2005 – just 2.9 per thousand lower than in 1991 (DoH 2006b). And the picture for teenage sexual health is even worse.

Almost across the board, young Britons' sexual health is considerably poorer than it was a decade ago. Between 1995 and 2004, the number of 16- to 19-year-old men diagnosed with syphilis increased nearly 16-fold; for women rates increased nearly 14-fold. Although the trends for other diseases are less dramatic, they are still worrying: levels of genital chlamydia rose by 508 per cent for men and 238 per cent for women in this age group and levels of genital herpes rose by 52 and 38 per cent respectively (HPA 2006). This may be partly because young people are becoming sexually active at younger ages (see chapter 7), but it may also reflect changing attitudes towards sexual health. Looking internationally, young people in Britain take greater risks with their sexual health than their peers in other countries, as shown in Figure 2.5. In 2001/02, just 70 per cent of British 15-year-olds used a condom the last time they had sex, compared to 89 per cent of their Spanish and 82 per cent of their French contemporaries, pointing to the importance of individual behaviour and self-control. As we argue, there are signs that many young people in Britain increasingly lack these abilities, partly because of widespread mental health problems.

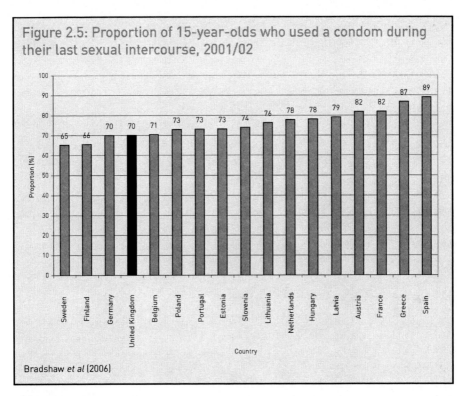

Figure 2.5: Proportion of 15-year-olds who used a condom during their last sexual intercourse, 2001/02

Bradshaw *et al* (2006)

Mental health

Newspapers regularly trot out the latest statistics on mental health among young people – for example, in the *Independent*: the 'huge rise in depression, self-harm and antisocial behaviour' (Goodchild 2006). Commentators and researchers have linked childhood depression to the growth in consumerism, changing family types, exam pressures and changes in rules set by parents. One of the most interesting observations about mental health is that rising problems seem to be related to improvements in economic conditions; commentators argue that rising affluence has led directly to deteriorating mental health. But is this empirically supported?

Perhaps surprisingly, there is little academic consensus as to whether young people's mental health has actually changed over the last few decades. Some research suggests that rates of mental disorder have remained stable – at least recently (Green *et al* 2005) – but other evidence suggests that rates may be rising. One detailed study comparing the experiences of 16-year-olds in three separate cohorts found that conduct problems more than doubled and emotional problems increased by more than 50 per cent between 1974 and 1999, with big changes occurring between 1986 and 1999, as shown in Figure 2.6. Boys remained far more likely than girls to show conduct and hyperactivity problems, and girls were more likely to experience emotional problems.

Yet other countries, such as the Netherlands and the United States, have

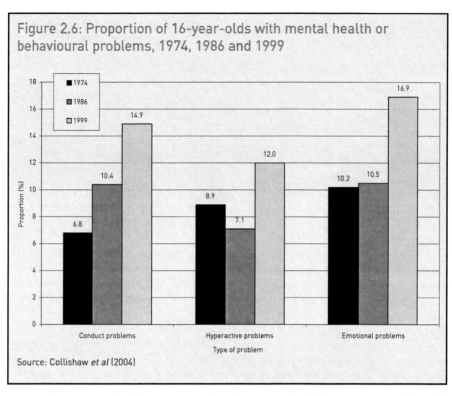

Figure 2.6: Proportion of 16-year-olds with mental health or behavioural problems, 1974, 1986 and 1999

Source: Collishaw *et al* (2004)

not undergone a similar increase in the rate of adolescent mental health problems (Green *et al* 2005; Rankin 2005).

If we look specifically at Autistic Spectrum Disorder (ASD), a similar lack of consensus is revealed. Although studies have reported year-on-year rises in the incidence of ASD, there is considerable dispute about whether this reflects changes in diagnostic criteria, the development of the concept of the wide autistic spectrum, different methods used in studies, growing awareness and knowledge among parents and practitioners, the development of specialist services, or the possibility of true increases in prevalence (Wing and Potter 2002; Pillai *et al*, forthcoming). Looking at the number of pupils with Special Educational Needs (SEN) shows similar ambiguities: in England, this increased from 195,000 in January 1994 to peak at an estimated 258,000 in 2001 but numbers then declined to around 243,000 in January 2005 (Babb *et al* 2006).

Regardless of trends, it is clear that mental health problems are relatively widespread and systematically underpinned by economic inequality and disadvantage. In 2003, such problems were more common among children in lone parent families (16 per cent) than those in two parent families (eight per cent) and in families with neither parent working (20 per cent), than those in which both parents worked (eight per cent) (Green *et al* 2005). In addition, 17 per cent of children whose interviewed parent had no educational qualifications had a mental disorder compared with four per cent of children where the interviewed parent had a degree level quali- fication (ibid). Evidence also suggests that young people from black and minority ethnic groups may be disproportionately affected by mental health problems because a larger than average number have a history of homelessness, school exclusion or residential care (Barrow Cadbury 2006).

One factor underpinning higher rates of mental health problems may be changing patterns of alcohol and drug use. We turn to these issues next.

Alcohol and drug use

In the 1920s and 1930s, young people were the lightest drinkers in the population. This picture has changed unrecognisably over the intervening decades and around 45 per cent of 15-year-old boys and girls had drunk in the last week when surveyed in 2005 (DoH 2006a). Trends in the preva- lence of young people's drinking show little change since the late 1980s, although there seems to have been a gradual decline in prevalence since 2001 (ibid). Yet this apparent stasis (or slight improvement) may be mis- leading. As Figure 2.7 shows, the signs are that for those who drink, con- sumption levels are steadily increasing, particularly at younger ages.

In England, the average weekly consumption of alcohol for drinkers aged 11 to 13 rose from 3.4 units in 1992 to 8.2 units in 2005. For boys

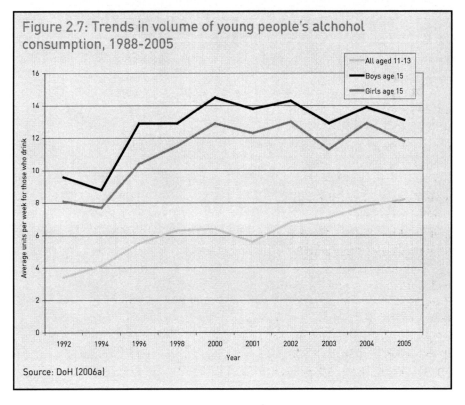

Figure 2.7: Trends in volume of young people's alchohol consumption, 1988-2005

Source: DoH (2006a)

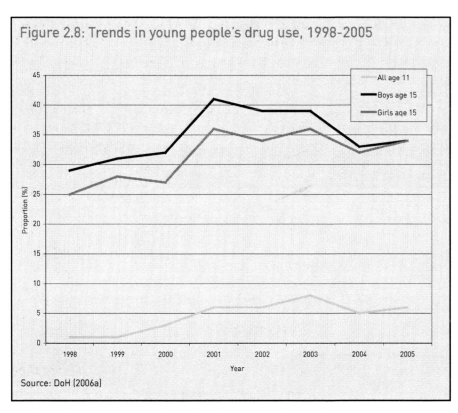

Figure 2.8: Trends in young people's drug use, 1998-2005

Source: DoH (2006a)

aged 15 the average number of units per week rose from 9.6 to 13.1 over the same period; for girls aged 15 the rise was from 6.0 to 10.5 (DoH 2006a). In an international context British adolescents are now ranked as the third-worst binge drinkers in Europe, coming close behind Denmark and Ireland (Bradshaw *et al* 2006): in 2003, 27 per cent of British 15-year-olds said they had been drunk 'more than 20 times'.

These trends have considerable implications for young people's health and well-being. Since the mid-1990s, binge-drinking among young women has increased and is now at the second-highest level in the EU (Bates *et al* 2005) (although boys still drink and get drunk more than girls), with important repercussions for public services. Research by the Royal Liverpool Children's Hospital Accident and Emergency Department shows a ten-fold increase in young people being admitted for alcohol poisoning between 1985 and 1996 (ibid).

This picture is broadly, though less dramatically, mirrored by recent trends in young people's drug use, as shown by Figure 2.8. In 2005, 34 per cent of 15-year-olds boys and girls had taken drugs in the last year, as had six per cent of 11-year-olds, significantly up from 1998 levels, although (as with drinking) down from a peak in 2001 (DoH 2006a).

Within these overall trends, different patterns in types of drug use can be clearly identified. Cannabis remains by far the most common drug among young people, with 12 per cent of 11- to 15-year-olds having used it in the last year. But while trends in cannabis use and class A drugs rose only slightly between 1998 and 2005, the use of stimulants (such as amyl nitrite or 'poppers') doubled from three to six per cent and the use of glue increased sevenfold from one to seven per cent (DoH 2006a).

Drug use among older groups is more common than among younger groups. The most accurate estimates suggest that, in 2003/04, 47 per cent of 16- to 24-year-olds had used one or more illicit drugs in their lifetime, 28 per cent had done so in the last year and 17 per cent had done so within the last month (Chivite-Matthews *et al* 2005). Trends over time appear to show that drug use for this group has remained relatively stable since 1996, although there have been large increases in cocaine use (up from 1.3 per cent of young people having taken it within the last 12 months in 1996 to 4.9 per cent in 2003/04) and substantial falls in the use of hallucinogens, such as LSD, and amphetamines (ibid).

Although a breakdown of young people's drug use by social class is currently unavailable, looking at trends in the population as a whole suggests that drug use is strongly skewed. The poorest households are much more likely to use class A and other drugs than any other group. More affluent households tend to take less drugs: those earning £20,000 to £30,000 had the lowest prevalence in 2003/04 (ibid). But households in the highest income bracket, earning above £30,000 a year, have a slightly higher rate of drug use than those immediately below them.

Smoking

Social class also cuts across young people's smoking habits. Although young people are less likely to smoke than at any point in recent history – 40 per cent of 16- to 19-year-olds smoked in 1974, compared to 24 per cent in 2005 (Ash 2006) – children from poorer and less advantaged backgrounds are slightly more likely to start smoking than their better-off counterparts. And crucially, they are much more likely to become addicted: by the time they reach their thirties, 50 per cent of smokers from an affluent background have stopped smoking while 75 per cent of those from poorer backgrounds continue to smoke regularly (ibid).

One reason for this is likely to be that children from less affluent households are more likely to be exposed to tobacco smoke at home as more of their parents or family members smoke. Parents act as role models: children are three times as likely to become regular smokers if both their parents smoke than if neither does (ibid).

So what is the overall picture of the health of young people? Taken as a whole, it is clear that the vast majority of young people are better off than ever before, largely as a result of better diet, higher living standards and medical advances. But this positive picture is undermined by worsening health for many of the most disadvantaged children, who are increasingly likely to be obese and suffer mental health problems. Considerable and sustained progress for the majority appears to have been tainted by worsening prospects in many areas for the worst-off.

Importantly, the greatest difference between those who are most disadvantaged and their more fortunate peers can be seen in areas in which personal choice and behaviour are paramount, such as smoking, obesity, drug use and teenage pregnancy. But can similar patterns be seen in other areas too?

Staying safe

Childhood mortality is much less common than it was even two decades ago. Compared to their counterparts in 1980, today's 10- to 14-year-olds are about half as likely to die from accidental causes during childhood (ONS 2006c). This is partly due to improvements in road safety and public awareness campaigns, which have resulted in the number of child pedestrians killed or seriously injured on Britain's roads falling considerably, from more than 4,600 in 1994/95 to fewer than 2,400 in 2004/05 (DfT 2006). However, children from disadvantaged backgrounds remain much more likely to die in road accidents: those from the poorest backgrounds were five times more likely to do so in 2002 than those from the most affluent (Dixon and Paxton 2005).

These indicators tell an overwhelmingly positive story. But accidental harm to children only plays a relatively small role in limiting life chances. Far more important is the impact of adults (and peers) on young people's lives, particularly in terms of victimisation, neglect and abuse.

Victimisation

Despite common perceptions of young people as solely perpetrators of crime, it is now clear that they are more likely to be victims than other age groups (Dixon et al 2006). The recent introduction of the Offending Crime and Justice Survey has provided an important boost to our knowledge in this area for children above the age of 10 (Wood 2005), although data for younger age groups remains scarce. The new evidence shows that victimisation appears to be a surprisingly common experience for many children: 35 per cent of children aged 10 to 15 were victims of crime in 2003, with 19 per cent experiencing five or more incidents (ibid), with children from disadvantaged backgrounds more likely to be victims. As many as 59 per cent of children from deprived 'On Track'[3] areas were victims of crime in 2004, with more than 25 per cent of boys and 10 per cent girls having been physically attacked in the last year (Armstrong et al 2005). Important risk factors seem to be poverty, difficult relationships with parents and having committed anti-social behaviour in the last year (Wood 2005).

---

3.   'On Track' is a long-term government initiative aimed at children at risk of getting involved in crime (see www.crimereduction.gov.uk/crpinit.htm)

These risk factors appear to become more marked for older groups, when gender in particular starts to dictate the kinds of crime young people experience. Young men are especially likely to be the victim (or perpetrator) of violent crime: in 2004/05, men aged between 16 and 24 were nearly three times as likely to be victims of violent crime as men aged 25 to 44 and seven times as likely as men aged 45 to 64 (Nicholas *et al* 2005); in England and Wales, nearly 450,000 young men were attacked by a stranger in 2004/05 (Dixon *et al* 2006). Lifestyle undoubtedly plays a part here: people who visit a pub at least three times a week are more than twice as likely to be victims of violent crime as those who never go (Nicholas *et al* 2005).

Similar age patterns can also be seen for other types of crime: just 1.5 per cent of people over retirement age were burgled last year, compared to 3.6 per cent of those aged 25 to 44 and 7.1 per cent of those aged 16 to 24 (ibid). And other research shows that young people, particularly those aged 10 to 15, are far more likely to be victims of repeat victimisation than other groups (Wood 2005).

Young people's physical safety is in an important end in its own right. But it also has considerable repercussions for other outcomes. ippr's analysis of British Crime Survey data shows that being a victim of crime, or having high levels of worry about crime, can have a significant impact on people's behaviour and engagement in the local community, particularly for the most disadvantaged. For example in 2003/04, nearly 20 per cent of victims of wounding started 'avoiding certain places' as a direct result of their experience, which may have meant they were less likely to make a positive contribution to wider society (Dixon *et al* 2006).

Personally being a victim of crime is important. But crime also affects young people's lives in less direct ways too (ibid). Perhaps the most important example is domestic violence. More than one in five women aged between 16 and 59 have been a victim of domestic violence at least once in their lifetimes and 17 per cent have been sexually victimised in some way (Walby and Allen 2004). Crucially, these crimes have higher rates of repeat victimisation than any other type of crime, especially when carried out on women, and have a profound impact on children's life chances (for a recent overview see Mills (2004)). Women who are abused during pregnancy are twice as likely to experience a miscarriage and more likely to experience stillbirth, premature birth, and foetal injury (including broken bones). Over the long term, exposure to violence or trauma before the age of five can alter the developing brain, which may partly explain why pre-school children who are exposed to domestic violence are at significantly higher risk of developing emotional, behavioural, speech and language problems (Refuge 2005).

In the longer term, children who have witnessed domestic violence suffer similar impacts as those who have been physically abused. They are also more likely to show aggressive and antisocial behaviour, suffer from low self esteem and tend to do less well at school (Mills 2004).

Neglect and abuse
Neglect and abuse usually involves someone in the immediate family circle, including parents, brothers or sisters, babysitters or other familiar adults (Royal College of Psychiatrists 2004). Official figures indicate a decline in the number of children suffering abuse and neglect by parents and carers. As Figure 2.9 shows, the number of children on the Child Protection Register fell from 35,000 in 1995 to 25,900 in 2005, with boys remaining slightly more likely to be on the register than girls.

However, research indicates that abuse and neglect are both under-reported and under-registered, suggesting that the prevalence of child abuse and neglect could be much worse than is currently believed. For example, research examining the childhood experiences of 2,869 young people found that 16 per cent of children had experienced serious maltreatment by parents, of whom a third experienced more than one type of maltreatment, and 38 per cent had experienced some degree of maltreatment (Cawson *et al* 2000).

A recent review of the literature, spanning 30 years, clearly shows that maltreated children perform less well at school, even controlling for socio-economic background (Veltman and Browne 2001). And other research has

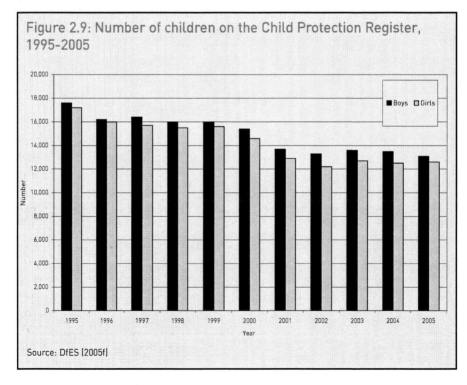

Figure 2.9: Number of children on the Child Protection Register, 1995–2005

Source: DfES (2005f)

shown that the earlier in their lives children are harmed, the more likely they are to exhibit behavioural problems in early adolescence, including self-harm (Keiley *et al* 2001).

Self-harm and suicide

In 2001, the UK had one of the highest rates of self-harm in Europe (Horrocks 2002). On average, young people who self-harm start to do so at around the age of 12 and by the end of the teenage years, an estimated one in ten young people will have self-harmed at some point (National Inquiry into Self-harm among Young People 2006). Girls are much more likely to do so than boys: in 2005, one in five girls aged 15 to 17 said they had self-harmed and nearly a quarter had considered doing so (Samaritans and the Centre for Suicide Research 2002; The Priory 2005).

Although breakdowns by social class are unavailable, young people with mental health problems – which are strongly linked to other forms of disadvantage – are much more likely to self-harm than others. In 2005, research showed that 28 per cent of those with an emotional disorder had previously self-harmed, as had 21 per cent of those with a conduct disorder and 18 per cent of those with a hyperkinetic disorder (Green *et al* 2005). Meaningful trends in young people's self-harm are difficult to ascertain, largely due to a lack of comparable data (National Inquiry into Self-harm among Young People 2006). But the evidence suggests that self-harm rose dramatically from the late 1960s to the early 1970s, decreasing in the early 1980s, before rising again in the 1990s. And over the past decade, there appears to have been a substantial increase in self-harm by young men (Horrocks 2002).

Only a small fraction of young people who self-harm receive medical treatment, largely because these young people are usually very secretive about their behaviour. Research published in 2005 suggests that most keep their behaviour hidden from their family, often for many years (National Inquiry into Self-harm among Young People 2006): seven per cent of children aged 11 to 16 said they had self-harmed but just two per cent of parents thought their child had done so (Green *et al* 2005). Although some forms of self-harm are fairly obvious, others can be much more discrete, such as ingesting toxic substances or objects. And at worst, self-harm can involve attempted suicide.

A conservative estimate is that there are 24,000 cases of attempted suicide by young people aged between 10 and 19 each year in England and Wales, the equivalent to one attempt every 22 minutes (Hawton *et al* 1999). Although young women are more likely to self-harm, young men are much more likely to commit suicide; this remains the most common cause of death in men aged under 35. As Figure 2.10 shows, while suicide rates for women have remained relatively constant since the early 1970s,

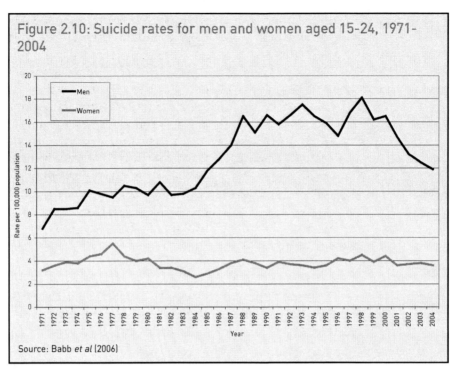

Figure 2.10: Suicide rates for men and women aged 15-24, 1971-2004

Source: Babb et al (2006)

there have been considerable changes in male suicide rates, which rose during the mid 1980s before falling again from 1998 (Babb *et al* 2006).

Making a positive contribution

Making a positive contribution to society is a key strand of the Every Child Matters framework. This is a deliberately broad and inclusive theme, incorporating spheres as diverse as civic engagement, respecting the law, developing positive relationships with peers and adults, developing self-confidence and personal and social skills, and developing enterprising behaviour (DfES 2004b). We start by assessing young people's political and civic engagement.

Trends in young people's interest and participation in mainstream political processes are not encouraging, showing marked declines over the last decade even: in 1994, 36 per cent of 12- to 19-year-olds said they had 'some' or 'a great deal of' interest in politics; by 2003 this had fallen to 31 per cent. Similarly, 21 per cent of young people said they supported a particular political party in 1994, compared to just eight per cent in 2003 (Park 2004).

But this does not necessarily mean that young people are becoming less interested in political issues. Rather, there has been a shift in the forms of political action that young people are becoming involved in. The anti-war marches in 2003 were the largest public demonstrations in British history and the 2005 Make Poverty History campaign resulted in more than 500,000 people contacting the Prime Minister and eight million wearing a white wrist band (Make Poverty History 2005). These campaigns are examples of a broader trend in British public life in which people are more likely to join single issue campaigns or groups and less likely to become involved in broader political movements or to use formal mechanisms such as contacting their MP (Dixon and Paxton 2005). Union and political party membership has fallen just as English Heritage and similar charities have experienced considerable increases in membership and support (ibid). People increasingly express their political preferences through personal, market-related activity, or through activity that generates an immediate response such as contacting the media rather than politicians, and boycotting products rather than signing petitions. These broader societal trends are reflected in the way younger people engage in civic society.

In 2005, young people were more likely to participate in voluntary activities than any other group. Around 50 per cent of 16- to 19-year-olds informally volunteered at least once a month, 32 per cent formally volunteered and 78 per cent had informally volunteered in the last year – an increase from 73 per cent in 2001 (Attwood *et al* 2006; Kitchen *et al* 2006). Trends in other kinds of civic participation are somewhat harder to track, but we know that these are much less common than volunteering. Last year, eight per cent of 16- to 19-year-olds had been involved in at least one form of civic activism, including being a councillor, a school governor, a magistrate or a special constable, or being involved in groups that had a decision-making role in local services; 16 per cent had been involved in some form of civic consultation, including consultation about local services or problems by completing a questionnaire, attending a public meeting, or being involved in a group set up to discuss local services or problems; and 28 per cent had undertaken at least one form of civic participation, such as contacting a local councillor, an MP or taking part in a public demonstration (Kitchen *et al* 2006).

These figures are encouraging. It seems clear that a large proportion of young people are actively engaged in their communities and political issues. Yet a small proportion of others are facing difficulties in engaging in a similarly positive way.

Behaviour and personal and social skills

Last year, more than 1,000 pupils were permanently excluded from primary school and more than 8,000 were excluded from secondary school (DfES 2006c). Exclusion is a last resort, often coming after persistent disruptive behaviour or violence against another pupil. But while there have always been concerns about young people's behaviour in schools, perhaps surprisingly the signs are that young people's behaviour is generally improving.

Research from a wide variety of sources suggests that poor behaviour is

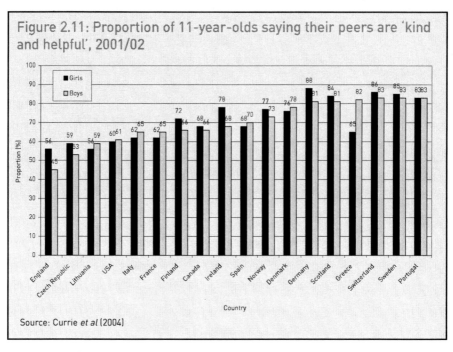

Figure 2.11: Proportion of 11-year-olds saying their peers are 'kind and helpful', 2001/02

Source: Currie *et al* (2004)

only a significant problem in a small minority of schools – Ofsted recently put the figure at one in ten (Ofsted 2005; Reed 2005). The number of pupils permanently excluded from school fell last year and remains far below the 12,300 peak of 1997/98 (DfES 2006c). Fewer teachers identify behaviour as a major problem now than they did at the beginning of the decade (Smithers and Robinson 2001, 2005). The pattern of steady improvement is reflected in parents' views and, with the exception of 2003/04, in Ofsted judgements over time (DfES and COI 2004; Ofsted 2005; Reed 2005). And, as the last chapter highlighted, antisocial behaviour is less widespread than a few years ago.

Yet these formal measures tell only part of the story and looking at young people's relationships with each other gives considerable cause for concern. Many will be familiar with tales of 'happy slapping' and whatever its current terminology, bullying remains stubbornly high, showing no change in prevalence over the last decade: surveys carried out between 1995 and 2003 consistently reveal that around 28 per cent of girls and 20 per cent of boys aged 12 to 13 say they are 'sometimes afraid of going to school because of bullying'. For children aged 14 to 15, the figures hover at around 22 per cent for girls and 15 per cent for boys (SHEU 2004). Other research shows that black children, looked-after children and children who have been excluded from school are all significantly more likely to be bullied by their peers (Armstrong *et al* 2005), with often devastating results. US research has shown that children who are bullied are more likely than those who are not to be depressed, lonely and anxious, have low self-esteem, feel

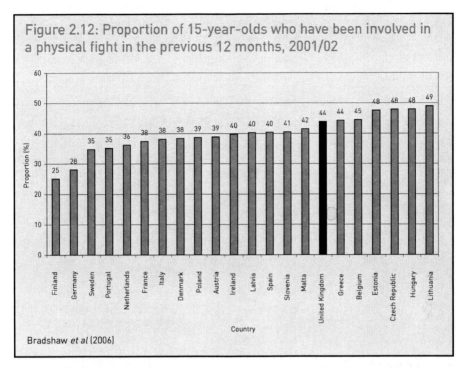

Figure 2.12: Proportion of 15-year-olds who have been involved in a physical fight in the previous 12 months, 2001/02

Bradshaw *et al* (2006)

unwell, have migraine headaches, and think about suicide (Limber 2002).

Benchmarking British children's experiences of relationships with their peers against those in other European countries gives considerable cause for concern. As Figure 2.11 shows, in 2001/02, just 45 per cent of boys and 56 per cent of girls aged 11 in England said their peers were 'kind and helpful', markedly less than in any other country – although Ireland and Scotland fared better.

This general picture is supported by a range of other data. As Figure 2.12 shows, young people in Britain surveyed in 2001/02 were more likely than the majority of their Continental counterparts to have been involved in a physical fight in the previous 12 months. Forty-four per cent of 15-year-olds in Britain had been involved in a fight, compared to just 25 per cent of those in Finland, 28 per cent in Germany and 35 per cent in Sweden (Bradshaw *et al* 2006).

The above gives a clear indication that British youth have poor personal and social skills when set in an international context. But there is little evidence to go on in this area. Although personal and social development is a key strand of the Every Child Matters framework, it appears to be the least well developed in policy or practical terms: in early 2006, this target remained the sole area for which no formal measure or indicator has yet been identified (DfES 2005a: 1).

The closest indicator that is currently available is achievement in 'personal, social and emotional development' at the end of school Foundation

Stage; after this point more formal testing measures take over. Although data collection and measurement are certainly more difficult in this area, these are not insurmountable difficulties; a number of measures in these areas have been developed over the past 40 years and have been incorporated in a wide range of other government-sponsored studies, such as the large cohort studies.

Criticism of how the original ideas and motivation behind Every Child Matters have been implemented in practice cuts deep. Although Every Child Matters has been an enormously welcome and positive development in child- and youth-related policy, and represents a considerable broadening of scope, it does not in practice go broadly enough to respond to concerns about the state of youth and its role in concerns about the civic order more generally. Recent piloted lessons in self-esteem as part of the school curriculum do not go far enough to address the factors essential to social and emotional development. To fully understand these factors we have to consider a wider range of indicators, assessing the state of young people's morality, values, attitudes and softer skills.

Morality and attitudes

Teenagers have distinct views and attitudes on a wide range of issues. They are more likely than older people to hold liberal views on questions of marriage, relationships and gender roles, and there is evidence that over the past decade, their attitudes have undergone faster changes than among older groups (Phillips 2004). ippr's analysis of the Young People's Social Attitudes Surveys show that between 1994 and 2003, young people's views became markedly more liberal on a range of issues: in 2003, 70 per cent agreed that one parent can bring up a child as well as two and 85 per cent said that it is fine for a couple to live together and not marry, compared to 55 per cent and 80 per cent respectively in 1994, as shown in Figure 2.13.

But there are some more worrying developments too. A greater proportion of young people now say that they would keep extra change given to them in error in both large and corner shops, which could be taken as an indicator of declining deference to authority and respect. Unfortunately, trends in youth attitudes and values are extremely difficult to analyse due to a pervasive shortage of solid data or evidence, reflecting the relatively minimal role that attitudes and values have played in policy development. Perhaps the best longitudinal evidence we have comes from cohort studies, which suggest that parents are now more likely than before to report problems with their teenage children in surveys – particularly in terms of lying and general disobedience, as shown in Figure 2.14.

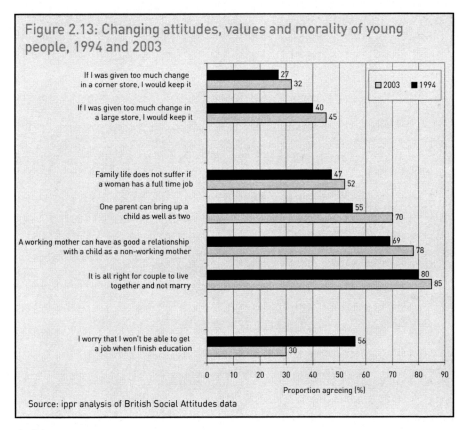

Figure 2.13: Changing attitudes, values and morality of young people, 1994 and 2003

Source: ippr analysis of British Social Attitudes data

Achievement

So there do seem to have been changes in youth culture over the last three decades. But what underpins these changes? One hypothesis, popular in the media and in academic literature on mental health, is that the educational and labour market experiences of young people have become more problematic.

Charting trends in young people's achievement in education is plagued with difficulty. There have been several major shifts in qualifications over the last 40 years, meaning that there are relatively few long-term comparable measures of attainment. Most measures look back around a decade and these show some encouraging signs of success: authorised pupil absences have fallen considerably over the past decade – from 8.01 per cent of all maintained secondary school half-days (one of the Government's preferred measures) in 1996/97 to 6.6 per cent in 2004/05, but these are qualified by rising levels of unauthorised pupil absences, which have increased from 1.01 per cent to 1.23 per cent of all half-days over the same period (DfES 2005d). But it is difficult to tell whether measures of attainment have shown similar patterns.

Comparable data for the latest set of targets for 11- and 14-year-olds

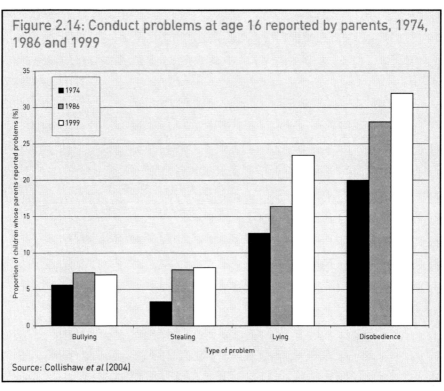

Figure 2.14: Conduct problems at age 16 reported by parents, 1974, 1986 and 1999

Source: Collishaw *et al* (2004)

only goes back to 2003, although these show marked improvements over even the last two years: at age 11, 74 per cent of boys and 84 per cent of girls reached level 4 in English at Key Stage 2 in 2005, compared to 70 per cent of boys and 81 per cent of girls in 2003 (DfES 2005b). And at age 14, 73 per cent of boys and 74 per cent of girls achieved level 5 or above at Key Stage 3 in 2005, compared to 70 per cent of boys and 72 per cent of girls in 2003 (DfES 2005b). Although helpful, these indicators are less useful in judging trends over time and do not fully capture the marked inequality in the outcomes of young people. International comparisons are perhaps more revealing here.

The most comprehensive international comparison of pupil achievement that includes the UK is the 2000 OECD PISA study, which compares the achievements of students aged 15 in reading and mathematics. This shows clearly that although young people in the UK perform well on average, with a mean score in reading literacy that sits well above that of most other countries in the OECD – including Sweden, France, Norway, Germany and the US – however, there is much greater inequality of outcome than in most other countries (OECD 2001). Figure 2.15 shows how different countries compare on these two measures of excellence and equity: countries to the right have higher achievement on average, and countries towards the top of the chart have higher levels of equity – student

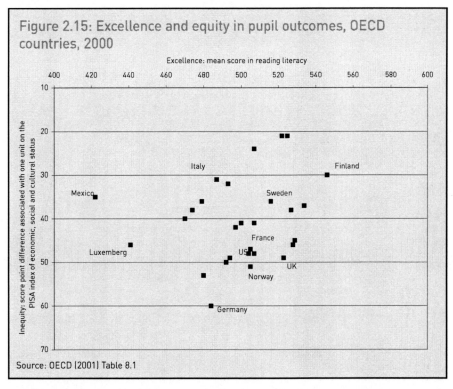

Figure 2.15: Excellence and equity in pupil outcomes, OECD countries, 2000

Excellence: mean score in reading literacy

Inequity: score point difference associated with one unit on the PISA index of economic, social and cultural status

Italy

Finland

Mexico

Sweden

Luxemberg

France

US

UK

Norway

Germany

Source: OECD (2001) Table 8.1

performance is less strongly determined by social disadvantage. The UK sits firmly in the bottom right hand corner, confirming its place as a high excellence, low equity country.

This high degree of inequity in achievement in the UK is well known and gives considerable cause for concern. It is often referred to as the 'long tail of underachievement' in the media and in a number of government reports and speeches (DfES 2006e). It has profound implications for the state of young people's achievement later in life.

Achieving economic well-being: educational attainment to employment

Performance at GCSE level largely determines whether young people stay on in education post-16. Although overall results have been improving rapidly for the past decade, there is some concern that current targets – which incentivise schools to focus on pupils at the five A*-C borderline – are disadvantaging the worst-off and exacerbating inequality in the education system. The proportion of young people achieving five or more A*-C grades at GCSE rose from 44.5 per cent in 1995/96 to 57.1 per cent in 2004/05, while the proportion of young people achieving five or more A*-G grades at GCSE rose from 86.1 per cent to 90.2 per cent over the same period

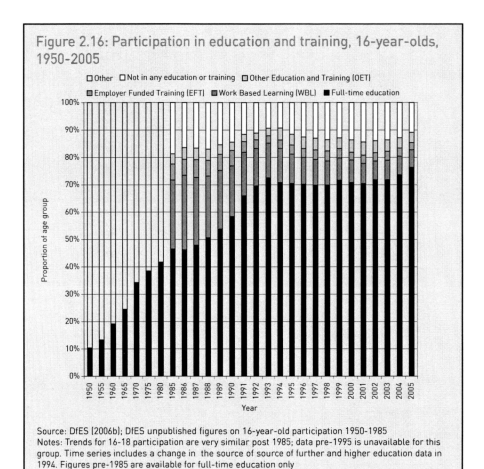

Figure 2.16: Participation in education and training, 16-year-olds, 1950-2005

Source: DfES (2006b); DfES unpublished figures on 16-year-old participation 1950-1985
Notes: Trends for 16-18 participation are very similar post 1985; data pre-1995 is unavailable for this group. Time series includes a change in the source of source of further and higher education data in 1994. Figures pre-1985 are available for full-time education only

(DfES 2006a). There has been much greater success in improving standards for the majority, at the possible expense of the minority who are most disadvantaged. For nearly half of young people with modest or poor GCSE attainment, further education provision is often poor, receiving less funding and offering fewer hours of teaching than that available to their higher achieving peers (Delorenzi and Robinson 2005).

This story plays out in a range of other indicators in other areas. Two of the most robust are the proportions of young people continuing in post-compulsory education and those entering higher education. As Figure 2.16 shows, following sustained increases in post-16 participation in education and training between 1950 and 1993, participation rates have almost flat-lined over the past decade with only very recent increases, and remain lower than in almost all other industrialised countries (ibid). Young people whose parents are 'higher professionals' are nearly 50 per cent more likely to be in post-compulsory full-time education than the children of those in 'routine' occupations, and more than twice as likely to be studying for an 'academic' qualification, such as an A-level.

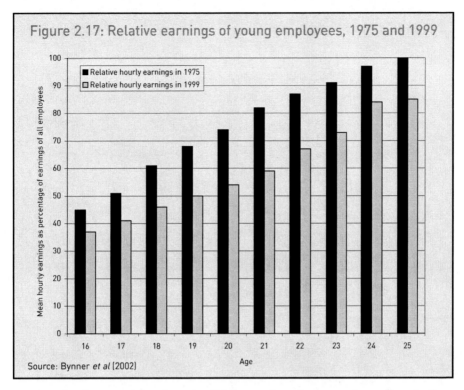

Figure 2.17: Relative earnings of young employees, 1975 and 1999

- Relative hourly earnings in 1975
- Relative hourly earnings in 1999

Mean hourly earnings as percentage of earnings of all employees

Age

Source: Bynner *et al* (2002)

Trends for participation in higher education are broadly similar. Between 1970 and 2003/04 the numbers participating in higher education grew from 416,000 men and 205,000 women to 1,054,000 and 1,392,000 respectively (Babb *et al* 2006), with the middle classes taking up the bulk of new places (Galindo-Rueda *et al* 2004). But this increase should not detract from the fact that over the past few years the Higher Education Initial Participation Rate (HEIPR) has flat-lined: it was 41 per cent in 1999/2000 and had risen by just one percentage point five years later in 2004/05 (DfES 2005c).

These trends suggest that most young people have never had it so good. A greater proportion participates in education for longer and receives greater wage premiums later in life: research shows that obtaining a degree consistently results in much higher earnings (see chapter 3). But what has happened to those young people who do not continue in education, either through choice or circumstance?

The picture for this group is relatively bleak. Unemployment rates for young people have remained consistently higher than for older age groups and have not fallen in line with national unemployment rates (ONS 2006b). The proportion of 16- to 18-year-olds not in education, employment or training (NEET) has remained at around 9 or 10 per cent since the early '90s – higher than in Sweden, Germany, the US, Canada and Spain (OECD 2005) – and now stands at record levels: around 220,000 16- to 18-

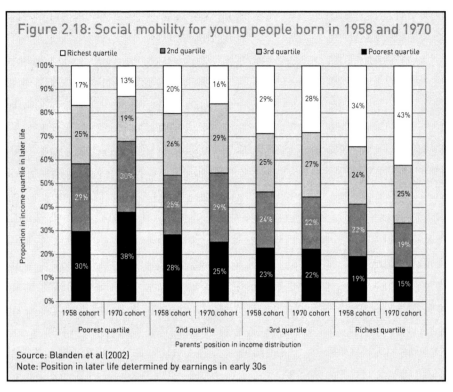

Figure 2.18: Social mobility for young people born in 1958 and 1970

Legend: ☐ Richest quartile ■ 2nd quartile ☐ 3rd quartile ■ Poorest quartile

Y-axis: Proportion in income quartile in later life (0% to 100%)

Poorest quartile:
- 1958 cohort: 30%, 29%, 25%, 17%
- 1970 cohort: 38%, 30%, 19%, 13%

2nd quartile:
- 1958 cohort: 28%, 25%, 26%, 20%
- 1970 cohort: 25%, 29%, 29%, 16%

3rd quartile:
- 1958 cohort: 23%, 24%, 25%, 29%
- 1970 cohort: 22%, 22%, 27%, 28%

Richest quartile:
- 1958 cohort: 19%, 22%, 24%, 34%
- 1970 cohort: 15%, 19%, 25%, 43%

X-axis: Parents' position in income distribution

Source: Blanden et al (2002)
Note: Position in later life determined by earnings in early 30s

year-olds fell into this group at the end of 2005 (DfES 2006b).

For those in work, earnings prospects have declined, following the collapse of youth labour markets in the early 1980s. As more young people entered further and higher education and labour markets shifted (see chapter 4), the relative earnings of young people in employment have declined significantly as employers shift their recruitment practices for higher-paid jobs away from younger people. As Figure 2.17 shows, in 1975 the average hourly earnings of young people grew from about 45 per cent of the national average at age 16 to 100 per cent at age 25; by 1999 the relative earnings of young people had declined significantly (Bynner *et al* 2002).

Partly as a result of these changes to the workplace, there has been a well documented fall in social mobility in recent years (Blanden *et al* 2004). Young people born in 1970 were more constrained by the circumstances of their birth and less likely to be upwardly mobile than those born 12 years before, as shown in Figure 2.18. This is a relatively complex and important chart and it is worth examining it in some detail.

Each bar in the chart represents all those born to parents in each income quartile in 1970 or 1958. So the bar on the far left represents all those born to parents in the lowest income quartile in 1958, and the bar on the far right represents all those born to parents in the richest income quartile in 1970. The shaded blocks and percentages show where in the income distribution these groups ended up in their early thirties. So the bar on the far left shows that 30 per cent of those born in the poorest income quartile in 1958 remained in this quartile by age 30, 29 per cent were in the second income quartile, 25 per cent were in the third quartile and 17 per cent were in the richest quartile. This measure is important because it shows how much family background determines people's life chances: if family background made no difference, then each bar would be equally split into four equal groups. But the chart clearly shows that starting off disadvantaged has a profound influence on later life chances.

The chart allows us to compare the changing pattern of social mobility between the two cohorts, clearly showing that social mobility has declined: family background has become a more important determinant of success. Thirty-eight per cent of those born to parents in the poorest income quartile in 1970 remained in that quartile by their early thirties, compared to 30 per cent of those born in 1958; and 43 per cent of those born to parents in the richest income quartile in 1970 remained in that quartile by their early thirties, compared to 16 per cent of those born in 1958.

This is perhaps the most damning evidence that young people's position in society has not improved dramatically over the last thirty years despite the unarguable context of greater opportunities and choice. Looking to other countries also reveals cause for concern about domestic youth: using data provided by Blanden *et al* (2005), ippr has calculated that the social mobility experienced by this cohort in Britain was 14 per cent lower than for contemporaries in West Germany; 17 per cent lower than in Finland; and 18 per cent lower than in Canada, Denmark, Norway and Sweden. Only the US had lower social mobility than the UK over this period, and even in the US, which has a similar political economy in many respects, there was nothing like as severe a decline in social mobility between previous cohorts and those born in 1970 (Blanden *et al* 2005).

Summary of features of youth attainment

In combination with the analysis in the rest of this chapter, this assessment of social mobility contributes to a picture of youth attainment with four key features:

1. Family background is becoming a more important determinant of outcomes across the board.
2. Indicators are improving almost across the board for the majority of young people, but for the most disadvantaged groups many indicators are getting worse.
3. Some indicators have stalled, particularly in areas where personal responsibility and young people's ability to make and carry out decisions (agency) is paramount, such as teen pregnancy, behaviour, drink-

ing and using drugs, obesity, self-harm and post-16 participation.

4. Softer personal and social skills and the ability to deal successfully with significant life changes and challenges (agency/capability) are systematically overlooked in current policy, despite key concerns about mental health and young people's ability to navigate an increasingly complex socio-economic environment.

The central findings of this report are that these four features are fundamentally interwoven, that they are compounded by underlying socio-economic change, and that policy can respond in a progressive way. In the following chapter we assess the links between these features of contemporary youth attainment, drawing out a new conceptual approach to understanding what lies beneath these confusing results.

References

Note: web references correct at September 2006

Action on Smoking and Health (Ash) (2006) *Factsheet No. 1: Who Smokes and how much?* Available at: www.ash.org.uk/html/factsheets/html/fact01.html

Armstrong D, Hine J, Hacking S, Armaos R, Jones R, Klessinger N and Armstrong A (2005) *Children, Risk and Crime: The On Track Youth Lifestyles Surveys* London: TSO www.homeoffice.gov.uk/rds/pdfs05/hors278.pdf

Attwood C, Singh G, Prime D and Creasey R (2001) *2001 Home Office Citizenship Survey: people, families and communities.* Home Office Research Study 270 London: TSO

Babb P, Butcher H, Church J and Zealey L (2006) *Social Trends* 36 London: TSO, available at: www.statistics.gov.uk/downloads/theme_social/ Social_Trends36/Social_Trends_36.pdf

Barrow Cadbury (2006) *Lost in Transition* London: Barrow Cadbury

Blair T (1999) 'Beveridge Revisited: A welfare state for the 21st Century', in Walker R (ed.) *Ending Child Poverty* Bristol: Policy Press

Blanden J, Goodman A, Gregg P and Machin S (2004) 'Changes in Intergenerational Mobility', in Corak M (ed.) *Generational Income Mobility* Cambridge: Cambridge University Press

Blanden J, Gregg P and Machin S (2005) *Intergenerational Mobility in Europe and North America. A report sponsored by the Sutton Trust* London: Centre for Economic Performance, London School of Economics

Bradshaw J, Hoelscher P and Richardson D (2006) 'An Index of Child Well-being in the European Union' *Social Indicators Research* 78(1): 1 – 45

Burchfield R (1998) *The New Fowler's Modern English Usage* Oxford: Oxford

University Press

Bynner J, Elias P, McKnight A, Pan H and Pierre G (2002) *Young people's changing routes to independence* York: JRF, available at: www.jrf.org.uk/bookshop/eBooks/184263108X.pdf

Cawson P, Wattam C, Brooker S and Kelly G (2000) *Child maltreatment in the United Kingdom: a study of the prevalence of child abuse and neglect* London: NSPCC, available at: http://server-uk.imrworldwide.com/cgi-bin/b?cg=informDN&ci=nspcc&tu=http://www.nspcc.org.uk/Inform/Publications/Downloads/ChildMaltreatmentInTheUKExecSummary_pdf_gf25453.pdf

Chivite-Matthews N, Richardson A, O'Shea J, Becker J, Owen N, Roe S and Condon J (2005) *Drug Misuse Declared: Findings from the 2003/04 British Crime Survey England and Wales.* HOBS 04/05 London: TSO, available at: www.homeoffice.gov.uk/rds/pdfs05/hosb0405.pdf

Collishaw S, Maughan B, Goodmand R *et al* (2004) 'Time trends in adolescent mental health' *Journal of Child Psychology and Psychiatry* 45: 1350-62

Currie C, Roberts C, Morgan A, Smith R, Settertobulte W, Samdal O, Barnekow Rasmussen V (2004) *Young people's health in context. Health Behaviour in School-aged Children* (HBSC) study: international report from the 2001/2002 survey. Copenhagen: World Health Organization Regional Office, available at: www.euro.who.int/Document/e82923.pdf

Delorenzi S and Robinson P (2005) *Choosing to Learn: Improving participation after compulsory education* London: Institute for Public Policy Research

Department for Education and Skills (DfES) (2004a) *Every Child Matters* London: TSO

DfES (2004b) *Every Child Matters: Change for Children* London: TSO, available at: www.everychildmatters.gov.uk/_files/F9E3F941DC8D4580539EE4C743E9371D.pdf

DfES (2005a) *Every Child Matters Outcomes Framework* London: TSO

DfES (2005b) *National Curriculum Assessments of 14 year olds in England, 2005* (Provisional). SFR32/2005 London: TSO

DfES (2005c) *Participation Rates in Higher Education: Academic Years 1999/2000-2004/2005.* SFR14/2006 London: TSO

DfES (2005d) *Pupil Absence in Schools in England: 2004/2005* (Revised). SFR56/2005 London: TSO

DfES (2005e) *Youth Matters: Next Steps. Something to do, somewhere to go, someone to talk to* London: TSO, available at: www.dfes.gov.uk/publications/youth/

DfES (2006f) *Youth Matters* Green Paper London: TSO

DfES (2006a) *GCSE and Equivalent Results and Associated Value Added Measures in England 2004/05* (Revised). SFR02/2006 London: TSO

DfES (2006b) *Participation in Education, Training and Employment by 16-18 Year Olds in England: 2004 and 2005.* SFR21/2006 London: TSO

DfES (2006c) *Permanent and Fixed Period Exclusions from Schools and Exclusion Appeals in England 2004/05.* SFR24/2006 London: TSO

DfES (2006d) Personal correspondence (unpublished)

DfES (2006e) *Social Mobility: Narrowing Educational Social Class Attainment Gaps* London: TSO

DfES (2006f) Referrals, assessments and children and young people on child protection registers, England - Year ending 31 March 2005 (Provisional), London: DfES, available at: www.dfes.gov.uk/rsgateway/DB/SFR/ s000614/SFR50-2005.pdf

DfES and COI (2004) *Stakeholder Tracking Study 2004 (Waves 7-9)* London: TSO, available at: www.dfes.gov.uk/research/programmeofresearch/ index.cfm?resultspage=11&keyword=parents-&keywordlist1=0&keyword list2=0&keywordlist3=0&andor=or&type=0

Department of Health (DoH) (2006a) *Drug use, smoking and drinking among young people in England in 2005: headline figures. A survey carried out for the Health and Social Care Information Centre and the Home Office by the National Centre for Social Research and the National Foundation for Educational Research* London: TSO, available at: www.ic.nhs.uk/pubs/drugsmokedrinkyoungeng2005/finalreport.pdf/file

DoH (2006b) *Health Statistics Quarterly 30 Summer 2006* London: TSO

DoH (2006c) *Health Survey for England 2004. Updating of trend tables to include childhood obesity data.* London: TSO, available at: www.ic.nhs.uk/pubs/hsechildobesityupdate

Department for Transport (DfT) (2005) *National Travel Survey 2004* London: TSO

DfT (2006) *Transport accidents and casualties. TSGB 2005 – List of Casualties by Type data tables* London: TSO

Department for Work and Pensions (DWP) (2005) *Households Below Average Income (HBAI) 1994/95-2004/05* London: TSO, available at: www.dwp.gov.uk/asd/hbai/hbai2005/contents.asp

DWP (2006) *Making a difference, Tackling poverty – a progress report* London: TSO, available at: www.dwp.gov.uk/publications/dwp/2006/poverty/tackling-poverty.pdf#search=%22poverty%20progress%20report%22

Dixon M (2006) *Rethinking Financial Capability: Lessons from economic psychology and behavioural finance* London: Institute for Public Policy Research, available at: www.ippr.org.uk/ecomm/files/financial_capabilities.pdf

Dixon M and Margo J (2006) *Population Politics* London: Institute for Public Policy Research, available at: www.ippr.org.uk/publicationsandreports/publication.asp?id=341

Dixon M and Paxton W (2005) 'The State of the Nation: An audit of social injustice', in Pearce N and Paxton W (eds) *Social Justice: Building a fairer Britain* London: Institute for Public Policy Research/Politico's

Dixon M, Rogers B, Reed H and Stone L (2006) *CrimeShare: The unequal impact of crime* London: Institute for Public Policy Research, available at: www.ippr.org.uk/members/download.asp?f=%2Fecomm%2Ffiles%2FCrimeSh are%2Epdf

Fabian Society (2006) *Narrowing the Gap, the final report of the Fabian Commission on Life Chances and Child Poverty* London: Fabian Society

GAD (2005) *Period and cohort expectation of life tables* London: TSO

Galindo-Rueda F, Marcenaro-Gutierrez O and Vignoles A (2004) *The Widening Socio-economic Gap in UK Higher Education* London: CEE

Goodchild S (2006) 'Happi (sic) lessons for all; Schoolchildren will take self-esteem classes to raise standards and cut crime. US guru called in to pioneer radical scheme that could enter the school curriculum', *Independent on Sunday* 9 July

Green H, McGinnity A, Meltzer H, Ford T and Goodman R (2005) *Mental health of children and young people in Great Britain, 2004* London: TSO, available at: www.dh.gov.uk/assetRoot/04/11/83/39/04118339.pdf

Hawton K, Houston K, Shepperd R (1999) 'Suicide in young people. Study of 174 cases, aged under 25 years, based on coroners' and medical records' *British Journal of Psychiatry*, 175: 271-276

Heckman J, Stixrud J and Urzua S (2006) 'The Effects of Cognitive and Noncognitive Abilities on Labor Market Outcomes and Social Behaviour' *NBER Working Paper* 12006 Cambridge, MA: National Bureau of Economic Research

Hirsch D (2006) *What Will it Take to End Child Poverty: Firing on all cylinders* York: JRF, available at: www.jrf.org.uk/bookshop/eBooks/9781859355008.pdf

Home Office (2006) *The Respect Action Plan* London: TSO

Horrocks J (2002) 'Self-poisoning and self-injury in adults' *Clinical Medicine* 2(6): 509-12

HPA (2006) *Supplementary Tables of Sexually Transmitted Infections in the United Kingdom* London: HPA, available at: www.hpa.org.uk/infections/topics_az/ hiv_and_sti/epidemiology/dataresource.htm#top

Jeffery A and Voss L (2004) 'Parents unable to weigh up childhood obesity' *Practical Diabetes International* 21(9): 319-20

Keiley M, Howe T, Dodge K, Bates J and Pettit G (2001) 'The timing of child physical maltreatment: a cross-domain growth analysis of impact on adolescent externalizing and internalizing problems' *Development and Psychopathology* 13(4): 891-912

Kitchen S, Michaelson J, Wood N and John P (2006) *Citizenship Survey, Topic report: active communities* London: TSO

Limber S (2002) *Bullying among children and youth* Proceedings of the Educational Forum on Adolescent Health: Youth Bullying, Chicago: American Medical Association, 12 August 2005, available at: www.ama-assn.org/ama1/pub/upload/mm/39/youthbullying.pdf

Make Poverty History (2005) *White Band* London: Make Poverty History

Marsh D (2006) 'We need a tsar to tackle our obese kids' *Yorkshire Evening Post,* June 14

Mills C (2004) *Problems at home, problems at school: The effects of maltreatment in the home on children's functioning at school: an overview of recent research* London: NSPCC, available at: http://server-uk.imrworldwide.com/cgi-bin/b?cg=informDN&ci=nspcc&tu=http://www.nspcc.org.uk/inform/publicatio ns/downloads/ProblemsAtHome_pdf_gf25321.pdf

National Inquiry into Self-harm among Young People (2006) *Truth Hurts: Report of the National Inquiry into Self-harm among Young People* London: Mental Health Foundation and Camelot Foundation

Nicholas S, Povey D, Walker A and Kershaw C (2005) *Crime in England and Wales 2004/2005* London: TSO

OECD (2001) *Knowledge and Skills for Life: First Results from PISA 2000* Paris: OECD

OECD (2005) *Education at a Glance* Paris: OECD

OECD (2006) *OECD Factbook 2006 – Economic, Environmental and Social Statistics* Paris: OECD

Office of the Deputy Prime Minister (ODPM) (2005) *Transitions* London: TSO

Ofsted (2005) *Managing Challenging Behaviour* London: Ofsted

Office of National Statistics (ONS) (2000) *Child Health Statistics* London: ONS

ONS (2006a) Gross domestic product (Average) per head, CVM market prices (IHXW): SA Not seasonally adjusted Constant 2003 prices Updated on 21/ 7/2006 London: ONS, available at: www.statistics.gov.uk/statbase/TSDdownload2.asp

ONS (2006b) *Labour Market Trends* 114 (6) London: TSO

ONS (2006c) *Mortality Statistics: Childhood, infant and perinatal.* Series DH3 no.37 London: ONS

Park A (2004) 'Has Modern Politics Disenchanted the Young?' in Park A, Curtice J, Thomson K, Bromley C and Phillips M (eds) *British Social Attitudes: The 21st Report* London: SAGE

Phillips M (2004) 'Teenagers on Family Values', in Park A, Curtice J, Thomson K, Bromley C and Phillips M (eds) *British Social Attitudes: The 21st Report* London:

SAGE

Pillai R, Rankin J, Stanley K, Bennett J, Heatherington D, Stone L and Withers K (forthcoming) *Disability 2020: Opportunities for the full and equal citizenship of disabled people in Britain in 2020*. A report by ippr trading ltd for the Disability Rights Commission London: DRC/ippr trading

Priory, The (2005) *Adolescent Angst* London: The Priory Group

Rankin J (2005) *Mental Health in the Mainstream* London: Institute for Public Policy Research, available at: www.ippr.org.uk/publicationsandreports

Reed J (2005) *Towards Zero Exclusion: An action plan for schools and policymakers* London: Institute for Public Policy Research, available at: www.ippr.org.uk/ecomm/files/toward_zero.pdf

Refuge (2005) *Refuge assessment and intervention for pre-school children exposed to domestic violence* August 2005 London: Refuge

Samaritans and the Centre for Suicide Research (2002) *Youth and self-harm: Perspectives* London and Oxford: Samaritans and the Centre for Suicide Research, University of Oxford

Royal College of Psychiatrists (2004) *Mental Health and Growing Up, Third Edition. Child abuse and neglect – the emotional effects* London: Royal College of Psychiatrists

SHEU (2004) *Emotional Health and Well-being (including Bullying) 1983-2003* Exeter: SHEU

Smithers A and Robinson P (2001) *Teachers Leaving* London: NUT

Smithers A and Robinson P (2005) *Teacher Turnover, Wastage and Movements between Schools* London: DfES

Taylor D (2006) 'The fitness babysitters: Parents are hiring personal trainers to get their children into shape' *Guardian*, June 15

UNICEF (2006) *Child Poverty in Rich Countries 2005. The proportion of children living in poverty has risen in a majority of the world's developed economies* Florence: UNICEF Innocenti Research Centre

Veltman M and Browne K (2001) 'Three decades of child maltreatment research: implications for the school years' *Trauma,Violence and Abuse* 2(3): 215-39

Walby S and Allen J (2004) *Domestic violence, sexual assault and stalking: Findings from the British Crime Survey* Home Office Research Study 276. London: TSO

Wing L and Potter D (2002) 'The epidemiology of autistic spectrum disorders: is the prevalence rising?' *Mental retardation and developmental disabilities research reviews* 8(3): 151-61

Wood M (2005) *Perceptions and experience of antisocial behaviour: findings from the 2003/2004 British Crime Survey* Home Office Online Report 49/04 London: TSO, available at: www.homeoffice.gov.uk/rds/pdfs04/rdsolr4904.pdf

3. What determines young people's outcomes? A capabilities approach

From the detailed youth audit in the last chapter it is now apparent that the flagship problem areas for young people are those in which personal and social skills determine individual success – where the ability to choose matters. In these areas – the continuation of post-16 education, drug and alcohol consumption, pregnancy and antisocial or civic behaviour – we can observe an emerging pattern. As the White Paper *Every Child Matters* notes, the majority of young people seem to be flourishing, making good the many and varied choices they now have to continue education, contribute to society and their community. But at the same time a particular group of young people, those from disadvantaged backgrounds, are consistently and increasingly failing, explaining at least in part the growing public sense that young people are 'in crisis'.

Yet looking at the raw evidence from the audit, it is difficult to understand why this group is failing so consistently just as the opportunities available to them dramatically increase. This is because, by focusing only on the traditional indicators of achievement and the availability of opportunities for young people, we will be unable to get to the heart of what really explains successful from unsuccessful youth outcomes. So a different strategy is called for.

ippr's analysis suggests that youth policy has too often been focused on the theoretical availability of opportunities, at the expense of what really matters in enabling young people to actually take up such opportunities. In reality, it is young people's personal and social skills and capabilities – for example their agency, capacity to plan for the future, moral maturity and self-control – that are more crucial determinants of their life chances across most domains than policy has recognised so far. Policy's failure to respond to the importance of personal and social skills underpins both concerns about the civic order and some young people's stalled attainment.

The 'capabilities approach' developed by Amartya Sen (Sen 1979, 1980, 1985, 1987, 1999; Vizard 2005) and Martha Nussbaum (Nussbaum and Sen 1993; Nussbaum 2000, 2006) provides a new way of thinking about what should matter for youth by placing a greater emphasis on the factors that are most effective in *enabling young people to take up opportunities,* as well as promoting the 'theoretical' availability of opportunities in themselves. This approach provides a better answer to the question of how far individuals' economic and social positions are the results of their preferences and how far these are the result of constraints individuals face (Le Grand 1984, 1991; Arneson 1989; Cohen 1989; Sen 1995; Roemer 1998; Burchardt and

Le Grand 2002).

In this chapter we outline the capabilities approach and show why this provides a more useful lens through which to view 'what matters' in young people's development. We argue that it provides a better way to think about the relative importance of economic and social structures; hard skills, qualifications and cognitions; and personal and social skills in determining young people's outcomes. We then use the best available data, including original analysis of cohort studies, to assess the relative importance and interplay between these, to draw out what matters for young people's outcomes in contemporary Britain.

The capabilities approach

The underlying idea behind the capabilities approach is that we should focus on what limits people's actual *capacity* to achieve a range of outcomes – their 'capabilities' – rather than on the outcomes people actually achieve – their 'functionings'. This may seem like a subtle and rather academic distinction but it has profound implications for policy in many areas, including gender, disability and unemployment (Burchardt and Le Grand 2002; Burchardt 2003, 2004). It is worth looking at what we mean by functionings and capabilities in more detail.

'Functionings' are states of being or outcomes, such as being employed or well-fed, or activities, such as voting or eating. At any given moment, individuals achieve several functionings simultaneously: you can be employed and in a good relationship while voting in London (and even eating). At the same time, there is a large group of other functionings that the individual could achieve instead, should he or she so wish, such as walking in Scotland. The whole set of functionings that an individual could achieve, or is currently achieving, is known as the 'capability set' – and this determines an individual's well-being: the broader the capability set, the better off the individual. According to capabilities theory, therefore, inequality should be thought of in terms of people's capability sets.

It is important to be precise about what we mean by 'opportunity' here, as the crux of capabilities theory is in the way it conceives of opportunity. A specific functioning is in an individual's capability set if the person:

> ...possess[es] the personal ability, resources, practical means, and the knowledge that is required to achieve the combination of functionings in question, and that the external circumstances (social, economic and physical environment) are such that he or she could do so.
>
> (Burchardt 2004: 738)

This highlights two distinct sets of issues. The first is that people's agency is partly determined by social and physical structures operating at different levels of causal depth. Agency then reproduces and/or transforms those structures (Schwartz 2004; Bynner 2005). This is importantly different to structuralism (which argues that only structures matter) or methodological individualism (which argues that the unit of analysis can only be the individual). The second point, and the one of concern to us here, is that agency is not rational in the classical sense: it is 'bounded'.

Bounded agency and the public ecology of decision-making

Bounded agency contrasts classical views of agency and rationality – in which people's decision-making capacity is seen as relatively independent of their environment – with situated conceptions of agency. As Professor Susan Hurley writes in a paper for ippr:

> Human agency and rationality are more ecological phenomena than previously thought; individual rational agency is profoundly embedded in and dependent on the individual's social environment [the public ecology].

> (Hurley 2006, forthcoming: 2)

Sociologists and psychologists have of course long understood the importance of the environment and experience. But emerging evidence from neuroscience is beginning to underline just how important this public ecology can be in influencing individual agency (Dixon 2006; Hurley 2006, forthcoming).[5] People are only rarely 'rational' in a traditional sense. As the sociologist Cass Sunstein and the economist Richard Thaler have put it:

> People fail to make forecasts that are consistent with Bayes' rule [which shows how we should update our beliefs in the light of new evidence], use heuristics that lead them to make systematic blunders, exhibit preference reversals (that is, they prefer A to B and B to A), suffer from problems of self-control, and make different choices depending on the wording of the problem.

> (Sunstein and Thaler 2003)

The point is that people's decisions are profoundly affected by their environment and experiences, as well as the way alternatives are presented or 'framed'. Therefore, young people's actual capacity to take up opportunities may be severely constrained by their background and softer skills such as their ability to relate to people, their motivation or confidence in their own abilities. Perhaps the most compelling evidence in this area comes from

---

5. Hurley (2006) gives a detailed analysis of the public ecology of rational agency and the implications that emerging scientific evidence has for our conceptions of personal responsibility and the appropriate role of government in influencing behaviour.

research investigating cognitive biases – the way people's decisions are systematically skewed by contextual factors. To take just a few illustrative examples:

- **Salience bias.** People tend to overestimate the probability of events that they can easily imagine – either because they are particularly memorable, recent, or have given a short-lived but extreme experience (Kahneman 2002). This means that familiar options, or the experiences of peers and the local community, are more likely to seem commonplace than they actually are. This also partly explains why community and parental expectations tend to influence people's lives so strongly.
- **Conceptual priming bias.** People are unconsciously influenced by conceptual priming. For example, people do better on test scores if they are encouraged to think about 'clever' stereotypes, such as university lecturers, than if they have no priming. And they do worse if they are encouraged to think about 'stupid' stereotypes, such as football hooligans (Hurley 2006). Similarly, people who are primed to think about elderly stereotypes, by exposure to words such as 'grey', 'sentimental', or 'bingo' show slower responses and poorer memories than those who are not primed (Banfield *et al* 2003).
- **Social priming bias.** People tend to unconsciously copy other people. On a very minor level this can be as simple as yawning in response to someone else's yawn, or mimicking body language.

These examples start to illustrate how people's agency is bounded by contextual factors. Although these focus on contemporaneous biases, similar processes operate in the longer term to shape the way people make decisions, based on expectations, the public ecology and previous experience. The implication of this emerging research is that we need to think about people's capacity for agency as being profoundly shaped by their environment and experiences, and the options open to them; as the poet John Donne put it, no man is an island.

Of course, policymakers have always aimed to facilitate people's agency. But the research outlined in this chapter reveals a shortfall in the traditional political Left's conception of what enables people to exercise their discretion. While the Left has focused on the importance of resources and qualifications for improving life chances, it has largely failed to take on board the importance of personal and social skills in the effective exercise of agency. We explore this idea in more detail in chapter 6 but the point here is that capability theory provides a useful lens by which to do this, as it stresses the broad range of capacities people need to develop to be able to take up formal opportunities, and the interdependence of agency and economic, environmental, social, cultural and psychological constraints.

Criticisms of capabilities

The capabilities theory is not uncontroversial (Burchardt and Le Grand 2002; Nussbaum 2006). Perhaps the most common cause for concern is that it is more prescriptive about what is important for a good life than a Rawlsian conception of social justice. While the Rawlsian approach deliberately avoids specifying how people should use their goods and faculties, the capabilities theory, while it does not specify a substantive set of goals or values that individuals should pursue, does specify more tightly than Rawls what particular functionings are necessary for freedom. For example, Martha Nussbaum provides a list of ten: life; bodily health; bodily integrity; senses, imagination and thought; emotions; practical reason; affiliation; living with concern for other species; play; and control over one's physical and political environment (Nussbaum 2006: 76-78).

This is unlikely, however, to cause much difficulty for policymakers. For example, the outcomes framework of *Every Child Matters* – described in the last chapter – could be seen as a form of capability set that policy aims to promote (DfES 2005). A more powerful criticism is that capabilities are too hard to measure. By definition, a capability set is a set of outcomes that an individual has not achieved. How, then, are we to use this in practice – how can we distinguish between voluntary and involuntary take-up of opportunities?

One approach is to simply ask people whether they face constraints in particular areas, and where these come from. But this suffers from a serious problem, known as 'adaptive preferences' – that people's analysis of their current situation is very determined by circumstances (Burchardt and Le Grand 2002; Dixon 2006). So, for example, a severely malnourished individual with scant experience of a normal diet may not assess his or her nutritional requirements in the same way as a very well fed individual.

This is a difficult issue but not an insurmountable one, particularly given new econometric techniques (Sugden 1998). For example, recent research in the UK has assessed how we can use a capabilities approach to distinguish between voluntary and involuntary employment (Burchardt and Le Grand 2002). And ippr's original analysis of cohort study data – in conjunction with groundbreaking research published earlier this year (Blanden *et al* 2006) – enables us to assess the relative importance of different factors in determining people's capabilities.

What determines capabilities? An empirical analysis

Four kinds of factors determine youth outcomes: 'harder' measures such as cognitive ability, qualifications and technical skills; 'softer' measures such as personal preferences, personal and social skills and personality traits (otherwise known as 'non-cognitions'); luck; and the external socio-economic context young people grow up in. These four sets of factors have been investigated in great detail by sociologists, economists and psychologists over the past few decades. Government has traditionally focused on the first and last of these, at the expense of 'softer' measures – although there have been recent moves to address the social and emotional development of young people through piloting cognitive behavioural therapy techniques in schools (affecting luck is clearly out of scope for government). But is this focus justified? In the rest of this chapter we outline what we know about the relative importance and the links between these four factors, and show how they explain the four key features of the state of British youth identified in chapter 2.

Detailed regression analysis of cohort data provides some answers. The British Cohort Study tracks a group of children born between 4 and 11 April 1970, collating detail on their family and economic background and their subsequent experiences. Because these cohort members are now in their thirties, this data allows researchers to track the impact of childhood and adolescent experiences on later life outcomes: we can therefore see what made a difference.

Recent research by Blanden *et al* (2006) has investigated the relative importance of qualifications, cognitions and non-cognitions (personal and social skills) on earnings in later life, and the interplay between these factors. This research provides compelling evidence that personal and social skills were particularly important in determining life chances for this cohort.

Figure 3.1 shows the association between various cognitive attributes measured early in life – such as reading ability at age 10 – and various non-cognitive attributes – such as application, internal locus of control[6] and self-esteem – on earnings at age 30 for the 1970 cohort. It shows that better[7] maths ability at age 10 was associated with 8.2 per cent higher earnings at age 30, better application aged 10 was associated with 8.9 per cent higher earnings and a more internal locus of control was associated with six per cent higher earnings. Another way of putting this is that better application may add approximately £68,500 to lifetime earnings and a more internal locus of control may add approximately £46,200 on average (in 2006 prices).[8]

---

6. 'Application' broadly captures young people's dedication and concentration (Blanden 2006). 'Locus of control' captures young people's agency – the degree to which they perceive events as within their control. People with a very 'internal' locus of control tend to see events as within their control: they have a strong sense of personal agency; whereas people with an 'external' locus of control tend to see events as beyond their control and determined predominantly be external forces (Rotter 1954, 1966).
7. 'Better' is defined here as an individual's score in a given domain increasing by one standard deviation in the overall distribution. This increase is roughly equivalent to moving from fiftieth place to sixteenth place out of 100.
8. Based on an estimated lifetime earnings of £770,000, calculated by uprating 2000 estimates for inflation (Hansard 2003; HM Treasury 2006).

Figure 3.1: Impact of cognitive attributes on earnings age 30, 1970 cohort

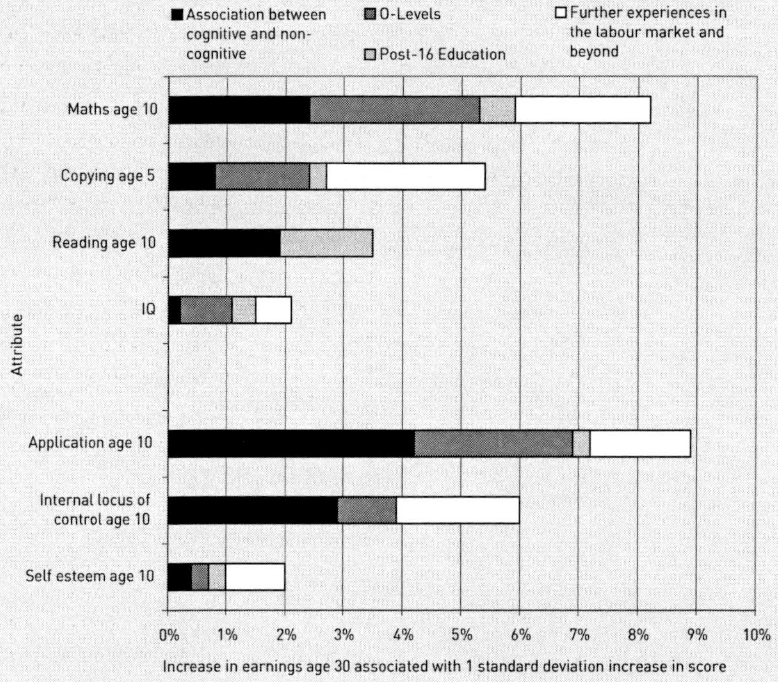

Association between cognitive and non-cognitive
O-Levels
Post-16 Education
Further experiences in the labour market and beyond
Maths age 10
Copying age 5
Reading age 10
IQ
Application age 10
Internal locus of control age 10
Self esteem age 10
Attribute
0%
1%
2%
3%
4%
5%
6%
7%
8%
9%
10%
Increase in earnings age 30 associated with 1 standard deviation increase in score

Source: Blanden *et al* (2006): Table 3

The figure also allows us to unpick the 'stages' through which these attributes impacted on earnings. The first of these is the interaction between developing cognitive and non-cognitive attributes, shown by the black sections within each bar. This happens in two ways: better cognitive attributes help people develop better non-cognitive attributes (and vice versa) and they also allow people to make more of their non-cognitive attributes. This interaction accounts for a substantial proportion of the benefit of both cognitive and non-cognitive attributes. So for example, slightly under a third of the impact of maths on earnings in later life is through its interaction with non-cognitive attributes.

The second stage is in terms of the impact on O-level attainment, shown by the dark grey sections within each bar. Just over a third of the impact of maths on earnings aged 30 occurs at this stage. The third stage accounts for the impact on post-16 attainment, shown by the light grey sections. Importantly, a greater proportion of the impact on earnings is accounted for in these two stages for cognitions than non-cognitions; it seems that non-cognitive attributes are most important in the labour market beyond education and subsequent experiences in life, and in helping people make the most of their cognitive abilities.

In many respects, these results confirm a substantial body of existing research. A well established literature on the wage returns to education convincingly shows that education levels make an enormous difference to future earnings (Blundell *et al* 2001; Walker and Zhu 2001; Sianesi 2003; Heckman *et al* 2006): on average in the UK each additional year of education adds around 7 per cent in earnings for men and 8 per cent for women. Although there are considerable differences between subjects and types of qualification, the broad picture is that GCSEs add around 10 per cent to wages compared to someone with no qualifications, A-levels add a further 15 per cent for women and 20 per cent for men, while a degree adds a further 25 per cent for women and 15 per cent for men (Walker and Zhu 2001). By contrast, returns to lower-level vocational qualifications are lower and vary. Some, such as Ordinary National Certificates (ONCs) and Higher National Certificates (HNCs), have significant positive returns. Others, such as NVQ Level 2, have little or no return, unless they are delivered in the workplace (for example). But the results in Figure 3.1 also cut against much received wisdom.

The importance of non-cognitions: agency and softer skills

The analysis reported in Figure 3.1 clearly shows that non-cognitive abilities – personal and social skills and personality attributes – are about as important as cognitive abilities in determining earnings in later life (Blanden *et al* 2006). Importantly, these non-cognitive attributes may be particularly significant in explaining why some young people 'buck the trend' – starting out from impoverished families and ending up well-off by age 30. Research shows that poor children who have high levels of application are 14 per cent more likely to be well-off by age 30, compared to the average poor child. The evidence suggests that application is in fact more important for these children than for their more affluent peers: for children who came from affluent backgrounds, having a high application score only makes affluence in later life four per cent more likely (Blanden 2006).

Until relatively recently, these findings about the centrality of agency in determining youth outcomes would have surprised many professional economists (Heckman and Rubenstein 2001). The relatively common-sense idea that personality traits such as persistence, motivation, confidence, acumen and old-fashioned gumption make a difference to youth attainment was widely discredited by most British economists, who resolutely argued that qualifications were almost the be-all and end-all. This started to change in 2000, with the publication of cohort analysis by Leon Feinstein (Feinstein 2000), and a subsequent article by John Goldthorpe that argued that middle-class children are protected against downward social mobility by their relative sophistication in verbal and interpersonal skills and greater self-esteem (Goldthorpe 2003). It is only now gaining ground as established orthodoxy.

The evidence is mounting fast (see Jackson (2006), Groves (2005), Dunifon and Duncan (1998), Farkas (2003) and Bowles and Gintis (2001) for good overviews). For example, recent US analysis of the *National Longitudinal Survey of Young Women* clearly shows that locus of control, aggression, and withdrawal are important determinants of wages for white women (Groves 2005). And a recent study of 5,000 young people in Britain and Germany found that unemployed young people tend to see education and qualifications as more important in influencing life chances, but were less likely than other groups to stress the importance of agency – measured in terms of interest, long-term goals, choice and planning – and were much more likely to attribute success or failure to chance, suggesting an external locus of control (Evans 2002). In contrast, young people with jobs tended to attribute their success to their own plans and efforts.

Other recent work in the US, looking at the academic performance of young people in school, finds that self-discipline is more than twice as important as IQ in predicting final grades in high school, high school selection, school attendance, hours spent doing homework, hours spent watching television and the time of day that students began their homework (Duckworth and Seligman 2005). Importantly, self-discipline also predicted which students would improve their test scores over the course of a school year, in contrast to IQ, which had little predictive power in this area.

This has profound implications for our understanding of existing research about the importance of formal qualifications for life chances: we may have simply miscalculated how important these are in determining outcomes by overlooking the way they act as a 'flag' for softer skills. Where research has not controlled for the impact of softer skills and agency, estimates of the impact of formal qualifications are likely to have been boosted by the hidden effect of softer skills (Jackson 2006, forthcoming), as those with good soft skills are more likely to go on to gain good formal qualifications.

Recent experiences with the Educational Maintenance Allowance (EMA) also seem to confirm the hypothesis that soft skills and agency matter more in Britain than had been thought previously. The initial pilot evaluation and later evidence from the national rollout revealed that providing educational training opportunities was not enough to ensure outcomes were improved. Making financial support available through the EMA led to increased participation post-16 by under-represented groups and had a particularly strong impact on key target groups such as low attainers and very low socio-economic groups, but made no statistically significant impact on *attainment*, suggesting that other factors are important in determining attainment levels. Importantly, in their analysis of why this might be, the researchers point to the importance of non-cognitive, agentic attributes, suggesting that:

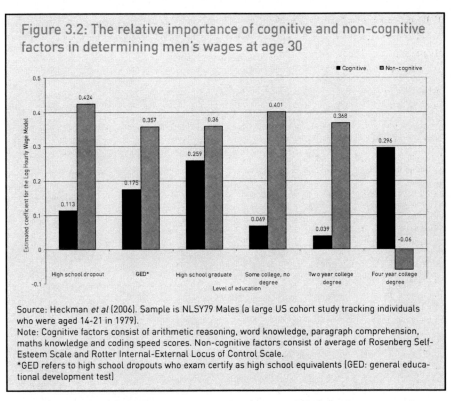

Figure 3.2: The relative importance of cognitive and non-cognitive factors in determining men's wages at age 30

Source: Heckman *et al* (2006). Sample is NLSY79 Males (a large US cohort study tracking individuals who were aged 14-21 in 1979).
Note: Cognitive factors consist of arithmetic reasoning, word knowledge, paragraph comprehension, maths knowledge and coding speed scores. Non-cognitive factors consist of average of Rosenberg Self-Esteem Scale and Rotter Internal-External Locus of Control Scale.
*GED refers to high school dropouts who exam certify as high school equivalents (GED: general educational development test)

These muted outcomes may indicate that young people who were encouraged to remain in full-time education by the availability of EMA differ substantively from those who traditionally take this route, *perhaps in terms of ambition, aptitude or temperament.*

(Middleton *et al* 2005: 125, emphasis added)

The debate in the US has been more advanced for some time and there is growing academic consensus that non-cognitions matter (Dunifon and Duncan 1998; Heckman 2000; Heckman and Rubenstein 2001; Farkas 2003; Heckman *et al* 2006): research published earlier this year has now quantified the difference in earnings that hard and soft skills can afford for different groups (Heckman *et al* 2006), as shown by Figure 3.2.

The figure clearly shows that non-cognitive abilities are crucial in determining men's incomes. Although the intuitive idea is relatively easy to grasp, this data is complex to understand in detail. The coefficient numbers show what percentage increase in hourly earnings could be expected by an increase of one standard deviation in an individual's score on the cognitive or non-cognitive measure. So a secondary school dropout could expect a 42.4 per cent increase in hourly wages if they were one standard deviation higher placed in the overall distribution of non-cognitive skills.

For low-skilled men, non-cognitions are four times as important as cog-

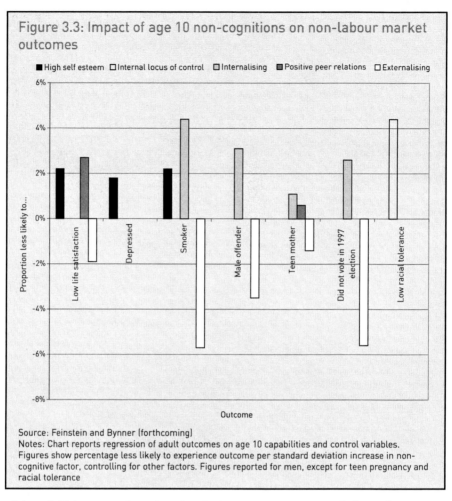

Figure 3.3: Impact of age 10 non-cognitions on non-labour market outcomes

■ High self esteem □ Internal locus of control □ Internalising ■ Positive peer relations □ Externalising

Source: Feinstein and Bynner (forthcoming)
Notes: Chart reports regression of adult outcomes on age 10 capabilities and control variables.
Figures show percentage less likely to experience outcome per standard deviation increase in non-cognitive factor, controlling for other factors. Figures reported for men, except for teen pregnancy and racial tolerance

nitive abilities. As education level rises, non-cognitive abilities become a less strong determinant of wages. (For women, non-cognitive abilities remain more important than cognitive abilities at all education levels beyond secondary school dropout.)

Non-cognitions, successful transitions and the civic order

Importantly, personal and social skills and personality attributes are also linked to the kind of behavioural outcomes the public and Government are most concerned with in the debate about social and moral decline. In understanding why some young people deviate towards antisocial behaviour, promiscuity and drug and alcohol use, the role of non-cognitions is key.

US research is again important here. Work by Heckman and colleagues shows that non-cognitions and cognitions are equally important determinants of a range of non-labour market outcomes, including smoking, drug use, likelihood of serving a jail term and participation in illegal activities (Heckman *et al* 2006).

Similar results can be seen in a British context too. Leon Feinstein and colleagues' analysis of the 1970 British cohort study finds that non-cognitions had a considerable effect in determining non-labour market outcomes for this cohort (Feinstein and Bynner, forthcoming). Young people with good communication skills and relationships with others (which is known as an 'internalising score') were four per cent less likely to smoke, three per cent less likely to offend, one per cent less likely to have been a teenage parent and three per cent more likely to have voted in the 1997 general election compared to the average, and considerably more likely than those with poor communication skills to do these things. Young people with an internal locus of control were four per cent less likely to be racially intolerant by age 30, and those with high self esteem were two per cent less likely to suffer low life satisfaction, experience depression or smoke.

These findings are powerful indicators that non-cognitions underpin both major concerns about young people identified in the previous chapters: that educational and economic progress appears to have stalled for the most disadvantaged, and that many young people lack the social, behavioural and non-cognitive capacity to engage successfully in adult life and

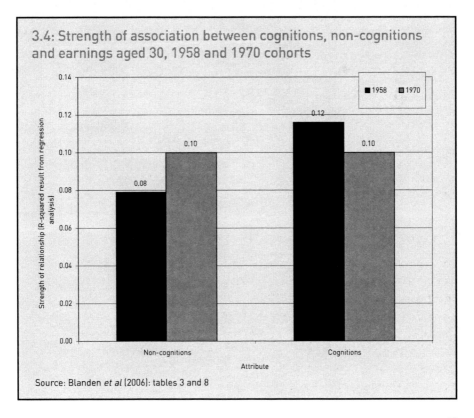

3.4: Strength of association between cognitions, non-cognitions and earnings aged 30, 1958 and 1970 cohorts

Source: Blanden *et al* (2006): tables 3 and 8

wider society in modern Britain. The widespread concerns about antisocial behaviour and moral decline thus appear more justified when we consider this evidence. But has this changed over time?

The increasing importance of non-cognitions

Comparing the 1958 and 1970 cohorts allows us to see whether the relative importance of personal and social skills and personality attributes has become more important. The evidence suggests that they have, as shown in Figure 3.4: for the 1958 cohort, the strength of the association between non-cognitions and higher earnings was 0.08,[9] whereas for the 1970 cohort it was 0.10. At the same time, the strength of the association between cognitions and earnings fell from 0.12 to 0.10.

Another way of putting this is that non-cognitions became 25 per cent more important in determining earnings later in life between the 1958 and 1970 cohort, while cognitions became 20 per cent less important. But what explains this shift? And has it continued for later cohorts? We turn to these questions in the next chapter.

References

Note: web references correct at September 2006

Arneson R (1989) 'Equality and equality of opportunity for welfare' *Philosophical Studies* 56 (1): 205-14

Banfield J, Pendry L, Mewse A and Edwards M (2003) 'The effects of an elderly stereotype prime on reaching and grasping actions' *Social Cognition* 21: 299-319

Blanden J, Gregg P and Macmillan L (2006) *Accounting for Intergenerational Income Persistence: Non-Cognitive Skills, Ability and Education* London: Centre for the Economics of Education, London School of Economics

Blundell R, Dearden L and Sianesi B (2001) *Estimating the Returns to Education: Models, Methods and Results* London: University College London and Institute for Fiscal Studies

Bowles S and Gintis H (2001) *Schooling in Capitalist America Revisited* Massachusetts: University of Massachusetts

Burchardt T (2003) *Being and becoming: Social exclusion and the onset of disability.* CASE Report 21. London: CASE

Burchardt T (2004) 'Capabilities and diability: the capabilities framework and the

---

9. On an r-squared measure

social model of disability' *Disability and Society* 19 (7): 735-51

Burchardt T and Le Grand J (2002) *Constraint and Opportunity: Identifying Voluntary Non-Employment.* CASE Research paper 55 London: CASE/LSE

Bynner J (2005) 'Reconstructing the Youth Phase of the Life Course; the Case of Emerging Adulthood' *Journal of Youth Studies* 8: 367-84

Cohen G (1989) 'On the currency of egalitarian justice' *Ethics* 99: 906-44

Department for Education and Skills (DfES) (2005) *Every Child Matters Outcomes Framework* London: TSO

Dixon M (2006) *Rethinking Financial Capability: Lessons from economic psychology and behavioural finance* London: Institute for Public Policy Research, available at: www.ippr.org.uk/ecomm/files/financial_capabilities.pdf

Donne J (1624) *Devotions Upon Emergent Occasions: Meditation 17* London: Printed by Augustine Mathewes for Thomas Iones

Duckworth A and Seligman M (2005) 'Self-Discipline Outdoes IQ in Predicting Academic Performance of Adolescents' *Psychological Science* 16(12)

Dunifon R and Duncan G (1998) 'Long-Run Effects of Motivation on Labor-Market Success' *Social Psychology Quarterly* 61 (1): 33-48

Evans K (2002) 'Taking control of their lives? Agency in young adult transitions in England and the New Germany' *Journal of Youth Studies* 5(3): 245-69

Farkas G (2003) 'Cognitive Skills and Noncognitive Traits and Behaviors in Stratification Processes' *Annual Review of Sociology* 29: 541-62

Feinstein L (2000) *The relative economic importance of academic, psychological and behavioural attributes developed in childhood* Brighton: University of Sussex, available at: www.sussex.ac.uk/Units/economics/dp/Feinstein2.pdf

Feinstein L and Bynner J (forthcoming) *The benefits of assets in childhood as protection against adult social exclusion: the relative effects of financial, human, social and psychological assets.* Unpublished mimeo, London: Institute of Education

Goldthorpe J (2003) 'The myth of education-based meritocracy ' *New Economy* 10 (4): 187-248

Groves M (2005) 'How Important Is Your Personality? Labor Market Returns to Personality for Women in the US and UK' *Journal of Economic Psychology* 26 (6): 827-41

Hansard (2003) *Lifetime Earnings: Graduates and the National Average. 25 Feb 2003: Column WA27* London: Parliament, available at: www.publications.parliament.uk/pa/ld200203/ldhansrd/vo030225/text/30225 w04.htm

Heckman J (2000) 'Policies to Foster Human Capital' *Research in Economics* 54 (1): 3-56

Heckman J and Rubenstein Y (2001) 'The Importance of Noncognitive Skills: Lessons from the GED Testing Program' *American Economic Review* 91 (2): 145-49

Heckman J, Stixrud J and Urzua S (2006) 'The Effects of Cognitive and Noncognitive Abilities on Labor Market Outcomes and Social Behaviour.' *NBER Working Paper* 12006 Cambridge, MA: National Bureau of Economic Research

HM Treasury (2006) *GDP deflators at market prices, and money GDP* London: TSO

Hurley S (2006 forthcoming) *The Public Ecology of Responsibility* London: Institute for Public Policy Research

Jackson M (2006) 'Personality Traits and Occupational Attainment' *European Sociological Review* 22 (2): 187-99

Jackson M (2006, forthcoming) *How Far Merit Selection? Social Stratification and the Labour Market.* Unpublished draft. Oxford: Nuffield College

Kahneman D (2002) *Map of Bounded Rationality: A perspective on intuitive judgement and choice* Nobel Prize Lecture, 8 December, available at: http://nobelprize.org/economics/laureates/2002/kahnemann-lecture.pdf

Le Grand J (1984) 'Equity as an economic objective' *Journal of Applied Philosophy* I: 39-51

Le Grand J (1991) *Equity and Choice: An Essay in Economics and Applied Philosophy* London: Harper Collins

Middleton S, Perren K, Maguire S, Rennison J, Battistin E, Emmerson C and Fitzsimons E (2005) *Evaluation of Education Maintenance Allowance Pilots: Young People Aged 16-19 Years Final Report of the Quantitative Evaluation* London: TSO, available at: www.dfes.gov.uk/research/data/uploadfiles/RR678.pdf

Nussbaum M (2000) *Women and Human Development* Cambridge: Cambridge University Press

Nussbaum M (2006) *Frontiers of Justice: Disability, Nationality, Species Membership* Harvard: Belknap Press

Nussbaum M and Sen A (1993) *The Quality of Life* Oxford: Clarendon Press

Roemer J (1998) *Equality of Opportunity* Cambridge, Mass.: Harvard University Press

Rotter J (1954) *Social learning and clinical psychology* New York: Prentice-Hall

Rotter J (1966) 'Generalized expectancies for internal versus external control of reinforcement' *Psychological Monographs* (80)

Schwartz B (2004) *The Paradox of Choice* New York: Harper Collins

Sen A (1979) 'Personal Utilities and Public Judgements: What's wrong with Welfare Economics?' *Economic Journal* 89: 537-58

Sen A (1980) 'Equality of What?' in McMurrin S (ed.) *Tanner lectures on Human Values* Cambridge: Cambridge University Press

Sen A (1985) *Commodities and Capabilities* Amsterdam: North Holland

Sen A (1987) *The Standard of Living* Cambridge: Cambridge University Press

Sen A (1995) *Inequality Re-examined* Oxford: Clarendon Press

Sen A (1999) *Development as Freedom* Oxford: Oxford University Press

Sianesi B (2003) *Returns to Education: A Non-Technical Summary of CEE Work and Policy Discussion* London: IFS/CEE

Sugden R (1998) 'The metric of opportunity' *Economics and Philosophy* 14: 307-37

Sunstein C and Thaler H (2003) *Libertarian Paternalism is not an Oxymoron* Working Paper 03-2 Washington, DC: AEI-Brookings Joint Center for Regulatory Studies

Vizard P (2005) *The Contributions of Professor Amartya Sen in the Field of Human Rights* CASE paper 91 London: CASE

Walker I and Zhu Y (2001) *The Returns to Education: Evidence from the Labour Force Surveys* DfES Research Report 313 London: TSO

4: Why agency and soft skills matter so much

In 1749 the German philosopher Gottfried Achenwall published the first volume of his *Statistik* (Achenwall 1749), collating for the first time a range of data about the activities and spread of the state. This was an early example of an enduring fascination for statistics: over the following decades his ideas and approach spread around the world on a tide of Enlightenment idealism as historians and political scientists embraced the emerging science of statistics in their efforts to identify the fundamental trends and drivers shaping the world (Johnson and Kotz 1997). By 1791 political econometrics had reached Britain, with the publication of the 21-volume opus *Statistical Account of Scotland*, which detailed the state of the nation 'for the purpose of ascertaining the quantum of happiness enjoyed by its inhabitants, and the means of its future improvement' (Sinclair 1749: XX, xiii).

Fast-forward more than two hundred years and evidence-based policy-making is firmly entrenched in the mechanics of government, and countless commentators and academic departments routinely chart societal shifts. This chapter draws on the best examples of this recent research to identify the major economic and social changes in Britain that have contributed to the growing salience of personal and social skills in determining life chances, and considers implications for the future. It argues that an unequal distribution of these skills, in combination with these shifts, can go a long way towards explaining the pattern of youth outcomes identified in chapter 2. In the final section we point towards a policy response, which we develop in the rest of this report.

There have been four major economic and social changes. The first is the changing structure of individual firms and the labour market as a whole – largely in its shift towards a service economy and a polarisation of jobs – which has increased the financial returns to softer skills for both employers and employees. This is relatively well charted and understood.

The second is that routes through life in education, employment and many other areas have become more open and preference based: the often oppressive but structured pathways that young people were expected to take have largely dissolved, with the result that most young people have more say over their lives than ever before. The typology of transitions has become more variegated as young people's experiences have become more diverse. This has resulted in young people's decision-making capacity becoming a more important determinant of their capabilities: as making the right choice from an ever wider field of options has become more important, so has the actual capacity to do so.

The third has been a shift in public policy that has emphasised choice, voice, personalisation and co-production in public services – partly in response to shifts in the private sector, which has increasingly concentrated on tailored, individual and customised services and delivery.

The fourth change has been a widening inequality in income, employment, the quality of jobs, wealth and civic participation. The last few decades – at least until very recently – have seen an unremitting widening of the gap between the best- and worst-off. This societal polarisation has exacerbated and amplified the divisions between those who succeed and those who do not – resulting in a larger gap between those who make successful transitions and those who do not. We chart these trends in more detail below.

The service economy and changing skill needs

As the last chapter showed, half of the impact of self-esteem, a third of the impact of an internal locus of control and a fifth of the impact of application on earnings aged 30 for the cohort of young people born in 1970 occurred post-education, in the labour market and beyond. But what made the labour market this group experienced so different from that of previous generations, and have the underlying trends continued?

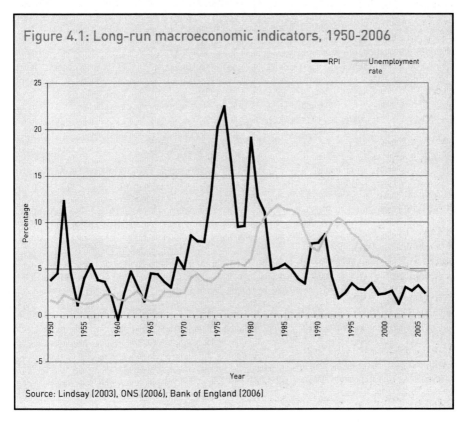

Figure 4.1: Long-run macroeconomic indicators, 1950-2006

Source: Lindsay (2003), ONS (2006), Bank of England (2006)

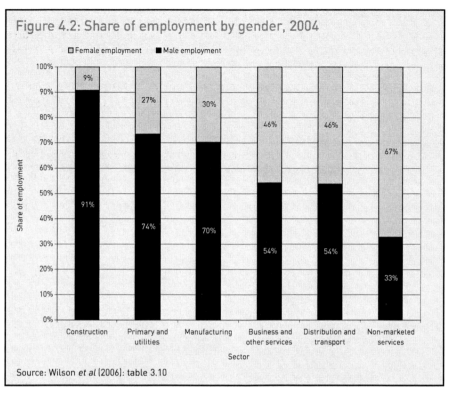

Figure 4.2: Share of employment by gender, 2004

☐ Female employment   ■ Male employment

Source: Wilson *et al* (2006): table 3.10

The last decade has certainly been one of almost unprecedented prosperity. As many Treasury reports note, unemployment is at a historic low, employment at a historic high and both inflation and interest rates remain low (HM Treasury 2006; Lindsay 2003). The economy is certainly in much better shape than it has been since the early 1970s, when inflation rose dramatically, and the mid 1980s and early 1990s which saw boom and bust macroeconomic cycles, as shown in Figure 4.1 (Lindsay 2003; Bank of England 2006; ONS 2006).

On these simple indicators, the labour market looks relatively similar today to that of the 1950s and early 1960s. But the picture is in fact radically different. The last few decades have seen some fundamental shifts to the structure of the British labour market, not least in the rising economic participation of women and a partly related shift to a service economy.

Although female employment had been rising throughout the early 20th Century, the Second World War catalysed a surge in women entering the labour market, causing American officials and employers to coin the term 'womanpower' to describe women's contribution to the civilian and military economy (Walsh and Wrigley 2001). Since then, female employment rates have continued to rise, from 45.9 per cent in 1955 to 70.1 per cent in early 2006 (Walsh and Wrigley 2001; ONS 2006). But despite this growing equality in participation, there are still considerable differences between the kinds of work women do and those that men do.

Women remain much more likely to work part time (Wilson *et al* 2006). And as Figure 4.2 shows, they are also more likely to work in service sectors than their male counterparts. In 2004, 67 per cent of employees in the non-marketed (public) services and 46 per cent of those in business and other services were women, compared to just 9 per cent in construction and 30 per cent in manufacturing.

This shift towards growing female employment in the service sector has had important implications for the structure of the economy and labour markets by stimulating demand for services over manufactured goods: many of the jobs that women were doing unpaid in the home and community have moved into the commercial rather than domestic sector. This has caused a kind of 'feedback effect': as more job opportunities open up in service industries, more women have taken up paid employment, creating more demand for services.

This trend towards greater female employment meant that the UK underwent a particularly strong industrial shakeout throughout the 1980s and now has one of the most service-orientated economies in the world (Dixon and Pearce 2005). This has been in combination with higher productivity growth in manufacturing than in services, leading to reduced relative demand for workers in manufacturing industries (Baumol 1967; Rowthorn 2004); the effects of 'globalisation', as some imports replaced domestic industries (McQuaid 2002; Rowthorn and Coutts 2004); and ris-

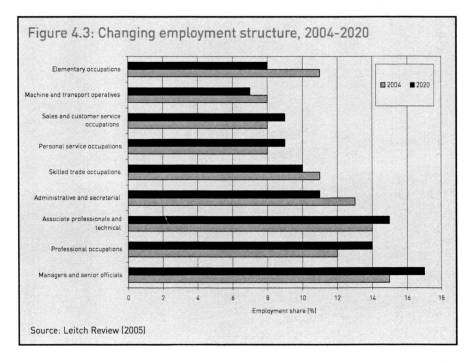

Figure 4.3: Changing employment structure, 2004-2020

Source: Leitch Review (2005)

ing GDP, which has led to a greater demand for services because as their income rises people tend to spend more on them (Hills 2004).

In 1982, 33.6 per cent of total UK employment was in the manufacturing, construction and utilities sectors and 65.4 per cent was in the service sector. Two decades later, in 2002, manufacturing employment had declined by 35 per cent and service employment had grown by 20 per cent (Wilson *et al* 2006). This is a shift that is ongoing and expected to continue over the next decade at least: by 2014 service sector employment is projected to be 82.1 per cent of all employment, with manufacturing, construction and utilities having declined to just 17.9 per cent (ibid). Looking in more detail at projected employment growth in the future shows this clearly (Leitch Review 2005), as shown in Figure 4.3. The jobs projected to show the fastest growth, such as professional and managerial occupations, are predominantly service-sector-based.

But why have these shifts meant that personal and social skills are more important in determining labour market outcomes? Our understanding of this issue is still in its infancy and there have been few detailed or conclusive economic analyses. Nevertheless there are many plausible theories.

Perhaps the most intuitive is that some service occupations simply require more human interaction than manufacturing ones; research consistently shows that skills do not transfer easily from many jobs within manufacturing to services (Iverson 2001). As the structure of professions has changed, so too has the skill requirement in favour of softer skills in some occupations (Jackson 2002; Jackson forthcoming). Even relatively highly technically skilled manufacturing workers often find it difficult to find acceptable employment in the service sectors (Hay 2004). In North East England, for example, rapid deindustrialisation has led to a considerable rise in inactivity and incapacity rates for older men and a corresponding rise in (largely female) public and service sector employment (Gibbons *et al* 2006). But similar effects can also be seen nationally.

A recent survey of nearly 75,000 companies revealed that employers are most concerned about gaps in 'soft skill areas, in particular team working and customer handling skills' (LSC 2006: 12), as shown in Figure 4.4. Nearly 40 per cent of British employers reported shortages in customer-handling skills and around 35 per cent reported shortages in oral communication and team-working skills.

Importantly, Figure 4.4 shows that employers' perceptions of soft skill shortages were more pronounced for elementary occupations than for higher-level occupations, suggesting that many disadvantaged workers are trapped in elementary occupations by their soft skills and that these often lie behind limited prospects for progression. This may partly explain why the shift to a service economy has exacerbated the impact of poor soft skills in limiting life chances and reducing social mobility.

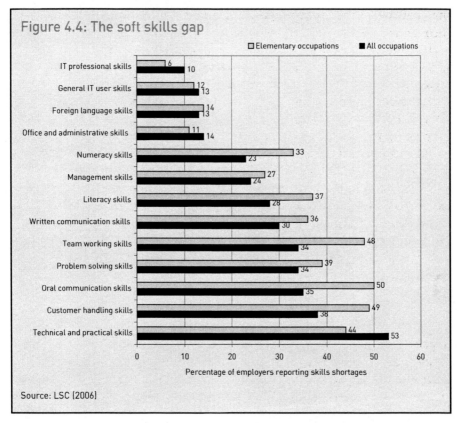

Figure 4.4: The soft skills gap

☐ Elementary occupations   ■ All occupations

Skill	Elementary occupations	All occupations
IT professional skills	6	10
General IT user skills	12	13
Foreign language skills	14	13
Office and administrative skills	11	14
Numeracy skills	33	23
Management skills	27	24
Literacy skills	37	28
Written communication skills	36	30
Team working skills	48	34
Problem solving skills	39	34
Oral communication skills	50	35
Customer handling skills	49	38
Technical and practical skills	44	53

Percentage of employers reporting skills shortages

Source: LSC (2006)

Business leaders also highlight the growing salience of personal and social skills. A report based on interviews with 1,656 senior executives earlier this year reveals that this group firmly believes that harnessing softer skills will become of increasingly paramount importance to successful companies:

> ...the focus of management attention [in 2020] will be on the areas of the business, from innovation to customer service, where personal chemistry or creative insight matter more than rules and processes ... [Value] will lie in hard-to-replicate personal relationships between employees, customers and suppliers.

(EUI 2006: 3)

These views stem from an awareness of macroeconomic shifts. But they are reinforced by senior executives' perceptions of changes to the internal structure of firms, technological change, and evolving working and management practices. Fifty years ago William Whyte's book *The Organisation Man* encapsulated the experience of corporate life for a generation – one in which long service, obedience and loyalty were the prerequisites for success. The contemporary corporate world was highly structured: lines of authority were clearly drawn on charts and decisions were taken at the top (Whyte 1956). But the last few decades have seen a sharp decline in this kind of organisational framework.

Companies have fundamentally changed their internal organisation, shedding layers of middle management and splitting into more autonomous teams that can work flexibly to suit particular projects or temporary requirements. This has meant that many employees have had to become better at shifting between roles, and develop the skills needed to work in more flexible and team-based structures. In management-speak 'decentralised', 'multi-skilled', 'multi-disciplinary' project teams now work autonomously, albeit bound together by a 'shared strategic overview' (Partington 1996; Thesmar and Theoenig 2000). The upshot for employees is that communication, learning and motivational skills have become far more valuable to firms (Egger and Grossmann 2004). This is particularly true in sectors where technological change has happened the fastest.

Recent research shows that the rise of information and communication technology (ICT) in firms has increased the return to general (softer) skills and reduced the relative importance of job-specific technical skills (Kirby and Riley 2006), partly because ICT has 'polarised' the labour market – widening the gap between 'lovely' and 'lousy' jobs as computers and technology replace labour in the middle of the labour market (Autor *et al* 2003; Goos and Manning 2004; Dixon and Pearce 2005).

The idea is simple: as computer technology – in both offices and manufacturing – has become cheaper and more widespread, it has replaced employment in the kinds of jobs that can be relatively easily automated. These jobs tend to be ones that are routine or require a high degree of precision and repetition: computers are very good at detail and reiteration but comparatively useless at tasks that require discretion or people skills (Goos and Manning 2004). Importantly, these 'technology-proof' jobs tend to be located at either end of the labour market: making sandwiches, serving coffee and taking board-level decisions require the kinds of skills that computers find difficult. As computers have become more ubiquitous, they have replaced the 'middle' of the labour market, where jobs were relatively routine, and so employment growth has come largely at the top and bottom of the labour market (Wilson *et al* 2006).

There have been at least two important implications of this process. The first and most obvious is that personal and social skills – the kinds of attributes technology cannot adequately replicate – have become more valuable to employers. The latest data appears to show that as the use of generic skills in the workplace has increased, high level communication and computer skills became much more strongly correlated with high returns (Dickerson and Green 2004).

A second important implication of this technological shift is that many of the 'stepping stone' jobs in the middle of the labour market, which people formerly used as a pathway from low-skill jobs to better pay and more responsibilities, have simply vanished from the labour market, potentially leaving those without good formal qualifications or the soft skills necessary to progress relatively stranded (Dixon and Pearce 2005).

These shifts help explain why personal and social skills have become more important once young people have entered the labour market. But what underpins their growing importance in determining educational attainment?

More diverse routes through education

As the last chapter showed, 30 per cent of the impact of application and 17 per cent of the impact of an internal locus of control on earnings aged 30 for the 1970 cohort was due to their importance in young people's O-level achievement. But the story of how the experience of navigating the British education system has changed over time and the implications for young people's personal and social skill requirements is a complex and nuanced one.

First, the introduction of the National Curriculum in the late 1980s has encouraged many commentators to assume that the role of personal choice in educational outcomes has become less important for today's young people. Yet it is also apparent, if we look a little further back, that developments since the 1960s have increased the importance of agency and personal skills for more recent generations, albeit within a more regulated system. Between 1944 and 1965, the 11-plus exam set the majority of young people down one of two paths. Those who 'passed' went on to a strictly academic education in a grammar school, while those who 'failed' attended a Secondary Modern school. Some grammar school pupils could be expected to continue post-16 and even to higher education; few of those who failed the 11-plus had similar prospects, as moving from one strand to the other was almost impossible (Sampson 1965)[10].

Although the system was intended to provide young people with the skills they would need later in life, its deterministic view of children's prospects and capabilities came to be resented by many parents and pupils, who regarded the system as oppressive and limiting. By the early 1950s, comprehensive schools – which had already been successful in Sweden – had started to spread across the country and in 1965 the newly elected Labour government requested, in Tony Crosland's famous circular, that all Local Education Authorities consider moving to a fully comprehensive system (Ministry of Education 1965). A decade later, the system was implemented throughout most of the UK and the pathways and educational

---

10. The 11-plus is still in force in a number of local authorities in England, such as Kent, and for some schools, such as those in Birmingham. Northern Ireland still has the 11-plus but it is about to be abolished.

options open to most young people had expanded considerably.

Marketising reforms under the Conservative government culminated in the 1988 Education Reform Act, which made considerable changes to the structure of the education system and introduced a National Curriculum – making it compulsory for schools to teach certain subjects and syllabuses for the first time. Importantly, it also reinstated 'open enrolment' and choice for parents, which meant that parental influences on which school their children went to became far more important (Timmins 2001).

Despite the dominance of the National Curriculum, Labour's education reforms since 1997 have arguably continued to emphasise choice and autonomy for parents and children alike, but with greater focus on meeting the personal needs of each child ('personalised learning'). The most recent round of reforms outlined in the 2005 White Paper *Higher Standards, Better Schools for All* continue this direction of reform (DfES 2005), arguably reinforcing the importance of agency, planning and motivation in determining which schools young people attend.

These structural shifts at the system level have been mirrored by changes to the way pupils are taught and examined. In response to growing dissatisfaction with an elitist examination system, the Certificate of Extended Education (CEE) was introduced in 1976 to meet needs of 'non-traditional' sixth formers, which was soon followed by the 1983 launch of Certificates of Pre-Vocational Education (CPVE). These rejected a single subject model of CEE for vocationally-based courses, allowing students to sample different 'vocational areas', expanding the range of qualification and subject options open to young people. But by the mid 1980s this division between 'certificate' and 'non-certificate' pupils was increasingly seen as restrictive and GCSEs were introduced in 1986, again opening up curriculum and subject choice (Wrights and Oancea 2005; Croxford *et al* 2006). Ongoing reforms to the National Qualifications Framework have extended this flexibility further.

At the same time, coursework and modular examinations became more prevalent, meaning that pupils were less able to ensure success through cramming in the summer term and making results more dependent on young people's concentration, application and self-discipline over longer periods. Pedagogy changed in parallel: rote learning, once the default in many schools, has been replaced by a variety of more interactive techniques, including co-construction, peer learning, peer mentoring and a focus on group work (DfES 2005).

Emerging evidence from the US shows that this may begin to explain why girls have begun to outperform boys in formal education almost across the board, as we highlighted in chapter 2. Recent longitudinal work tracking the performance of girls and boys in US high schools has shown that girls tend to be more self-disciplined and that this explains between 40 and 54 per cent of the difference in attainment between genders (Duckworth and Seligman 2006). But the analysis in chapter 3 shows that soft skills are now more important in determining successful transitions post-16 too.

Education to employment

From the post-war period to the mid-1970s, the pathways young people followed from compulsory education to work were relatively straightforward and homogenous. For the majority of young people, leaving school was swiftly followed by getting a job – usually involving some form of apprenticeship, at least for boys (Ferri 1993). Relatively few continued on to higher education – just three per cent in 1950 – but for those that did, relatively stable employment soon followed. But by the end of the 1970s, transition routes were beginning to be more diverse: as youth labour markets collapsed under the pressures of rapid deindustrialisation, it became increasingly difficult to move directly into work (Bynner *et al* 2002), and rising unemployment set school-leavers in direct competition with more experienced workers in the hunt for jobs. By the early 1980s, a deep recession compounded the difficulties young people faced in labour markets as large-scale unemployment followed (see Figure 4.1 above).

The rest of the 1980s saw continued declining prospects for young people attempting to go directly into employment from school (Banks *et al* 1992). The Government introduced a national Youth Training Scheme, which aimed to give all school-leavers one year's training (subsequently extended to two) and incorporated existing apprenticeships[11] (Bynner *et al* 2002). But this scheme met with limited success. By the end of the 1980s, many young people underwent a long period of diverse training schemes and short-term jobs before finding a niche in the adult labour market (Evans and Furlgon 1997; Bynner *et al* 2002).

For increasing numbers of others who continued in higher education, the transition from education to the labour market had become similarly heterogeneous. Graduates now commonly take non-graduate jobs while searching for employment that could make use of their degree skills and knowledge. And there is some evidence that the transition to graduate employment after qualification is taking longer for women, suggesting greater complexity in pathways (Elias and Purcell 2003). Sociological research has also pointed to a more complex typology of graduate jobs, as the traditional destinations of established professions have been complemented by the emergence of 'modern graduate occupations' in new professions such as management, IT and creative vocational sectors; 'new' and 'niche' occupations in marketing, sales, advertising and social work; as well

---

11. This has since evolved through modern apprenticeships into the current foundation and advanced apprenticeship.

as growing numbers of graduates occupying 'non-graduate' occupations (ibid).

These changes have meant that the experiences of young people moving from education to the labour market are becoming less certain, less predictable, more diverse and increasingly heterogeneous. Young people are decreasingly able to rely on formal organisational structures to guide them straightforwardly into a job, and more dependent on their own agency and motivation. But these shifts have not been limited to education and labour markets. As the analysis in the previous chapter showed, 53 per cent of the impact of non-cognitions on social mobility occurs later in life – part of which is due to changes in the way people interact with the private sector.

The new private sector

In 1923, Henry Ford, the paragon of cutting-edge contemporary manufacturing, famously wrote that 'any customer can have a car painted any colour that he wants so long as it is black' (Ford and Crowther 1923: IV). Eighty-three years later the new Ford Focus – the modern Model T and Europe's best-selling car – comes in 12 colours. Potential customers can also choose from four body styles, nine 'series', 13 engines, two interior trims, and 21 further 'options' (Ford 2006) – a bewildering array of more than 230,000 possible combinations. In post-Fordist modern capitalism, the most successful firms have been those which have responded best to consumer preferences and adapted their products and services to individual requirements (Amin 1994; Wigfield 2001; Koch 2006).

For much of the twentieth century, (predominantly male) workers took home their cash in a weekly pay packet; relatively few had need of bank accounts. As living standards increased and people's disposable income grew – partly due to women entering the labour market, creating dual-earner households – people began to turn to intermediaries to help secure and manage their money. And over the last few decades there has been a shift in people's personal financial portfolios (Kempson and Whyley 1999; FSA 2003).

Following the deregulatory 'big bang' of 1986 and subsequent reforms that increased competition in financial markets, there was a large expansion in the scale, scope and range of financial services offered to consumers. Building societies demutualised and raised finance through share offerings, increasing the range of providers, and financial service institutions began to offer a much wider range of products than before. Total lending more than doubled from £531 billion in 1993 to £1,077 billion in 2005 and consumer credit expanded even faster, by 167 per cent over the same period (Babb et al 2006).[12]

These structural shifts meant that people's ability to manage their finances and choose between complex financial products – their 'financial capability' (FSA 2003) – has become more important (Dixon 2006; FSA 2006). Yet in early 2006 just 17 million adults in the UK were successfully making ends meet, keeping track, planning ahead, choosing products and staying informed about financial products. As many as 10.5 million were experiencing considerable difficulty in one of these areas, 3.8 million faced severe problems in two, 6.2 million lacked capability in three areas, 8.6 million in four, and 1.4 million were succeeding in none (Dixon 2006).

And younger generations are far less likely to be coping well: recent research shows that even accounting for age, affluence and experience, young people are faring worse on all indicators of financial capability (Atkinson *et al* 2006) – with severe problems occurring relatively frequently among the most deprived young people.

Cognitive skills are of course particularly important here: without basic levels of numeracy and literacy, financial capability is impossible, so initially we should acknowledge the increasing important of 'hard skills'. But non-cognitions are central too, as financial problems often result from behavioural and agentic problems – finding it difficult to resist impulse purchases or plan ahead for the longer term.

Importantly, there is growing consensus among key industry players, consumer groups and policymakers that unless people's softer financial management skills improve, there will be serious consequences for their own well-being, the British economy and future prosperity. Policymakers in this area are beginning to promote a strategy aimed at empowering people to change their behaviour, through improving their softer skills, by making use of the latest emerging evidence from the behavioural and cognitive sciences (Dixon 2006).

The state of debate is particularly advanced in financial services sector because the expansion of choice and resulting complexity has clearly created substantial market failure and exacerbated social exclusion. But recent shifts in this industry are not isolated; they are indicative of wider trends in the private sector – towards personalisation, choice and the importance of discretion and preference – which have made softer skills and agency more important in getting a good deal and appropriate products. The shift to a service economy has meant that good personal and social skills are important in getting a good job; but it has also meant that they are also crucial in getting a good deal *from* the private sector. And they are increasingly important in engaging with public services too.

---

12. Prices indexed to 2004

Choice, agency and public services

As the last chapter showed, personal and social skills are important in making the most of 'harder' attributes, such as IQ or qualifications. Nearly half the benefit of good application and an internal locus of control occurs through this interaction, which highlights the importance of softer skills and attributes in helping people make suitable choices. This has arguably been particularly important in public services over the last three decades in the light of a concerted expansion of both 'responsibility' and 'choice' in the welfare state (Timmins 2001; Stanley *et al* 2004; Pearce and Paxton 2005), and a growing consensus that personal responsibility will be important in determining service delivery (Halpern *et al* 2004), prompted by moral and political arguments as much as fiscal concerns.

As family structures became more complex over the course of the latter half of the 20th century, benefit receipt became increasingly tied to conditions, particularly through expanded active labour market policy as a way of incentivising individuals to take up employment (Stanley *et al* 2004; Mulgan 2005). The driving motivations have been varied, including increasing economic efficiency; reducing poverty, and particularly child poverty, through higher employment; and an appeal to fairness in the face of the growing injustice and inequity of a contribution-based system – it became increasingly apparent that people should be able to access benefits without having made any prior contributions, but that they should have to fulfil certain obligations in return.

'New Public Management' and subsequent shifts in thinking have led to a conception of citizens as active consumers of public services, in which personal 'choice' is more important, as both a delivery mechanism and a valuable end in itself (Pearce and Paxton 2005; Byrne *et al* 2006). And the 'empowerment agenda' steadily gaining ground across government similarly sees more active citizens as crucial to more effective governance (Miliband 2006).

Similar philosophical shifts have altered the underlying structure of public services over the last few decades. Bevan's NHS was built on the foundations of a command and control war economy in which conscription and rationing had homogenised experiences through shared risk and pooled hardship. Collective action to solve national problems was deeply embedded in the national psyche and the state had become the focal point for national solidarity. But the last few decades have seen a shift against this model: as the private sector has become better at providing increasingly personalised, tailored public services, public expectations of public services have shifted in a similar direction and policymakers have become increasingly cognisant of the need for public services to be user-friendly and responsive (Hills 2004; Mulgan 2005; Taylor 2006) – to be driven by user 'choice'.

In this context, choice means tailored services that are flexible, available at times and in places to suit citizens, and responsive to user needs (Hills 2004; Taylor 2006). Sometimes this view shades into a broader narrative of 'personalisation' but the key is simply that services are better aligned to individual requirements. Some have pushed for more radical reform, for a full-blooded concept of marketised public services, in which competition drives change and national targets, the role of commissioners and local democracy all become increasingly redundant and individual choices determine resource flows and patterns of service delivery. Under this conception, all that is required to support choice are clear, impartial information, a funding framework in which money follows users and a robust inspection regime.

The impact of these shifts in public service delivery for the importance of agency and personal and social skills is not yet entirely clear. One commonly cited concern is that expanding personal choice does not always deliver socially equitable outcomes because the middle classes are better able to make use of soft networks, greater knowledge and 'pushiness' to secure the best places in the best schools and treatment with the best specialist (Pearce and Paxton 2005; Farrington-Douglas and Allen 2005). This has led to a concerted policy effort to promote 'empowerment strategies' for disadvantaged groups, such as providing additional support to make sure everyone understands their entitlement to choice and voice and how to exercise that entitlement (Farrington-Douglas and Allen 2005; Taylor 2006).

These empowerment strategies are important in the context of greater personalisation and user voice within public service reform – a direction that shows little sign of altering. But they are in a sense merely palliative: we also need to recognise that public service reform is just one area in which agency and soft skills are becoming more important.

Explaining youth outcomes

By 2006, clear differences can be seen between the experiences of today's young people and their counterparts in the early 1970s or earlier. The analysis in this chapter has shown that *fundamental structural trends and drivers*, arising from global and domestic socio-economic and cultural shifts, are making these factors more important in determining outcomes throughout people's lives – in education, in the labour market and in interactions with the state. Youth pathways from education to work have become more protracted than they were previously; more complex, in that younger people pass through more states on average; more heterogeneous, in that there is greater diversity across all young people; and these pathways are subject to influence of greater diversity of factors (Dixon and Pearce 2005). In combination, these shifts mean that young people now have 'available, at least in principle, a more extended set of opportunities than at any other time' (Bynner 2005: 15) and go a long way towards explaining why young people's agency and softer skills have become more important in determining whether they flourish or flounder (Schwartz 2004).

They also go some way towards explaining the pattern of youth outcomes observed in chapter 2. In many of the areas in which there is entrenched disadvantage, or growing inequality between the experiences of most young people and their less fortunate peers, agency, behaviour and choice are crucial determinants of success. From teen pregnancy to obesity to post-compulsory educational participation, young people's early choices now reverberate through their lives to a greater degree than ever before.

Developing personal and social skills

The key idea here is that as pathways through education to work became less structured (and often less oppressive), making the right decision, having long-term plans and being able to see them through became more important in shaping success. The decline of educational and economic structures that traditionally shaped young people's lives was an inevitable result of deeper, underlying shifts in the domestic and global economy (Dixon and Pearce 2005). This was in many ways a positive development. But the gradual removal of the constraints of traditional pathways meant that those with the capacity to take advantage of formal opportunities had unprecedented chances to succeed in education and the emerging labour market.

These trends would inevitably lead to greater inequality if people did not have equal opportunities to develop the personal and social capabilities that were vital for success in this changing world (Bynner 2005). As the research outlined in this report shows, Britain remains deeply unequal when viewed from this perspective – perhaps more so than from traditional measures. By glossing over the way young people develop agency and personal and social skills, policy has left a legacy of entrenched inequality of life chances. Policy needs to move beyond providing advice and guidance to a broader approach that makes better use of the best research, experience and theory about how people develop agency, motivation and personal and social skills. We examine this evidence from the behavioural sciences – psychology and sociology – in the next chapter.

References

Note: web references correct at September 2006

Achenwall G (1749) *Abriß der neuen Staatswissenschaft der vornehmen Europäischen Reiche und Republiken* Göttingen: University of Göttingen

Amin A (1994) *Post-Fordism: A Reader* Oxford: Blackwell Publishing

Atkinson A, McKay S, Kempson E and Collard S (2006) *Levels of financial capability in the UK. Results of a baseline survey* Bristol: University of Bristol

Autor D, Levy F and Murnane R (2003) 'The Skill Content of Recent Technological Change: An Empirical Exploration' *Quarterly Journal of Economics* 118 1279-333

Babb P, Butcher H, Church J and Zealey L (2006) *Social Trends* 36 London: TSO, available at: www.statistics.gov.uk/downloads/theme_social/Social_Trends36/Social_Trends_36.pdf

Bank of England (2006) *Statistical Interactive Database – official bank rate history* London: Bank of England

Banks M, Breakwell G, Bynner J, Emler N, Jameson L and Roberts K (1992) *Careers and Identities* Buckingham: Open University Press

Baumol W (1967) 'Macroeconomics of Unbalanced Growth: The Anatomy of Urban Crisis' *American Economic Review* 57

Bynner J (2005) 'Reconstructing the Youth Phase of the Life Course; the Case of Emerging Adulthood' *Journal of Youth Studies* 8: 367-84

Bynner J, Elias P, McKnight A, Pan H and Pierre G (2002) *Young people's changing routes to independence* York: York Publishing Services

Byrne L, Purnell J and Taylor M (2006) *Power to the People: Next steps for New Labour* London: Progress, available at: www.egovmonitor.com/reports/POWER%20TO%20THE%20PEOPLE.pdf

Croxford L, Howieson C, Iannelli C, Raffe D and Shapira M (2006) 'Trends in Education and Youth Transition Across Britain 1984-2002' *Education and Social Change: England, Wales and Scotland 1984-2002* Edinburgh: Centre for Educational Sociology, 12 May 2006

Department for Education and Skills (DfES) (2005) *Higher standards, better schools for all* White Paper, London: TSO

Dickerson A and Green F (2004) 'The growth and valuation of computing and other generic skills' *Oxford Economic Papers* 56 (3): 371-406

Dixon M (2006) *Rethinking Financial Capability: Lessons from economic psychology and behavioural finance* London: Institute for Public Policy Research, available at: www.ippr.org.uk/ecomm/files/financial_capabilities.pdf

Dixon M and Pearce N (2005) 'Social Justice in a Changing World', in Pearce N and Paxton W (eds) *Social Justice: Building a fairer Britain* London: Institute for

Public Policy Research/Politico's

Duckworth A and Seligman M (2006) 'Self-Discipline Gives Girls the Edge: Gender in Self-Discipline, Grades, and Achievement Test Scores' *Journal of Educational Psychology* 98 (1): 198-208

Egger H and Grossmann V (2004) *Noncognitive Abilities and Within-Group Wage Inequality.* IZA Discussion Papers, Bonn: Institute for the Study of Labor (IZA), available at: ftp://repec.iza.org/RePEc/Discussionpaper/dp1024.pdf

Elias P and Purcell K (2003) *Measuring change in the graduate labour market. Research paper No. 1: Researching Graduate Careers Seven Years On.* A research project jointly funded by the Economic and Social Research Council and the Higher Education Careers Services Unit, Warwick: Institute for Employment Research

EUI (2006) *Foresight 2020: Economic, Industry and corporate trends* London: Economist Intelligence Unit

Evans K and Furlgon A (1997) 'Metaphors of youth transitions: niches, pathways, trajectories and navigations', in Bynner J, Chisholm L and Furlong A (eds) *Youth, Citizenship and Social Change* Aldershot: Ashgate

Farrington-Douglas J and Allen J (2005) *Equitable Choices for Health* London: Institute for Public Policy Research

Ferri E (1993) *Life at 33: The Fifth Follow-up of the National Child Development Study* London: National Children's Bureau

Ford (2006) 'Ford Focus Online Configurator': www.ford.co.uk/foc_c307/-/-

Ford H and Crowther S (1923) *My Life and Work* SI: Heineman

Financial Services Authority (FSA) (2003) *Towards a National Strategy for Financial Capability* London: FSA

FSA (2006) *Financial Capability in the UK: Delivering Change* London: FSA

Gibbons S, Green A, Gregg P and Machin S (2006) 'Is Britain Pulling Apart? Area Disparities in Employment, Education and Crime', in Pearce N and Paxton W (eds) *Social Justice: Building a Fairer Britain* London: Institute for Public Policy Research/Politico's

Goos M and Manning A (2004) *Lovely and Lousy Jobs: The rising polarisation of work in Britain.* CEP Discussion Paper 0604, London: Centre for Economic Perfomance (CEP)

Halpern D, Bates C, Mulgan G, Aldridge S, Beales G and Heathfield A (2004) *Personal Responsibility and Changing Behaviour: the state of knowledge and its implications for public policy* London: Prime Minister's Strategy Unit, available at: www.strategy.gov.uk/downloads/files/pr2.pdf

Hay C (2004) 'Common Trajectories, variable paces, divergent outcomes? Models of European capitalism under conditions of complex economic interdependence' *Review of International Political Economy* 11(2)

Hills J (2004) *Inequality and the State* Oxford: OUP

HM Treasury (2006) Budget press release, 22 March, available at: www.hm-treasury.gov.uk/budget/budget_06/press_notices/bud_bud06_press01.cfm

Iverson T (2001) 'The dynamics of welfare state expansion', in Pierson P (ed.) *The New Politics of the Welfare State* Oxford: Oxford University Press

Jackson M (2002) *Meritocracy, Education and Occupational Attainment: What do employers really see as merit?* Thesis. Oxford: Nuffield College

Jackson M (forthcoming) *How Far Merit Selection? Social Stratification and the Labour Market.* Unpublished draft. Oxford: Nuffield College

Johnson N and Kotz S (1997) *Leading Personalities in Statistical Sciences from the Seventeenth Century to the Present* New York: Wiley

Kempson E and Whyley C (1999) *Kept out or opted out? Understanding and combating financial exclusion* Bristol: Policy Press

Kirby S and Riley R (2006) *The Returns to General versus Job-Specific Skills: the Role of Information and Communication Technology.* NIESR Discussion Paper 274 London: National Institute of Economic and Social Research

Koch M (2006) *Roads to Post-Fordism: Labour Markets and Social Structures in Europe* London: Ashgate

Leitch Review (2005) *Skills in the UK: The long-term challenge. Interim report of the Leitch review* London: TSO

Lindsay C (2003) 'A century of labour market change: 1900 to 2000' *Labour Market Trends* March: 133-44

LSC (2006) *National Employers Skills Survey 2005: Key Findings* London: LSC, available at: http://readingroom.lsc.gov.uk/Lsc/2006/research/commissioned/nat-nationalemployersskillssurvey2005keyfindings-re-june2006.pdf

McQuaid R (2002) *Employability and Employment Change – some lessons for the future* Professorial Lecture, Edinburgh: Napier University

Miliband D (2006) 'Empowerment and Respect: Building change from the bottom up.' Speech by David Miliband at the Cleaner, Safer, Greener Conference, A Vision of Respect on 13 March 2006 London: TSO, available at: www.odpm.gov.uk/index.asp?id=1164236

Ministry of Education (1965) Circular 10/65 London: TSO

Mulgan G (2005) 'Going with and against the grain', in Pearce N and Paxton W (eds) *Social Justice: Building a Fairer Britain* London: Institute for Public Policy Research/Politico's

Office of National Statistics (ONS) (2006) 'Labour market analysis and summary' *Labour Market Trends* 114 (7): 213-40

Partington D (1996) 'The project management of organizational change'

International Journal of Project Management 14 (1): 13-21

Pearce N and Paxton W (eds) (2005) *Social Justice: Building a fairer Britain* London: Institute for Public Policy Research/Politico's

Rowthorn R (2004) *The impact on advanced economies of North-South trade in manufacturing and services* Paper presented at the First International Forum for Development, New York City, 18 October

Rowthorn R and Coutts K (2004) *Commentary: De-industrialisation and the Balance of Payments in Advanced Economies* Paper presented at an international conference on 'De-industrialisation and Industrial Re-structuring', Seoul, South Korea, 5 December

Sampson A (1965) *Anatomy of Modern Britain Today* London: Hodder and Stoughton

Schwartz B (2004) *The Paradox of Choice* New York: Harper Collins,

Stanley K, Asta Lohde L and White S (2004) *Sanctions and Sweeteners: Rights and responsibilities in the benefits system* London: Institute for Public Policy Research, available at: www.ippr.org.uk/publicationsandreports/publication.asp?id=242

Taylor M (2006) 'Empowerment: a Labour vision for public services', in Byrne L, Purnell J and Taylor M (eds) *Power to the people: Next steps for New Labour* London: Progress

Thesmar D and Theoenig M (2000) 'Creative Destruction and Firm Organization Choice' *The Quarterly Journal of Economics* 115 (4): 1201-37

Timmins N (2001) *The Five Giants: A biography of the welfare state.* Second edition London: Harper Collins

Walsh M and Wrigley C (2001) 'Womanpower: The Transformation of the Labour Force in the UK and the USA Since 1945' *Recent Findings of Research in Economic and Social History* 30: 1-4

Whyte W (1956) *The Organisation Man* New York: Simon and Schuster

Wigfield A (2001) *Post-Fordism, Gender and Work* London: Ashgate

Wilson R, Homenidou K and Dickerson A (2006) *Working Futures 2004-2014 National Report* Warwick: Institute for Employment Research, University of Warwick, available at: www.ssda.org.uk/ssda/pdf/Working%20Future%2020042014%20National%20R%20060215.pdf

Wrights E and Oancea A (2005) 'Policies for 14-19 Education and Training in England, 1976 to the present day: a chronology' Nuffield Foundation Review of 14-19 Education and Training Working Day, Nuffield Foundation 25 May 2004, available at: www.nuffield14-19review.org.uk/files/documents93-1.pdf

5. Raising youth: family matters

The research in this report suggests that if we wish to offer all young people an equal chance to succeed, we should start by identifying what encourages the development of soft, non-cognitive skills and then intervene to ensure all young people have access to the relevant factors. Yet despite being more concerned with enhancing equality of opportunity than any government before it, the current Labour government knows and thinks surprisingly little about personal and social skills and how these are developed; our audit of youth in chapter 2 shows clearly how inadequately such skills are currently measured and assessed.

This chapter assesses the importance of family and parental background in determining personal and social skills – or 'non-cognitions' as they are known in psychology – and outlines the most important processes by which these are developed. The next chapter asks what other factors can counterbalance the impact of families for young people who would be otherwise unlikely to develop good personal and social skills.

Parent power: parental background is key

Research consistently highlights that the home environment and parenting have the biggest impact on children's outcomes across many domains (Feinstein 2000; Bynner *et al* 2002; Blanden *et al* 2004; Feinstein *et al* 2005; Blanden 2006). A long tail of compelling evidence proves that parental background has traditionally been able to predict a range of capabilities and functionings, including educational and labour market outcomes as well as health and well-being, as our audit of youth indicators clearly shows. And the evidence outlined in chapter 3 shows that personal and social skills are crucial determinants of outcomes.

Taken together, these findings suggest that parents have the strongest influence socialising young people's non-cognitive skills. But we need not rely on conjecture: recent quantitative research presents strong evidence in favour of this hypothesis. Figure 5.1 presents the results of Leon Feinstein and John Bynner's regression analysis of the 1970 Youth Cohort Study, showing the factors that develop and undermine two areas of non-cognitive development.

Because self-esteem and locus of control are both measured on a continuum, these results are presented in terms of the distribution of scores (or standard deviations). In a normal distribution, an improvement of one standard deviation is equivalent to moving from fiftieth place out of 100 to

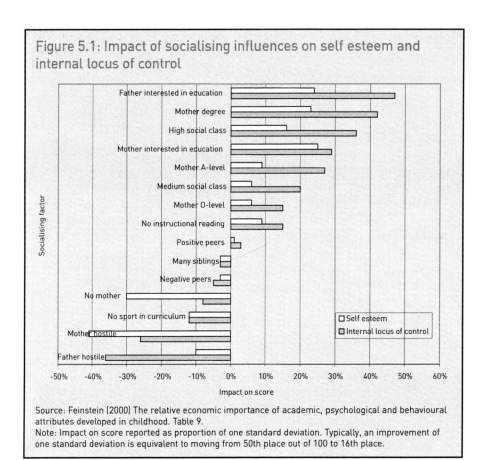

Figure 5.1: Impact of socialising influences on self esteem and internal locus of control

Socialising factor

Father interested in education
Mother degree
High social class
Mother interested in education
Mother A-level
Medium social class
Mother O-level
No instructional reading
Positive peers
Many siblings
Negative peers
No mother
No sport in curriculum
Mother hostile
Father hostile

-50% -40% -30% -20% -10% 0% 10% 20% 30% 40% 50% 60%

Impact on score

☐ Self esteem
☐ Internal locus of control

Source: Feinstein (2000) The relative economic importance of academic, psychological and behavioural attributes developed in childhood. Table 9.
Note: Impact on score reported as proportion of one standard deviation. Typically, an improvement of one standard deviation is equivalent to moving from 50th place out of 100 to 16th place.

sixteenth place. This means that, for example, a father being interested in education is associated with moving from fiftieth place to thirty-second place out of 100 (47 per cent of one standard deviation) in terms of self-esteem and to forty-first place in terms of internal locus of control (24 per cent of one standard deviation). Although this may seem like a relatively small change, it is significant in terms of the impact of public policy and later life chances.

The apparent power of parental attributes – parental education, social class, hostility and interest in education – to predict non-cognitive development for this cohort of young people is clear: the two most important factors in undermining an internal locus of control were maternal and paternal hostility. In contrast, peers and characteristics of a person's school, such as whether teachers emphasised reading for pleasure or whether there was sport in the curriculum, mattered far less for non-cognitive outcomes for this cohort. And worryingly, international evidence shows that the influence of family background – in the form of the possession of 'classical culture' in the home, for example – is higher in the UK than many other countries (OECD 2001).

But what lies behind this powerful influence and what can policy do about it? Before we can explore this question fully we must first examine the extent to which parental contribution to non-cognitions is merely genetic and thus beyond the realm of policymakers.

Is it all in the genes?

Recent advances in genetic science have largely answered the perennial nature versus nurture debate (Gray 2002; Nuffield Council on Bioethics 2002; Dixon 2005). It is clear that both genes and environment are important in personality development; not *all* behaviour is learnt, modelled or innate. For example research has proven that genes are partly responsible for many different personality attributes, such as neuroticism, agreeableness and conscientiousness (Dixon 2005). But while they may contribute to personality outcomes, genes do not determine how the brain grows independently of experience, but influence how the brain grows in *response* to experience (Wilson 1998). There is wide consensus that the difference in personality between individuals is 30 to 50 per cent determined by genes and 50 to 70 per cent determined by environment and experience (Gray 2002).

Research that has looked at antisocial behaviour also flags up the role of genes in social and emotional skills: the identical twin of someone who has displayed antisocial behaviour is nearly twice as likely as the average to show similar signs themselves controlling for other factors (Rhee and Waldman 2002). One controversial study[13], published in August 2002, investigated the link between the gene encoding Monoamine Oxidase A (MAOA), which affects the production of a protein involved in the metabolism of serotonin in the brain, and antisocial behaviour in a group of 500 male children in New Zealand (Caspi *et al* 2002). The study examined the genotypes of the boys and identified a variant in the MAOA gene that was associated with high levels of MAOA activity in the brain, and another that was associated with low levels.

The researchers found that by age 11, 36 per cent of the children in their study had been maltreated (eight per cent severely). Of these, the 12 per cent that had the gene associated with low levels of MAOA accounted for 44 per cent of their generation's total convictions for assault and other violent crimes. As adults, 85 per cent of the severely maltreated children who also had the gene for low MAOA activity experienced antisocial outcomes, such as violent criminal behaviour. Importantly, the combination of maltreatment and the genetic variation magnified the odds by nine times.

---

13. Some care should be taken when interpreting this study, as it has been the subject of criticism in the scientific community, and its results are somewhat controversial. It has been noted, for example, that low levels of MAOA are associated with impaired cognitive ability, and that it may be this that correlates more generally with antisocial behaviour.

(Those children who were maltreated but had the other version of the gene were relatively unlikely to develop behavioural problems.) However, those with the gene who received warm and consistent parenting were no more likely to develop antisocial behaviour than those without the gene and similar parenting: so environment and experience do matter greatly, suggesting there is a role for policy or external factors in equalising non-cognitive development.

The challenge for policymakers is to understand the details of socialising influence parents exert. This is no easy task: contemporary political accounts of family influence largely fail to grasp fully how this socialising influence works, meaning policy is unlikely to be able to intervene effectively (DfES 2006; Home Office 2005; ODPM 2005). But what are the crucial aspects of parenting that make a difference for children? Is positive parenting about time spent with children, interactions with children, access to facilities, money, helping children get into a good school or a combination of these? We examine the evidence here.

Understanding family influence

The regression analysis on the Youth Cohort Studies reported in Figure 5.1 helps us to unpick exactly what it is about parents that impacts on non-cognitive outcomes. A useful distinction here is between 'structural' factors, such as social class and parental education, and 'micro-level' factors and processes, such as parental hostility, warmth or interest.[14]

Looking at the chart suggests that although both are important, micro-level processes seem to have a stronger influence on non-cognitive development than structural factors: paternal interest in education matters most for developing an internal locus of control and high self-esteem; and maternal and paternal hostility matter most for developing an external locus of control, with maternal hostility particularly linked to developing low self-esteem. The child psychologist Urie Bronfenbrenner – who was one of the co-founders of the Head Start scheme in the US, which has formed the basis for the UK Government's Sure Start programme – has argued powerfully that micro-level factors can be understood as mediating the impact of structural factors, as well as influencing these factors in return (Bronfenbrenner 1979). A version of his 'ecological systems model' is presented in Figure 5.2.

In this model, the micro-level processes are factors that enable the child to 'buck the trend' and overcome disadvantage, but they are also determined in part by whether the parent will have the time and resources to undertake them well. So for example, having a warm and loving relation-

---

14. This analysis draws heavily on Bronfenbrenner's model of development, which distinguishes between 'distal' (structural) and 'proximal' (micro-level) factors (Bronfenbrenner 1979).

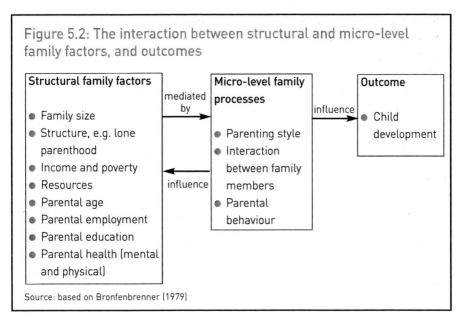

Figure 5.2: The interaction between structural and micro-level family factors, and outcomes

Structural family factors		Micro-level family processes		Outcome
● Family size ● Structure, e.g. lone parenthood ● Income and poverty ● Resources ● Parental age ● Parental employment ● Parental education ● Parental health (mental and physical)	mediated by → ← influence	● Parenting style ● Interaction between family members ● Parental behaviour	influence →	● Child development

Source: based on Bronfenbrenner (1979)

ship with a parent can override the impact of living in a lone-parent family, but this depends on whether that lone parent is able to spend quality time with the child.

This developmental model provides a useful framework by which to analyse the most important factors and processes in socialising non-cognitions. In the sections below we assess the interaction and importance of structural and micro-level factors, drawing on the best empirical work to substantiate Bronfenbrenner's ideas.

Structural family factors

A large body of research shows that structural factors, such as family size, parental age, social class, marriage and family income are important determinants of how young people develop non-cognitions. Perhaps the most compelling recent research has been undertaken by Leon Feinstein and John Bynner in a hitherto unpublished paper analysing the 1970 cohort (Feinstein and Bynner forthcoming). Table 5.1 reports the results of a regression analysis that shows the links between various structural factors and both cognitions and non-cognitions. The table clearly shows that family income in childhood, social class and poverty, parental education, family size and age, and peer social class and academic ability are all significantly related to all age-10 cognitions and non-cognitions, controlling for other factors.

Three further important findings stand out: the first is that the link between structural factors and both cognitions and non-cognitions is relatively weak, as shown by the R-squared scores for income. This shows that

Table 5.1: Regression analysis of age-10 cognitions and non-cognitions on structural family factors

	Maths	Reading	Self-esteem	Internal locus of control	Externalising	Internalising	Peer relations
Income per week (compared to highest income group)							
£35 to £49	-0.932	-0.816	-0.472	-0.639	0.586	0.299	-0.325
£100 to £149	-0.585	-0.507	-0.274	-0.403	0.276	0.155	-0.061
£200 to £249	-0.152	*-0.099*	-0.156	*-0.131*	*0.092*	*0.001*	*0.084*
R-squared	0.06	0.05	0.01	0.02	0.02	0.01	0.01
Social class and poverty (compared to highest social class)							
Free school meals	-0.100	-0.090	-0.114	-0.056	0.208	0.115	-0.125
Medium SES	-0.202	-0.206	-0.083	-0.135	0.070	0.098	*-0.044*
Low SES	-0.267	-0.325	*-0.064*	-0.192	0.130	0.082	*-0.076*
Parental education (compared to highest parental education)							
Low parental education	-0.363	-0.348	-0.110	-0.267	0.167	*0.071*	*0.019*
Medium parental ed.	-0.243	-0.195	-0.074	-0.165	0.095	0.021	0.058
Family size and age (compared to smallest families and oldest mothers)							
Number of older siblings	-0.059	-0.097	-0.050	-0.034	0.037	-0.042	0.023
Young mother	-0.204	-0.216	*-0.089*	*-0.035*	0.202	*-0.005*	0.259
Mother age 25-34	-0.074	-0.117	*0.047*	*-0.020*	*0.015*	-0.110	0.148

Source: Feinstein and Bynner (forthcoming): Table 5

Note: Figures in italics are not significant at 10 per cent

many children from low-income homes have high levels of both kinds of skills and vice versa, as might be expected.

The second finding is that income is a much more powerful determinant of cognitions (maths and reading) scores than non-cognitions. Within non-cognitions, locus of control and externalising behaviour appear to be most strongly affected by parental income.

The third finding is that this research gives an important context to claims advanced by the political Right that an 'intact, two-parent family' is absolutely essential for children's successful development, and those by the political Left that family structure is unimportant.

Much of the US research reports a consistent overarching finding that children who grow up in an 'intact, two-parent family' with both biological parents do better on a wide range of outcomes than children who grow up in a single-parent family (Amato 2005). Single parents, it has been shown, can be less emotionally supportive, have fewer rules, dispense harsher discipline, are often more inconsistent in dispensing discipline, provide less supervision, and engage in more conflict with their children (ibid).

While this research may be instinctively difficult for those on the Left to accept, the British evidence seems to support it. For example, research by Feinstein shows that, controlling for all factors up to the age of 16, and comparing to children from 'intact, two-parent families', those with a single parent at age 16 were, by age 30, four per cent more likely to smoke, 5 per cent more likely to be single, separated or divorced, 1 per cent more likely to be a single parent, 2 per cent more likely to be in social housing, 4 per cent less likely to achieve level 3 qualifications, 4 per cent more likely to have a low income, 2 per cent more likely to receive benefits, 3 per cent more likely to be in a workless household and 1 per cent more likely to be in a workless household with children (Feinstein *et al* 2005).

Evaluations have also suggested that certain relationship support interventions, particularly those involving couple therapy, have led to positive effects on children in terms of school performance and sustained increased involvement by fathers (Cowan and Cowan 2002). We consider the most promising interventions in the concluding chapter.

So lone parenthood does matter, and this will have policy implications, but what about marriage versus cohabitation? Very new research in a British context indicates that marriage may be important. Research using the Millennium Cohort Study has shown that, controlling for other factors, children of cohabiting couples do worse than those of married couples (Benson 2006). This is largely because of the increased risk of separation for cohabiting couples. The implication is that 'being married' encourages couples to work through difficulties, whereas cohabiting is fundamentally less secure.

These findings have been taken to suggest that marriage promotion is the answer, and, for example, the Bush administration in the US is investing US$1.5 billion in 2005/06 in programmes that aim to promote 'healthy marriage' among low-income unmarried couples by providing services to improve relationship skills and increase union stability (Stanley 2005), while in the UK Cameron's Conservatives are investigating the potential of marriage promotion as part of their Social Justice Policy Review.

But there are four problems with this response. First, it is simply not realistic to think that we might substantially lower the rates of divorce, cohabitation and single-parenthood. These are economically- and culturally-driven trends and unlikely to reverse; research claiming to prove a link between benefits systems and family structures is consistently unconvincing, as we show in our concluding chapter. Second, focusing support on traditional family types regardless of need skews much-needed resources towards those who require them less (as single-parent families tend to be most in need of financial support), and is unnecessarily morally prescriptive – telling people how they should live, rather than enabling them to choose. Third, financial incentives are unlikely to work: the introduction of the Married Couples Allowance in the 1970s famously coincided with the greatest number of moves away from marriage that century. And fourth, research shows that although family structure has an impact on how parents interact with their children, it far from determines micro-level processes.

The research throughout this chapter shows that children growing up in non-traditional family forms can succeed if warmth, stability and other micro-level factors are also present. In addition, the research using the Millennium Cohort found that marital status matters much less than many other factors in determining whether couples stay together. A good example here is income: the richest 20 per cent of cohabiting couples are more likely to stay together than the poorest 20 per cent of married couples (Benson 2006). Age also matters: the chance of a couple in their teens and twenties splitting up is twice that of a couple in their thirties.

Therefore, rather than penalise single parenthood or cohabitation or attempt unrealistic policies, we should consider instead how best to support those parents – through the traditional routes of better childcare and more flexible working arrangements as well as increased investment in parenting education, relationship education and support. But first, we consider the evidence of micro-level factors versus structural, below.

Micro-level family processes

The first clear indication of how micro-level processes can be more important than structural ones is that the link between income and non-cognitive development is strongly mediated when we take micro-level factors into account. Advanced statistical techniques allow us to examine this. Although the details are quite complex, the idea is relatively simple: by comparing the link between income, cognitions and non-cognitions before and after controlling for micro-level factors such as parental interest and warmth, we can quantify the extent to which these make a difference.

Table 5.2 shows the percentage fall in the regression scores for the link between age 10-cognitions and non-cognitions on income reported in table 5.1 above, after controlling for micro-level processes. Figures in bold show relationships that are statistically significant only before controlling for micro-level processes – that is, those that are almost entirely mediated by micro-level processes. The table shows that income as a structural factor is only significant for maths ability and self-esteem once micro-level processes are taken into account, clearly indicating the central importance of these micro-level processes in children's development.

Other British empirical research shows that there is a systematic association between the quality of parent-child relationships and young people's subjective well-being (Quilgars *et al* 2005). For example, recent work by the Home Office has found that in 2005 young people who got on badly with

Table 5.2: Extent to which micro-level processes mediate structural factors in the development of non-cognitions: percentage fall in regression scores of age-10 cognitions and non-cognitions on structural family factors, after controlling for micro-level processes

	Maths	Reading	Self-esteem	Internal locus of control	Externalising	Internalising	Peer relations
Income per week (compared to highest income group)							
£35 to £49	**85%**	**98%**	**70%**	**77%**	**82%**	**76%**	**93%**
£100 to £149	**78%**	**87%**	**53%**	**67%**	**68%**	**63%**	115%
£200 to £249	**87%**	120%	*14%*	*44%*	**46%**	n/a	*11%*

Source: Authors' analysis of figures presented in Feinstein and Bynner (forthcoming)
Note: Figures in bold report relationships only statistically significant before controlling for micro-level processes. Figures in italics are not significant at 10 per cent before controlling for micro-level processes.

at least one parent were 2.1 times as likely as those who got on well with both parents to engage in antisocial behaviour (Wood 2005). Similarly, those who spent little or no time with parents were 1.6 times as likely, and those who said their parents were favourable to delinquent behaviour twice as likely to engage in such behaviour.

This point is increasingly understood by psychologists in the US in particular, where research looking at why many affluent families produce children with high rates of drug and alcohol problems, depression and anxiety disorders has shown that children from upper-middle-class US families (with an income of more than £63,000 a year) are not necessarily better off than those from less affluent backgrounds in terms of their non-cognitive attributes. In some cases children appeared to be substantially worse off as a result of their parents' successful careers (Levine 2006). And a particularly important empirical study in the US, carried out with low-income families in 2004, looking at the impact of family structure and micro-level processes on young people's participation in positive extra-curricular activities[15], revealed that good quality family communication is more important than family income, structure or parental working hours for predicting whether children participate in activities and educational opportunities that will help them succeed (Orthner *et al* 2004).

Although Table 5.2 only reports results for income, similar, although smaller, effects can be seen for other structural factors such as marital status of parents, lone-parenthood and age of parents. So what are the most important micro-level processes?

---

15. We present the results of our cohort analysis in the next chapter, which shows how important certain kinds of extra-curricular activities can be for the development of personal and social skills

Unfortunately, our understanding of micro-level processes and interactions is much less advanced, partly because surveys and quantitative techniques are less suitable for capturing and assessing the way parents interact with their children than they are for measuring structural factors. Nevertheless, analysing cohort data provides a considerable degree of insight. Table 5.3 reports the results of a regression analysis that shows the links between various micro-level processes and both cognitions and non-cognitions.

The table clearly shows that parental hostility and interest make a considerable difference to all cognitive and non-cognitive outcomes by age 10, controlling for other factors including single-parenthood. As with structural factors, cognitive attributes are more strongly determined by micro-level processes than non-cognitive attributes. There are considerable differences by gender role: maternal interaction appears to be more important in developing both self-esteem and internal locus of control than paternal interaction.

This analysis is revealing and makes a strong case for the importance of micro-level processes. But it does little to reveal the details of how these work. To understand better the processes through which non-cognitions are socialised and developed in the family, we need to turn to a different academic literature.

Consistency matters

Psychological research has shown consistently that children who have an

Table 5.3: Regression analysis of age-10 cognitions and non-cognitions on micro-level family factors

	Maths	Reading	Self-esteem	Internal locus of control	Externalising	Internalising	Peer relations
Mother hostile	-0.265	-0.392	-0.449	-0.348	0.846	0.195	-1.051
Father hostile	-0.615	-0.219	0.388	-0.332	0.525	0.639	-0.344
Mother's interest very low	-0.634	-0.701	-0.198	-0.362	0.562	0.333	-0.483
Mother's interest low	-0.485	-0.595	-0.249	-0.382	0.353	0.063	-0.511
Mother's interest moderate	-0.213	-0.284	-0.068	-0.182	0.171	0.061	-0.183
Father's interest very low	-0.316	-0.377	-0.221	-0.291	-0.047	-0.284	-0.503
Father's interest low	-0.190	-0.189	-0.183	-0.089	0.199	0.108	-0.377
Father's interest moderate	-0.090	-0.080	-0.128	-0.079	0.036	0.021	-0.179

Source: Feinstein and Bynner (forthcoming)
Note: Figures in italics are not significant at 10 per cent

internal locus of control are more likely to have parents who treat them consistently and give them more autonomy. For example, Carton and Nowicki (1994) found that the research supports the assumption that consistent parental use of reward and punishment as well as parental encouragement of autonomy are associated with the development of generalised internal control expectancies.

Warmth matters

A wide consensus now exists among psychologists and policymakers that children do better when parents provide a warmer, more supportive and secure relationship, regardless of material resources or family structure (Stanley 2005; Waldfogel 2006). Table 5.3 supports this with hard empirical evidence. But perhaps more interesting is the evidence on what enables warm parenting. Some have argued that parental warmth is much less likely in low-income families or single-parent families. But there is a marked lack of empirical research to support this finding. We base our analysis on areas where high quality, reliable research exists.

An extensive literature shows that the quality of relationships between parents is linked to positive parenting and better outcomes for children (see for example, Cummings and Davies 1994; Emery 1999). Young people have been found to be very aware of this too: in 2005, seven out of ten teenagers said that parents getting on well together was one of the most important factors in determining the nature of the relationship between parent and child and in raising happy children (Stanley 2005). The most extensive evidence on the impact of parent's relationships on parent-child relationships and parenting, and on the impact of interventions, is from the US and was reviewed in Stanley (2005).

This research showed that relationships between family members do affect both individuals and other relationships between family members in many ways. The 'spill-over hypothesis' argues that there is emotional spill-over of positive affect or stress from one family relationship to another. The research provides strong evidence for a positive association between parents' relationship quality and parent-child relationship quality.

In particular, greater levels of supportiveness in the mother-father relationship appear to increase fathers' involvement, at least around the time of a non-marital birth (Carlson and McLanahan 2005). UK evidence has found that fathers who are relatively satisfied with their marriages were likely to report more positive relationships with their children than those who are less satisfied (Pike et al 2005). Older children in this study also reported less anger and hostility from those fathers who were more satisfied with their marriages. For mothers, their own personal characteristics were closely linked with the quality of relationships with their children, whereas for fathers, contextual factors such as the marital relationship were key.

Stability matters

Stability at home also features strongly. Research shows that experiencing stressful life events, particularly if disruptive and occurring when young, seems to be associated with a greater likelihood of poor behaviour in children (Carton and Nowicki 1994).

Research also shows that poorly handled conflict can be detrimental to children's sense of well-being (Stanley 2005). The child-rearing years tend to be the times of greatest marital discord, with conflict escalating during the time of infancy and early childhood and reaching a peak between early childhood and pre-adolescence. Frequent conflict appears to deter fathers' positive engagement with their children and at times of marital distress fathers may become more withdrawn, especially from daughters, and mothers may become more involved with children (Reynolds *et al* 2001). Childhood mental health problems associated with parental conflict include behavioural problems such as aggression and anti-social behaviour, and emotional problems such as depression and withdrawal. Children from highly discordant homes are also more likely to fare worse at school, and have problems establishing good relationships with peers, siblings and adults, than those from more stable homes (ibid).

Research also shows that family processes – such as how conflict is handled – can explain children's non-cognitive development better than family structures (Reynolds 2001; Amato 2005; Rodgers and Pryor 1998). Conflict can be constructive when children can learn about negotiation and resolution. For example, research conducted at the University of Leeds on post-divorce family life has shown that people can learn how to manage processes like divorce as a life event and move on in ways that are enabling rather than constraining of their family relationships. People do get through conflict and it is more helpful to consider what support can be provided for people to help them to get through it, than to make the process of divorce difficult or focus solely on preventing divorce. 'Good families' are those with good quality relationships in place, regardless of family structure, and we are now beginning to learn from ordinary divorced families 'what works' in different circumstances (Neale and Smart 2001; Smart *et al* 2001; Stanley 2005).

This is not to say family structure does not play a role. For example, Stanley (2005) explains how children in step-families may be exposed to two sources of conflict between parents: between biological parents living apart and between parent and step-parent. However, she argues that this can be mitigated by the different ways in which step-families can function from first-marriage families: for example, adults can be more influenced by children in step-families (Reynolds 2001; Stanley 2005). In these ways the structure of a family is likely to have a role in influencing a child's non-cognitive development but it is only one element of a wider set of processes and circumstances.

Sociological research shows that children who have experienced disruption and multiple family structures are more likely to experience poor outcomes, such as poor mental health, than children living continuously in single-parent or step-families (Rodgers and Pryor 1998). However, the *Enduring Families* project has shown that there is nothing inherently harmful about multiple changes in family life; just as conflict has to be managed if harm is to be avoided, so change, too, is a challenge that can be managed well or poorly. Much depends on how effectively children are prepared for the changes in their family lives, the pace of change, and the ways in which they are supported through them (Flowerdew and Neale 2003). The key to conferring benefits to children appears to be the continuity of loving relationships and this can be achieved through all family forms and sustained through changes in family structure over time.

Multiple problems and factors such as economic stress can exacerbate the effect of conflict on children (Cummings and Davies 1994). Links between marital conflict and children's difficulties appear to be stronger in families experiencing a range of other problems, than in more stable families. Parental depression and family stresses such as poverty may increase the likelihood of conflict, as well as reducing parents' ability to engage positively with each other and their children (Reynolds 2001). There is strong evidence that parents' experience of multiple, overlapping and cumulative problems including poverty, disability, poor-quality housing, access to services, long-term health difficulties and debt can contribute significantly to relationship breakdown (Ghate and Hazel 2002).

Finally, research in the UK has illuminated the impacts of divorce or separation on children (Stanley 2005). The risks that children face in relation to divorce are often less to do with actual parental separation and more to do with the context. The key factor is the conflict that can occur before, during and after separation and the impact that poorly managed conflict has on parents and parent-child relationships (Stanley 2005).

The key point for policymakers deriving from this research is that differentiated family forms are likely to remain a feature of 21st century Britain, so rather than pursuing unachievable and unpalatable aims such as to promote marriage, we must instead orientate policy towards first, supporting people to live together in stable, loving homes and second, enabling children to succeed whatever their family form. We consider the appropriate policy response in the concluding chapter.

Timing matters

The above analysis starts to explain how parents influence non-cognitive development through micro-level processes and gives some indication of where the policy focus should lie. But there are two things it is missing. First, it fails to explain why the parental influence is so enduring: why is it so able to predict adult outcomes when young people come into contact with many other institutions in the course of their lives? And second, it fails to identify which of these other institutions may be relevant in socialising young people: while the regression analysis undertaken by Feinstein and Bynner indicated parents were more important than peers or school characteristics, it does not look in detail at the latter two factors, or examine the influence of other factors such as the local area, or attendance at various extra-curricular activities.

But obviously there would be little point in examining these if, as recent theorists have argued, it is overwhelmingly what happens in the first few years of life that matters to developmental outcomes. So how much does timing matter?

Recent interest in children's development has focused on the early years, often characterising this stage as 'make or break' in developmental terms. This theory is still supported by a range of research. For example a cross-disciplinary examination of research in economics, developmental psychology, and neurobiology by Knudsen *et al* (2006, cited in Waldfogel 2006) found that early experiences have a uniquely powerful influence on the development of cognitive and non-cognitive skills, as well as on brain architecture and neurochemistry.

Neuro-developmental research indicates that, unlike other organ systems, the human brain is embryonic at birth; it completes the majority of its development, including the production of necessary and destruction of unnecessary neural architecture, in response to environmental stimuli – such as interaction with parents and other humans, manipulation of environmental elements like blocks or sand, and creative, problem-solving activities – over the first 18 to 24 months of life (Waldfogel 2006). There is thus a wide consensus that the first year of life is the most important in terms of ensuring the right environment and experiences for development (ibid) and this is already recognised and appreciated by the Government, as we showed in chapter 2.

But what about the parenting and other experiences that occur when children are older? Specific empirical evidence of the impact of other factors on child development in subsequent years (after the ages of three to four years) is as yet inconclusive. There is some indication that attendance in pre-school programmes can assist in non-cognitive development even when parental effects are negative and other evidence has shown that children raised in relative neglect can overcome developmental problems to some extent if they are removed to more supportive environments. For example, research comparing the development of 165 severely maltreated adoptees from Romania at age four with that of 52 healthy children adopted within the UK before they were six months old shows that, although complete recovery was rare, the majority of mistreated adoptees were able to dramatically overcome their initial deprivation in terms of their cognitive and non-cognitive development (O'Connor *et al* 2000).

In contrast to the limited empirical evidence, theoretical work on child development beyond the early years is abundant, and informative – certainly suggesting that while what happens early in life is important, what happens later matters too. A vast psychological and medical literature on stages of human social and emotional development has been constructed around the early work of Erikson (1950, 1958, 1964, and 1968). Such work aims to understand the process through which social and emotional, as well as cognitive skills, develop in individuals *across the life course* and the ongoing interaction between genetics, experience and environment in enabling this.

Stages of non-cognitive development

Erikson argued that the socialisation process consists of eight phases. Each stage is regarded as a 'psychosocial crisis', which arises and demands resolution before the next stage of non-cognitive development can be satisfactorily negotiated. These stages are conceived in an almost architectural sense: satisfactory learning and resolution of each crisis is necessary if the child is to manage the next and subsequent ones satisfactorily.

Table 5.4 highlights the key stages. The first is now commonly known in psychology circles as 'early attachment' – the child must feel secure and nurtured by the caregiver or he will develop a sense of insecurity. Stage two involves the child grasping self-control, but requires support and nurture from the caregiver to overcome the psychosocial crisis. Although Erikson's stages of development seem mainly to describe the process of gaining independence and autonomy, he emphasises the need for security, protection, support and structure throughout.

This analysis suggests that while the early years are particularly important, social and emotional development is an ongoing process that extends well into adulthood. It is also important to recognise that there are some developmental differences between girls and boys in this respect: one influential US study found significant gender differences in 'ego development' – essentially emotional and psychological maturity – with girls tending to display more ego development at each grade, with the gap beginning to close by the end of high school (roughly age 18) (Cohn 1991).

Cohort analysis has also shown important gender differences in the development of non-cognitions. While girls do better than boys in avoiding anti-social behaviour, they tend as a rule to have lower self-esteem throughout adolescence (Feinstein 2000). These psychological and behavioural gender differences are stronger than differences in academic abilities, which may explain why boys fare worse at school in the current socio-economic climate, as we argue in the previous chapter. Interestingly, the biggest gender difference is for attentiveness at the age of ten, at which

Table 5.4: Erikson's eight stages of psychosocial development

Stage	Ages	Basic conflict	Important event	Summary
1. Oral-sensory	Birth to 12-18 mths	Trust vs. mistrust	Feeding	The infant must form a loving, trusting relationship with the caregiver, or he will develop a sense of mistrust and insecurity.
2. Muscular-anal	18 mths - 3 yrs	Autonomy vs. shame /doubt	Toilet training	The child's energies are directed towards the development of physical skills, including walking and grasping. The child learns control but may develop shame and doubt if not handled well.
3. Locomotor	3-6 yrs	Initiative vs. guilt	Indep'dence	The child continues to become more assertive and to take more initiative, but may be too forceful, leading to feelings of guilt.
4. Latency	6-12 yrs	Industry vs. inferiority	School	The child must deal with demands to learn new skills or risk a sense of inferiority, failure and incompetence.
5. Adolescence	12-18 yrs	Identity vs. role confusion	Peer r'ships	The teenager must achieve a sense of identity in occupation, sex roles, politics, and religion.
6. Young adulthood	19-40 yrs	Intimacy vs. isolation	Love r'ships	The young adult must develop intimate relationships or suffer feelings of isolation.
7. Middle adulthood	40-65 yrs	Generativity vs. stagnation	Parenting	Each adult must find some way to satisfy and support the next generation.
8. Maturity	65 to death	Ego integrity vs. despair	Reflection on and acceptance of one's life	The culmination is a strong sense of agency and fulfilment.

Source: Adapted from Erikson (1950, 1958, 1964, 1968)

point boys do particularly badly. These developmental differences are important beyond the educational sphere as slower social and emotional development of boys may help to explain the disproportionately large percentage of serious crimes committed by male juveniles (Cohn 1991).

Beyond the family

But perhaps the most important finding of developmental psychology and related research is that parental influence wanes as children become older. Detailed analysis of the 1970 cohort study by Feinstein and Bynner has shown that 'parenting factors are not particularly important [in the development of non-cognitions] once age ten capabilities are controlled for' (Feinstein and Bynner, forthcoming: 2). We present a range of recommendations related to how government and the voluntary sector can provide better support for families in the concluding chapter of this report. Yet there is still considerable scope for development in personal and social skills beyond the family.

ippr's analysis of the 1970 cohort has shown that there is only a 5 per cent correlation between young people's locus of control aged 10 and aged 16, and a 3 per cent correlation between their extroversion/introversion aged 10 and aged 16 (see Appendix 2). This has two important implications, particularly given the fact that parental influence to non-cognitions makes relatively little difference after the age of 10 (and that other factors are important in early childhood). First, it highlights the developmental importance of early adolescence in shaping personal and social skills and other non-cognitions. And second, it shows that we need to look beyond the family to understand how personal and social skills can be fostered throughout childhood and adolescence. We turn to this issue in the next chapter.

References

Note: web references correct at September 2006

Amato P (2005) 'The Impact of Family Formation Change on the Cognitive, Social and Emotional Well-being of the Next Generation' *Marriage and Child Well-being* 15 (2), Fall, Princeton: Brookings

Benson H (2006) *The conflation of marriage and cohabitation in government statistics - a denial of difference rendered untenable by an analysis of outcomes* Bristol: Harry Benson Bristol Community Family Trust, available at: www.bcft.co.uk/Family%20breakdown%20in%20the%20UK.pdf

Blanden J (2006) *'Bucking the trend': What enables those who are disadvantaged in childhood to succeed later in life?* DWP Working Paper No 31 London: TSO

Blanden J, Goodman A, Gregg P and Machin S (2004) 'Changes in Intergenerational Mobility' in Corak M (ed.) *Generational Income Mobility* Cambridge: Cambridge University Press

Bronfenbrenner U (1979) *The ecology of human development* Cambridge, MA: Harvard University Press

Bynner J, Elias P, McKnight A, Pan H and Pierre G (2002) *Young people's changing routes to independence* York: York Publishing Services/JRF

Carlson M and McLanahan S (2005) *Strengthening unmarried families: could enhancing couple relationships also improve parenting?* Working Paper #02-16-FF, Princeton, NJ: Center for Research on Child Well-being

Carton JS and Nowicki S (1994) 'Antecedents of individual-differences in locus of control of reinforcement – a critical review' *Genetic Social and General Psychology Monographs* 120: 31-81

Caspi A, McClay J, Moffitt TE, Mill J, Martin J, Craig IW, Taylor A and Poulton R (2002) 'Role of genotype in the cycle of violence in maltreated children' *Science* (297): 851ff, available at: www.med.umich.edu/hg/EDUCATION/COURSES/HG803/Burmeister/CaspiMaoAmaltreatment.pdf

Cohn LD (1991) 'Sex differences in the course of personality development: A meta-analysis' *Psychological Bulletin* 109: 252-266

Cowan P and Cowan C (2002) 'Strengthening couples to improve children's well-being' *Poverty Research News* 3: 18-20

Cummings E and Davies P (1994) 'Maternal depression and child development' *Journal of Child Psychology and Psychiatry* 35: 73-112

Department for Education and Skills (DfES) (2006) *Youth Matters* Green Paper, London: TSO

Dixon M (2005) *Brave New Choices: Behavioural genetics and public policy, a discussion document* London: Institute for Public Policy Research

Dixon M and Paxton W (2005) 'The State of the Nation: An audit of social injustice', in Pearce N and Paxton W (eds) *Social Justice: Building a fairer Britain* London: Institute for Public Policy Research/Politico's

Emery R (1999) *Marriage, divorce, and children's adjustment* London: Sage Publications

Erikson EH (1950) *Childhood and Society* New York: Norton

Erikson EH (1958) *Young Man Luther* New York: Norton

Erikson EH (1964) *Insight and Responsibility* New York: Norton

Erikson EH (1968) *Identity: Youth and Crisis* New York: Norton

Feinstein L (2000) *The relative economic importance of academic, psychological and behavioural attributes developed in childhood* Brighton: University of Sussex, available at: www.sussex.ac.uk/Units/economics/dp/Feinstein2.pdf

Feinstein L and Bynner J (forthcoming) *The benefits of assets in childhood as protection against adult social exclusion: the relative effects of financial, human, social and psychological assets* Unpublished mimeo London: Institute of Education

Feinstein L, Bynner J and Duckworth K (2005) *Leisure contexts in adolescence and their effects on adult outcomes* London: Centre for Research on the Wider Benefits of Learning

Flowerdew J and Neale B (2003) 'Trying to stay apace: children with multiple challenges in their post divorce family lives' *Childhood* 10 (2): 147-161

Ghate D and Hazel N (2002) *Parenting in poor environments: stress, support and coping* London: Jessica Kingsley Publishers

Gray J (2002) *Behavioural Genetics Research in the Field of Personality* London: Nuffield Council on Bioethics

Home Office (2005) *The Respect Action Plan* London: TSO

Levine M (2006) *Ready or not, here life comes* New York: Simon & Schuster

Moran P, Ghate D and van der Merwe A (2004) *What Works in Parenting Support? A Review of the International Evidence* Research Report 574 London: Department for Education and Skills

Neale B and Smart C (2001) *Caring, earning and changing: parenting and employment after divorce* CRFKC Working Paper 24

Nuffield Council on Bioethics (2002) *Genetics and Human Behaviour: The Ethical Context* London: Nuffield Council on Bioethics

O'Connor T, Rutter M and The English and Romanian Adoptees Study Team (2000) 'Attachment disorder behavior following early severe deprivation: Extension and longitudinal follow-up' *Journal of the American Academy of Child and Adolescent Psychiatry* (39): 703-12

Office of the Deputy Prime Minister (ODPM) (2005) *Transitions* London: TSO

OECD (2001) *Knowledge and Skills for Life: First Results from PISA 2000* Paris: OECD

Orthner D, Jones-Saupei H and Williamson S (2004) 'The resilience and strengths of low income families' *Family Relations* (53): 159-67

Pike A, Dunn J and Stevenson J (2005) *Consistency in parent-child relationships: comparisons across mothers and fathers, siblings and family type* York: JRF

Quilgars D, Searle B and Keung A (2005) 'Mental health and well-being', in Bradshaw J and Mayhew E (eds) *The Well-being of Children in the UK*, 2nd ed. London: Save the Children

Reynolds J, Harold G, and Pryor J (eds.) (2001) *Not in front of the children? How conflict between parents affects children* London: One Plus One Marriage and Partnership Research

Rhee SH and Waldman ID (2002) 'Genetic and environmental influences on antisocial behaviour: a meta-analysis of twin and adoption studies' *Psychological Bulletin* 128: 490-529

Rodgers B and Pryor J (1998) *Divorce and separation: The outcomes for children* York: JRF

Smart C, Neale B, and Wade A (2001) *The changing experience of childhood: families and divorce* Cambridge: Polity Press

Stanley K (2005) *Daddy Dearest: Active fatherhood and public policy* London: Institute for Public Policy Research

Times Higher Education Supplement (1998) 'Out of a barren cradle: Perspective' April 1998

Thompson RA and Nelson CA (2001) 'Developmental science and the Media: Early Brain Development' *American Psychologist* 56:5-15

Waldfogel J (2006) 'What Children Need' *Public Policy Research* 13 (1)

Wilson EO (1998) *Consilience: The Unity of Knowledge* New York: Knopf

Wood M (2005) *Perceptions and experience of antisocial behaviour: findings from the 2003/2004 British Crime Survey* Home Office Online Report 49/04, London: TSO, available at: www.homeoffice.gov.uk/rds/pdfs04/rdsolr4904.pdf

6. Raising youth: beyond the family

In the final years of the 18th Century, churches and chapels around the country began to introduce Sunday Schools. This was the first formal attempt in Britain to provide young people with moral education and constructive activities on any kind of large scale or using innovative approaches: the most progressive Sunday Schools introduced more informal ways of working and later developed a range of activities including team sports and day trips (Smith 2006).

These early experiences catalysed a growing recognition of the importance of non-familial influences to young people's development and socialisation, leading to the first formal youth organisation – the Young Men's Christian Association (YMCA) – being set up in 1844 (ibid). The emerging field of 'youth work' was rapidly gaining credibility among opinion leaders and by 1863 it had a groundswell of political advocacy, led by the Reverend Arthur Sweatman, who had been involved in setting up and running one of the first Youth Institutes in Britain. In a highly influential and widely cited lecture to the Social Science Association in Edinburgh, he argued that young men have 'special wants and dangers', which call for dedicated institutions:

> Their peculiar wants are evening recreation, companionship, an entertaining but healthy literature, useful instruction, and a strong guiding influence to lead them onward and up-ward socially and morally; their dangers are, the long evenings consequent upon early closing, the unrestraint they are allowed at home, the temptations of the streets and of their time of life, and a little money at the bottom of their pockets.
>
> In the case of most of these lads, their own homes afford no supply for these peculiar wants .... But all these wants the Youths' Institute is specially designed to supply – recreation, companionship, reading, instruction, and all of a pure and healthy kind.
>
> (Sweatman 1867: 4)

Sweatman's analysis and ideas resonated strongly with his Victorian contemporaries and have subsequently fed into the common sense of the modern era. It is hard to imagine society without specific provision for young people outside formal education and the home: in mid 2006, there were more than 32,000 charities dedicated to the needs of children and young people, aiming to support families and provide beneficial opportunities to young people (Guidestar UK 2006). These practical initiatives have been accompanied by a parallel and growing interest in the theory of what socialises young people beyond the family; a substantial psychological literature has now produced a plethora of hypotheses and models explaining young people's development.

Yet it is only relatively recently that social scientists have been able to empirically test whether participation in extracurricular activities and civic institutions can actually aid young people from disadvantaged backgrounds to overcome early deprivation and develop good personal and social skills, or to rigorously assess the impact of other factors, such as consumerism, peers or the media.

In this chapter we explore how influential other processes beyond the family may be in child development – undertaking original analysis of the British Cohort Study to assess the impact of broader socialising factors affecting young people's development of personal and social skills – and the way in which family background mediates children's interactions with external bodies and institutions. In the following chapter we assess how the role of these socialising factors has changed over the past few decades and the challenges this raises for policy.

Interdependence

Previous research with young people provides a good idea of the kinds of activities and institutions they participate in at different ages, suggesting which factors may be important, and when. Table 6.1 illustrates these in some detail, cutting across traditional academic silos to incorporate emerging research strands – such as the importance of children's interaction with media and advertising – in recognition of an emerging literature on the socialising effects of these, as well as the impact of more traditional institutions.

This short overview indicates the degree of inter-dependence between different socialising factors: for example, the impact of peers cannot be understood in isolation from the effects of advertising, which is in turn mediated by participation in structured activities. This creates a considerable theoretical and research challenge; many commentators have lamented the degree to which academic research on the processes of socialisation tends towards subject isolationism, rather than drawing links across disciplines (Bronfenbrenner 1979; Palmer 2006), thereby creating significant difficulties for policy development. This makes Bronfenbrenner's ecological systems model of child development – outlined in the previous chapter – particularly salient here, as it provides a useful framework for analysis that captures the importance of interdependence.

Figure 6.1 draws on Bronfenbrenner's ideas to outline a way of thinking about the interaction between different socialising factors, highlighting the

Table 6.1: Socialising factors beyond the family, by developmental stage	
Early years	There are multiple influences on development in the early years, which can be assigned to three main categories: child endowment or social class (affluence and access to material resources); parents and the home environment (including parental engagement and the nature of the local community); and pre-school care and education.
Childhood	Most children spend a large proportion of their lives in school, mixing with peers and accessing extra-curricular activities. This again is dependent on social class and resources both locally and in the home.
	The role of advertising becomes increasingly important as children grow up. On average children spend half their time watching television, playing computer games and using the internet, even before the age of 10.
Adolescence	By the teenage years the influence of the local community – local resources such as activities and cultural institutions, the nature of local peer groups and demographic makeup of the area – may become more pronounced as young people spend decreasing amounts of time with parents and more time with peers, often in unstructured activities.
	The role of advertising and the media in young people's lives probably peaks at this point as young people have the freedom and opportunity to spend more time with media and more disposable income to do with as they please.
Late adolescence and early adulthood	In late adolescence we can expect peer influences to be mediated as young adults enter into love-relationships and continue education to university level, or enter early employment. Social class may again define the socialisation process as greater numbers of disadvantaged young people may enter early parenthood or early employment than their more affluent peers, who are more likely to pursue education and delay marriage and having children. Some young people will remain in the parental home until adulthood.
Adulthood	Marriage, parenthood and employment will by this stage have strong normative influences on most individuals.

interdependence between spheres. While this is not meant to be a definitive statement, it provides a useful structure by which to analyse the various impacts on young people's development without descending into obfuscation or endless cross-referencing.

The key insights highlighted by this model are that micro-level processes are most crucial in determining child development, that these are influenced by and mediate wider structural factors and that micro-level processes impact on wider structural factors in their turn. Of course, for each specific area, the balance of importance between structural and micro-level processes differs.

Below, we assess these areas in turn, considering the structural and micro-level processes within each area and the interaction between areas.

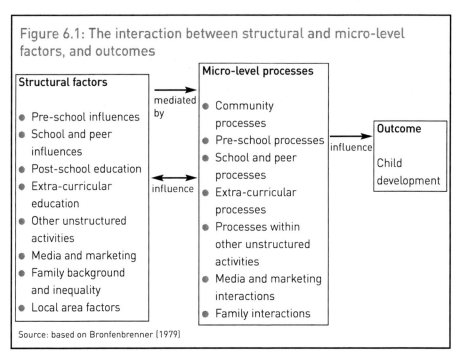

Figure 6.1: The interaction between structural and micro-level factors, and outcomes

Structural factors

- Pre-school influences
- School and peer influences
- Post-school education
- Extra-curricular education
- Other unstructured activities
- Media and marketing
- Family background and inequality
- Local area factors

mediated by →

Micro-level processes

- Community processes
- Pre-school processes
- School and peer processes
- Extra-curricular processes
- Processes within other unstructured activities
- Media and marketing interactions
- Family interactions

← influence →

influence →

Outcome

Child development

Source: based on Bronfenbrenner (1979)

We start with the importance of the local area: how much difference does this make, and how does its influence manifest?

Structural local area and community factors

There are a host of structural factors affecting young people's socialisation at the local area and community level. Some of the most important include the relative affluence of the local area and the opportunities it provides both parents and young people to gain skills – through local employment, training, services and activities, the demographic makeup and size of the area.

A range of research has shown how structural factors such as the physical quality of the area, the standard of housing, the level of social housing, the availability of services, and levels of income and deprivation interact to make some areas more predisposed to young people's cognitive and non-cognitive development than others (Delorenzi 2006). It is, for instance, well established that young people living in disadvantaged neighbourhoods tend to have less access to information, support and connections in the labour market than their more affluent counterparts, which can make it harder for them to access the social and human capital necessary for development (Buck and Gordon 2004). We also know that disadvantaged young people may face financial barriers to moving where these things exist (Gregg and Machin 2004).

Demographic factors such as the ratio of children to adults in these areas also matter. Unpublished regression analysis by the Home Office shows

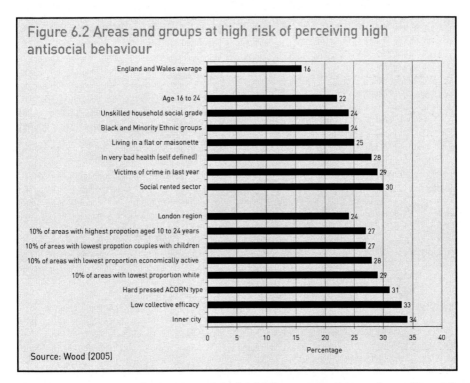

Figure 6.2 Areas and groups at high risk of perceiving high antisocial behaviour

	Percentage
England and Wales average	16
Age 16 to 24	22
Unskilled household social grade	24
Black and Minority Ethnic groups	24
Living in a flat or maisonette	25
In very bad health (self defined)	28
Victims of crime in last year	29
Social rented sector	30
London region	24
10% of areas with highest propotion aged 10 to 24 years	27
10% of areas with lowest propotion couples with children	27
10% of areas with lowest proportion economically active	28
10% of areas with lowest proportion white	29
Hard pressed ACORN type	31
Low collective efficacy	33
Inner city	34

Source: Wood (2005)

that the 10 per cent of UK areas with the highest proportion of couples with children are 32 per cent less likely to have high levels of antisocial behaviour as the 10 per cent of areas with the lowest proportion of couples with children (Wood 2005). Figure 6.2 shows the structural characteristics of areas suffering antisocial behaviour. Ethnic diversity, age structure and proportion of home owners all impact noticeably on rates.

Similar research in the US has consistently shown how living in particular areas, notably disadvantaged areas with a high proportion of public housing, is a risk factor that increases the likelihood of antisocial behaviour (Sampson *et al* 1997). Studies that have measured the relationship between individual risk factors, neighbourhood characteristics and juvenile offending show that children and young people with high risk factors were significantly more likely to seriously offend in the most disadvantaged neighbourhoods. But in more affluent neighbourhoods, predictions of future delinquency based on risk factor assessment – including the state of the family and relations with parents – did not materialise (Smith and McVie 2003; Macdonald and Marsh 2005; Sampson and Laub 1993; Furlong *et al* 2003). This suggests that structural neighbourhood factors can override micro-level processes in some cases (Macdonald and Marsh 2005; Sampson and Laub 1993).

However, the notion that all disadvantaged areas are prone to high levels of crime and disorder, or that all young people hailing from affluent areas are well-behaved is misleading; there are clearly disadvantaged areas that thrive and that do not suffer serious antisocial behaviour. Social disorganisation theory sees the explanation for these variations in terms of whether or not a community has the culture and micro-level processes to implement and express the values of its own residents.

Robert Sampson has argued that those neighbourhoods with high crime levels lack 'collective efficacy' – the ability of the community to control the precursors of crime, levels of trust, respect and self-esteem within and between community members (Sampson 1999). Broadly, this is the ability to socialise the young and maintain norms of respect for the law, and for one another (ibid). The factors that make for collective efficacy – dense friendship networks, community supervision of teenagers and high levels of civic participation – make 'collective efficacy' a very close cousin of 'social capital' (Dixon et al 2006). But the concept is a more action-orientated one, focusing in particular on how communities mobilise for the achievement of public goods (Sampson and Groves 1989). The key point here is that collective efficacy, at the micro level, is more important in determining whether an area will suffer from antisocial behaviour than almost all other measures.

Micro-level community factors

Recent empirical work has begun to substantiate this hypothesis, in part by showing how community-level processes influence other micro-level process. For example, collective efficacy within a community has been associated with increases in authoritative parenting (Simons et al 2005). This may be because local networks of parents tend to set behavioural norms within a community, deciding what behaviour is appropriate, how it should be dealt with and supporting each other in doing so (Jones 2005).

Other recent work has indicated that social order and high social capital in local areas is associated with lower crime rates (Cote and Healy 2001; Green et al 2000; Halpern 1999; Sampson et al 1997). As Figure 6.3 shows, low collective efficacy is one of the most accurate predictors of high levels of antisocial behaviour in England and Wales. The most detailed research, though, has been carried out in the US. In Chicago neighbourhoods, mutual trust and neighbourly altruism were key factors in explaining inter-neighbourhood differences in crime rates: communities characterised by anonymity and limited acquaintance, unsupervised teenage peer groups and low levels of civic participation face an increased risk of crime and violence (Sampson et al 1997; Cote and Healy 2001). The central idea here is that collective efficacy does not make residents more likely to intervene in serious crimes, but rather it enhances their preponderance to intervene in the precursors of crime, for example by discouraging the gathering of teenage gangs or drug taking (Halpern 2001).

The importance of stability and order within communities is now widely supported by scientific research. For example Gould (Lehrer 2006) has shown, using marmoset monkeys, that poverty can damage the brain by stunting the growth of neurons, as the brain diverts energy towards survival rather than creating new cells and connections. Importantly, it was not poverty in itself but the disorder and instability associated with it that caused the difficulties (ibid).

Supporting this, other recent research shows that the major environmental factor influencing serotonin secretion patterns in the brain (which partly determines the level of self-control an individual can exert) is social instability (Robinson 2004). Others have found that peer-raised monkeys have lower concentrations of serotonin than those raised in the more structured, nurturing and secure environment of parents (Bennett *et al* 2002; Kreamer *et al* 1998), due to the insecurity and instability of peer groups. The question, then, is how policy can better support communities in undertaking civic reinvention: what would enable them to develop stronger civic bonds, collective efficacy and trust? We consider this in chapter 7.

Of course, parents and the community are not the only influence on young people, who spend a large proportion of their time in school and, increasingly, pre-school institutions. But what is the potential of these institutions to positively influence cognitive and non-cognitive development?

Pre-school influences

Much of the work by economists and social policy researchers investigates the impact of participation of children in early childhood programmes like the US Head Start (see Currie 2001) or its British equivalent Sure Start on cognitive and non-cognitive development. It is clear from this literature that cognitive test score gaps emerge across children from different family backgrounds at early ages. Perhaps the best known example is Leon Feinstein's analysis showing that high early achievers from disadvantaged backgrounds are overtaken between the ages of five and ten by poor early achievers from advantaged backgrounds (Feinstein 2003). As two influential academics have recently stated: 'like it or not, the most important mental and behavioural patterns, once established, are difficult to change once children enter school' (Heckman and Wax 2004: XX).

This research has been a powerful force behind the recent policy focus on the early years. Debate has so far focused primarily on questions of access and affordability of childcare – Labour proudly stated in its 2005 manifesto that it has funded an additional 520,000 sustainable childcare places (The Labour Party 2005). One motivation for this has been the concern that differing pre-school enrolment rates have partly underpinned inequality in development (Meyers *et al* 2004), a challenge that still remains considerable. For example, in the most recent assessment of Sure Start, researchers found that it was not the most severely disadvantaged children that were benefiting from the services, but increasingly those from relatively less disadvantaged backgrounds that were making use of the facilities (Glennie *et al* 2005). Policy going forward must ensure that facilities are attractive to (and used by) those who need them most (Stanley *et al* 2006). But these structural solutions need to be accompanied by equal recognition of the importance of micro-level processes too: not all childcare is good childcare.

The evidence regarding the impact of *high quality* childcare on cognitive development is clear. Research shows that attendance at high quality pre-school activities confers a cognitive advantage on children before they enter school with no adverse effect on behaviour (Magnusson *et al* 2004; Sammons *et al* 2002; Currie 2001) and that early childhood education programmes have narrowed gaps in cognitive ability between ethnic minority children and white children in the US (Currie 2001).

The evidence on behaviour and personal and social skills is also compelling. Participation in high-quality pre-school activities is beneficial for non-cognitive outcomes including socialising, emotional and behavioural skills (Waldfogel 2006; Pearce and Paxton 2005; Stanley *et al* 2006).[16] Indeed, many evaluations have shown that the most enduring gains – reductions in delinquency and crime, and reductions in teen births – were in the area of social and emotional development, with particularly strong gains for the most disadvantaged children (Carneiro and Heckman 2003). For example, the Infant Health and Development Program (IHDP) in the US, an early intervention programme for low-birth-weight children that provided centre-based care for children starting at the age of one, boosted IQ at age three by 20 points for children whose mothers had less than a high school education, 10 points for children whose mothers had graduated from high school only, and no points for children whose mothers had graduated from college (Brooks-Gunn *et al* 1992; Ramey and Ramey 2000).

This research shows just how important both structural and micro-level processes in early years settings are for children's cognitive and non-cognitive development (Stanley *et al* 2006). Ensuring that all parents have fair access to high quality services must underpin a successful youth policy. But we also need to recognise the limitations of an exclusive focus on the early years: as the last chapter showed, influences in later life make an enormous difference, particularly to non-cognitive development. There is a growing concern that the recent huge investment in the early years agenda will be substantially mitigated without better policies supporting childhood and

---

16. Of course, children should not start pre-school too early – although exactly when is 'too early' remains a matter for debate. Some studies have shown that children who entered care earlier had more behaviour problems (NICHD ECCRN 2003; Sammons *et al* 2002).

adolescence, particularly in terms of school and peer effects.

School influences

Schools are undoubtedly important for both cognitive and non-cognitive development, although their impact can be easily overstated: family background, raw talent and parental interest remain by far the best predictors of formal educational attainment (Currie 1995; Gregg and Machin 1999, 2001).[17]

The evidence is much stronger for cognitive development than non-cognitive development, reflecting previous policy priorities. But recent analysis of the 1970 cohort has begun to shed light on the potential impact of schools in fostering personal and social development. Once again, micro-level processes are paramount. Children attending schools that emphasised reading for pleasure were much more likely to develop an internal locus of control and have high self-esteem, for example. Schools without sport in the curriculum significantly reduced the chance of children developing an internal locus of control or having high self-esteem (Feinstein and Bynner forthcoming). And attending school activities can significantly reduce the likelihood of smoking (by 4 per cent), being a single parent, living in social housing (by 4 per cent), and being homeless, and dissatisfied with life (Feinstein *et al* 2005). Other research corroborates these findings, albeit without as much empirical rigour. For example, teacher warmth (interacting well with children, without hostility) in the classroom can assist the development of perceived control in children (Skinner *et al* 1998).

Education Secretary Alan Johnson has recently made direct moves to address the potential of schools to assist in non-cognitive development, primarily through cognitive behavioural techniques (CBT), in the form of the Social and Emotional Aspects of Learning (SEAL) programme. This offers a whole-curriculum framework for teaching social, emotional and behavioural skills to all children and is organised into seven themes, which can be covered within a school year (DfES 2006).

The techniques are based on role play and teacher-led discussions aiming to help children raise self-esteem and confidence and are borrowed from 'Positive Psychology' techniques pioneered in the US by Martin Seligman through his Penn Resiliency Programme (PRP) (Reivich *et al* 2006). The PRP teaches assertiveness, problem-solving and decision-making strategies in schools. The US evaluations of PRP have found positive results for school-age children although they are yet to be evaluated in the British context. The result from evaluations found that the techniques can

---

17. For example, at Key Stage 3 just 8.8 per cent of the difference in progress between the best and worst performing pupils is accounted for by differences between schools once prior attainment and socio-economic factors are taken into account (Gibbons 2006).

reduce by 22 per cent the likelihood of a child developing depressive symptoms two years after treatment; by 23 per cent the likelihood of developing anxiety symptoms a year after treatment and can also reduce the likelihood of developing behaviour disorders (ibid).

These moves are a welcome step in the right direction. But as we argue in the concluding chapter, they do not go far enough: we need to ensure that personal and social skills are integrated properly into mainstream pedagogy, rather than being seen as an additional bolt-on to the curriculum.

Peer effects

Peers are clearly important. Recent analysis from the OECD has even argued that pupils at independent schools do better because they are surrounded by other privileged children, not because of the schools themselves (OECD 2004). But we still understand relatively little about how these processes work. Recent work in the UK has tended to convince policymakers that peer effects are relatively unimportant, finding that positive or negative peers make only a two per cent difference in either direction once family background is controlled for, in the development of internal locus of control. This is still a statistically significant result, but we can draw from a long history of literature from the US to show why the results may be somewhat misleading.

Peter Bearman's work on American high schools has shown that schools have different hierarchies of cliques: of athletes, 'druggies', 'eggheads' and so on (Bearman and Bruckner 1999). Where the 'eggheads' secure a place high up the hierarchy, he found that children do better academically; where 'druggies' reach the top they do less well, indicating the role of peer effects in setting norms of behaviour. However, the research showed that the wider peer context (friend group) is much more important than the prevailing school culture in influencing young people. For example, it was shown to be important in determining whether and when young people engage in sexual activity while the school culture is much less so (ibid).

Peer influence, the same study found, operates at many levels, and the network of close friends and the larger peer group have more significant effects on the female adolescent than do best friends. Some characteristics of friends appear to be of equal or greater importance as those of the individual in determining sexual debut and pregnancy risk. For instance, friends' risk status is a better determinant of pregnancy risk than the adolescent's own risk status, and the same holds true for friends' ages and sexual debuts. Further, friends' relationships with their parents are as important as a girl's relationship with her own parents.

Male and female friends have different influences on sexual debut and pregnancy risk. Female best friends' risk status is associated with sexual debut while male friends' risk status is associated with pregnancy risk.

Similarly, drawing from a sample of tenth-graders from the National Educational Longitudinal Survey, US researchers Gaviria and Raphael (1997) tested the influence of peer groups in the classroom on the propensity to engage in five activities: drug use, alcohol drinking, cigarette smoking, church going and the likelihood of dropping out of education. Moving a teenager from a school where none of her classmates used drugs to one where half used drugs increased the probability that the student would use drugs by approximately 13 per cent. Similar effects have been detected for alcohol consumption (with a 9 per cent increase in probability), cigarette smoking (8 per cent), church attendance (11 per cent) and dropping out of school (8 per cent). Harnessing peer effects should therefore be an important policy goal.

It is also possible to glean useful information from previous studies of how peer effects operate. For example, two influential pilot studies have focused on the processes by which students and their peers reciprocally influence each other (Kindermann 1993, 1996). These suggest that young people with poor motivation tend to form friendships with others who share similar motivation levels, while the same is true for those with better non-cognitive skills. The impact of these different peer groups is predictable: in groups where the motivation level is poor, children do even worse as a result of their association, while the opposite is true for the motivationally 'richer' peers.

One key factor thought to explain how peers influence each other is 'peer selection'. Childhood peer contexts have the characteristic that children are able to select their friend groups for themselves (within reason). These self-selected affiliations are based on mutual liking, shared interests, or shared activities. Thus, children tend to form friendships with those who are very similar to them in terms of development and skills (Kandel 1978). The key to mitigating the negative impact of peers, then, is to ensure children have the chance to mix more often with peers of different abilities.

Other research has shown that several aspects of the school may make a difference to peer effects. Influences outside the context of the peer group, such as influences from teachers or parents, can cause individuals within a group to become more similar and groups to become more different from one another. For example, teachers have been found to interact differently with students who enter a classroom with a high level of motivation than with students who enter the classroom motivationally 'poor' (Skinner and Belmont, 1993), and this in turn affects how students change across time. Teachers may treat in the same way students whom they perceive to be similar, and the students may change in a similar way even when they are not influencing each other at all.

There is also some early evidence that a certain structure of class may also be able to harness peer effects positively. One strand of research from the early 1990s examined the extent to which class composition can influence non-cognitive development, peer relations and behaviour, finding that when multi-aged children study together, the non-cognitive benefits can be large. Anderson and Pavan (1992), Ford (1977) and Miller (1990) reported improvements in children's attitude towards school from groups in multi-age classes. Anderson and Pavan (1992), Pratt (1986) and Way (1981) also detected a strengthening of children's self-concept and higher self-esteem. Children also demonstrated better attitudes towards their classmates in multi-age classes (Miller 1990; Pavan 1977) and showed less anxiety when at school (Katz et al 1990). In addition, Pavan (1992) claimed that the longer children are exposed to multi-age classes, the more positive their school-related attitudes became. There is also some evidence to show that multi-age classes may affect children's behaviour. Some (Furman et al 1979; Katz et al 1990; Pratt 1986) claim that social skills, particularly those of withdrawn, older children, improved in composite classes.

Other research looking at harnessing peer effects in schools has shown that within-class grouping that cuts across friendship groups can be particularly effective in forming new peer groups and improving personal and social skills (Kutnick et al 2005). But it remains clear that policymakers have much to learn in this area and that fresh approaches and thinking are necessary. A particularly important strand should be in terms of the way peer effects are mediated and influenced by extra-curricular activities and institutions.

Extra-curricular activities and institutions

During the teenage years, leisure activity takes on increasing significance in young people's lives, signalling the growing role of peer groups as an influence on young people. The nature of the activity changes across the teenage years, as does the company kept. Initial family leisure activities in early adolescence will later give way to single-sex activities, followed by mixed groups. Activity groups such as Scouts and Guides organised by adults are also prominent in the early- to mid-teens and are often an extension of schooling. In the late teens these tend to be replaced increasingly by commercially-run venues such as cafes, pubs and discos as the setting for social life.

But why should taking part in sport, community projects or after-school activities matter? There is a range of evidence showing benefits to young people attending these activities in attainment, behaviour and personal and social skills. A large body of research shows that participation in extracurricular activities promotes *educational attainment*, including low rates of school failure and dropout (Mahoney and Cairns 1997). Participation is associated with heightened school engagement and attendance, better academic performance and interpersonal competence and higher aspirations for the future (Barber et al 2001; Mahoney et al 2003).

Other work also shows that participation in organised activities is associated with reduced *problem behaviour* across adolescence and into young adulthood. Recent research shows that involvement reduces the likelihood of drugs and alcohol problems (Grossman and Tierney 1998), aggression, antisocial behaviour and crime (Mahoney 2000) or becoming a teenage parent (Allen *et al* 1997). This is explained by the opportunities presented to mix with non-deviant peers, to be mentored by adult activity leaders, and the fact that organised activities represent a conventional endeavour that is highly valued, challenging and exciting (Larson 2000).

Participation in organised activities has also been associated with improved mental health and personal skills, including low levels of negative emotions such as depressed mood and anxiety during adolescence (Barber *et al* 2001), heightened motivation for learning and self-efficacy (Mahoney *et al* 2005), the promotion of initiative – which involves the application of extended effort to achieve long-term goals (Larson 2000; Mahoney *et al* 2005), and maintaining or increasing self-esteem and sense of identity (Mahoney *et al* 2005). Some research has also shown that participation is related to developing a civic-minded identity (McIntosh *et al* 2005). The opportunities for social relationships and belonging presented by participation are thought to impact on these psychosocial processes. But what kinds of activities are best? And how important are micro-level processes?

Positive youth activities: organisation and structure

Recent research has shown that not all youth activities confer positive benefits: structural factors such as access and cost are important determinants of whether young people attend, but micro-level processes, such as the type of activity, organisational structure and goals are paramount. Analysis of the 1970 cohort study has shown that some youth activities such as sporting, uniformed and church activities were associated with positive adult outcomes by age 30, controlling for other relevant factors including outcomes up to age 10, while attendance at youth clubs was found to predict negative adult outcomes (Feinstein *et al* 2005).

By age 30, young people who participated in sports or community centres at age 16 were three per cent less likely to be depressed; five per cent less likely to be single, separated or divorced; three per cent less likely to be in social housing; two per cent less likely to have no qualifications; four per cent less likely not to have achieved level two qualifications; and three per cent less likely to be on a low income, than those who did not.

Attending uniformed activities meant you were three per cent less likely not to achieve level two qualifications, three per cent less likely to be on a low income and less likely to be depressed in adulthood than if you did not.

Young people who attended church were two per cent less likely to smoke in adulthood, three per cent more likely to experience psychological distress in adulthood and less likely to have no qualifications, low income or be an offender than those who did not.

These findings stand in marked contrast to those for youth club attendees, who were six per cent more likely to smoke in adulthood, one per cent more likely to be a single parent, one per cent more likely to be a victim of crime, five per cent more likely to have no qualifications and seven per cent more likely not to have reached level two qualifications than non-attendees. They were also five per cent more likely to be an offender and two per cent more likely to be on a low income. But what explains these differences?

Structural factors, such as the cost and availability of activities and institutions, are important. Cohort analysis shows that young people from disadvantaged backgrounds or who had high risk factors for poor attainment later in life were much more likely to attend unstructured activities, such as youth clubs (Feinstein et al 2005; Stattin et al 2005). But micro-level factors – particularly young people's existing personal and social skills – also played an important role in predicting attendance.

Attendance at uniformed youth organisations was associated with young people lacking internalising behaviour problems and internal locus of control, hailing from high-income to medium-income and high socio-economic status families. Attendance at church groups was associated with high internal locus of control, but low self-efficacy, and these young people hailed from low-income, middle-class families with parents showing high interest in their children's progress at school. Participation in sports and attendance at community centres was associated with a good, non-hostile relationship with mother, engagement in antisocial but not criminal acts and a higher internal locus of control score.

This stands in marked contrast to those participating in unstructured activities. Attendance at youth clubs for this cohort was associated with antisocial behaviour or mixing with antisocial peers in young adulthood, and was not associated with positive personal and social skills. But even accounting for these biases in participation – controlling for all other factors – it is clear that some forms of activity are much more beneficial than others. So the real question for policymakers is: why do organised activities have a positive impact on development? What is it about these activities that provide positive development opportunities for young people?

Understanding why some activities are beneficial: cohort analysis

ippr's analysis of the 1970 cohort study shows for the first time how different activities impact on young people's development of non-cognitions and other personal and social skills (see Appendix 2 for methodological details). Controlling for young people's locus of control and application scores at age 10 – and for other relevant factors such as parental background, educational attainment and parental interest – allows us to see

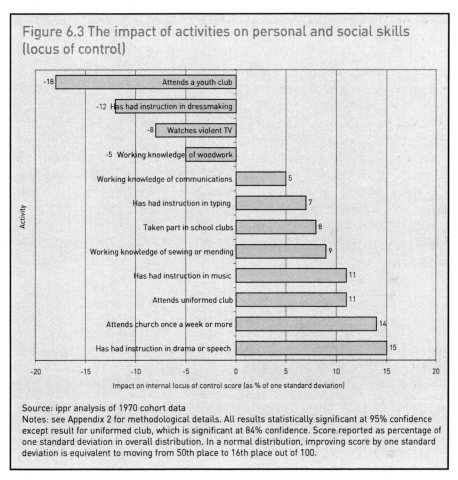

Figure 6.3 The impact of activities on personal and social skills (locus of control)

Activity

- Attends a youth club: -18
- Has had instruction in dressmaking: -12
- Watches violent TV: -8
- Working knowledge of woodwork: -5
- Working knowledge of communications: 5
- Has had instruction in typing: 7
- Taken part in school clubs: 8
- Working knowledge of sewing or mending: 9
- Has had instruction in music: 11
- Attends uniformed club: 11
- Attends church once a week or more: 14
- Has had instruction in drama or speech: 15

Impact on internal locus of control score (as % of one standard deviation)

Source: ippr analysis of 1970 cohort data
Notes: see Appendix 2 for methodological details. All results statistically significant at 95% confidence except result for uniformed club, which is significant at 84% confidence. Score reported as percentage of one standard deviation in overall distribution. In a normal distribution, improving score by one standard deviation is equivalent to moving from 50th place to 16th place out of 100.

which extracurricular activities at age 16 are positively associated with improved non-cognitions between the age of 10 and 16. Although this analysis does not prove causality, it is the best evidence we have available concerning the (potential) impact of activities on personal and social skills.

Broadly speaking, this analysis shows that those activities associated with positive outcomes in later life have a significant association (impact) in improving non-cognitions between the ages of 10 and 16, whereas those that are associated with worsened outcomes are also associated with reduced non-cognitions. This suggests that an important part of the benefit of participating in extra-curricular activities is in terms of developing good non-cognitive personal and social skills.

Our results are presented in more detail in Figure 6.3. This shows clearly that extracurricular activities that take place in a group setting, with a clear hierarchy, clear and well-defined aims – in that the group is working towards something, such as a final performance – and consistent meetings are positively associated with developing a more internal locus of control. Because locus of control is a continuum, our results are presented in terms of the distribution of scores (or standard deviations). In a normal distribution, an improvement of one standard deviation is equivalent to moving from fiftieth place out of 100 to sixteenth place. This means that, for example, having instruction in drama or speech is associated with a locus of control that is 15 per cent of one standard deviation more internal – the equivalent of moving from fiftieth place to fourty-fourth place out of 100. Although this may seem like a relatively small change, it is significant in terms of the impact of public policy and later life chances.

By way of contrast, those activities that are worst for developing an internal locus of control between the age of 10 and 16 are those that have limited hierarchy or group work. Importantly, watching violent TV is also associated with a more external locus of control at age 16 than at age 10.

These findings are intuitively attractive. And they go a long way towards confirming emerging theoretical work in evolutionary psychology and other fields that aims to shed light on the processes through which the beneficial impact of such activities occurs.

Understanding why some activities are beneficial: theory

Young people are profoundly influenced by each other's unmediated behaviour. For example, one of the most important predictors of an individual engaging in antisocial behaviour is whether their friends also engage and approve (Mahoney *et al* 2005; Wood 2005). This goes a long way towards explaining why youth clubs have such a distinctively negative impact on young people's life chances: they are often settings in which young people are free to interact with each other in unstructured, unmediated ways. While this can be a positive influence in some cases, this kind of setting can also become an environment in which negative peer influences proliferate. Given that those attending youth clubs tend to have poorer non-cognitions than those who attend other activities, it seems likely that a significant part of the club's impact is through these negative peer effects in the absence of adult authority, clear hierarchies and set goals. Evolutionary psychology and sociology can add deeper insight into how this influence operates through looking at how norms of altruism develop in communities.

These disciplines try to explain how the structure of communities results in patterns of behaviour. For example, the US sociologists Samuel Bowles and Herbert Gintis model three mechanisms by which 'communities' raise the net benefits to individual pro-social behaviours: reputation, retaliation and segmentation (Bowles and Gintis 1997). Reputation and retaliation are important in communities for obvious reasons: once someone develops a reputation for non-cooperation they lose out on benefits and opportunities from other community members, who retaliate. Segmentation is less self-explanatory but relies on the idea that communities naturally congregate along similarities, so those who also act more altruistically will tend to come into greater contact with others who act altruistically (ibid).

These mechanisms can promote pro-social behaviours even when people are not naturally pre-disposed to act altruistically – and the restricted mobility associated with communities (parochialism) enhances these mechanisms. This partly explains why structured activities such as local football clubs or drama groups have positive benefits: they tend to involve the same groups of people over time, which means that your reputation within the group becomes increasingly important. This tends to mitigate against taking short-term decisions that aggravate relationships with peers – thereby developing personal and social skills.

In the same way that communities help people to develop strong identities by being part of a bounded group, structured activities, by their emphasis on team involvement and an end-goal, do something similar. A range of sociological research empirically supports this theory (Barber *et al* 2001; McIntosh 2005). In addition, research has shown the beneficial impact of wearing a uniform for such activities (Feinstein *et al* 2005), which provides a similar function in terms of enforcing a group identity.

Professor Cass Sunstein has written in support of this idea, citing research examining the behaviour of students arriving at university for the first time (Sunstein 2003). In one study, students were told that their peers on campus were tee-total and the university culture was hostile to drinkers. These students are much less likely to subsequently drink, even when others do so in their presence: they were concerned their reputation within the student community would be undermined if they broke with social convention (Bearman and Bruckner 1999). This helps to explain why negative peer effects can easily proliferate in youth clubs, where there is limited adult mediation or structure and those who attend often have less developed personal and social skills, but are less present in uniformed activities or sports. But this raises the question of why these processes often do not occur in schools, considering they share the features of security, stability, authority and familiarity with uniformed extra-curricular activities.

It is likely that organised activities taking place outside of compulsory schooling, with an element of choice, the mixing up of age groups and freedom from exam pressures and other concerns about attainment, are what enable these contexts to be more beneficial to non-cognitive development. There is also a question mark over whether we actively want schools to be the main provider of opportunities for non-cognitive development or whether we should recognise the limits of their ability to do this due to the negative connotations schooling tends to have for the young people most in need of help. Replacing what currently counts as 'hanging out' with a more structured curriculum is not necessarily going to appeal. The risk is that it may stimulate all the negative connotations of schooling that put these young people off education in the first place. The solution is therefore not simply to promote church and sport. Rather, these contexts may offer good models of engagement with and between young people that could be replicated elsewhere. So what points can we draw from the evidence about the features of activities that promote positive development?

Features of contexts that promote positive development

Summarising much recent youth work, Eccles and Goodman developed a list of eight features of organised activities that are proven to promote development, summarised in Table 6.2.

This table enables us to assess the potential of different kinds of activities to assist in young people's development. But there are also important differences to communities and organised activities that we need to think

Table 6.2. Features of organised activities that promote positive development

Feature	Description
Physical and psychological safety	The context provides secure and health-promoting facilities and practices, allows for safe and appropriate peer interactions, and discourages unsafe health practices and negative or confrontational social interchanges
Appropriate structure	The context provides clear, appropriate and consistent rules and expectations, adult supervision, guidance and age-appropriate monitoring in a predictable social atmosphere where clear boundaries are known and respected
Supportive relationships	The context offers stable opportunities to form relationships with peers and adults wherein social interchanges are characterised by warmth, closeness, caring and mutual respect and where guidance and support from adults is available, appropriate and predictable
Opportunities for belonging	The context emphasised the inclusion of all members and maintains a social environment that recognises, appreciates and encourages individual difference in cultural values, gender, race/ethnicity and sexual orientation
Positive social norms	The context maintains expectations and requirements for socially appropriate behaviour and encourages desirable and accepted values and morals
Support for efficacy and mattering	The context allows for and supports autonomy, values individual expression and opinions, concentrates on growth and improvement rather than absolute performance, encourages and enables individuals to take on challenging responsibilities and to carry out actions aimed at making a difference
Opportunity for skill building	The context offers opportunities to learn and build physical, intellectual, psychological, emotional and social skills that facilitate well-being in the present and prepare individuals for health and competent functioning in the future
Integration of family, school and community efforts	The context provides opportunities for synergistic experiences that integrate transactions across family, school and community

Source: Eccles and Goodman in Mahoney et al (2005)

about when developing policy responses, drawing on the evolutionary psychological literature: after all, you cannot decide to opt out of your local community or school, but you can choose not to participate in a form of structured activity. This returns us to the challenge of how to encourage young people, particularly those from disadvantaged backgrounds, to participate in structured activities in the first place. But at the very least, policy and practice should work to ensure that youth contexts do not add to the processes of risk in ways that make the likelihood of adult social exclusion worse, on average, than it would otherwise have been. We develop these ideas in detail in the concluding chapter.

Increasingly unequal socialisation

The overview of developmental theory presented above and in the previous chapter provides a good indication of the most important factors in young people's development of personal and social skills. It is clear that the most crucial factor in developing these non-cognitive skills will always be micro-level processes within the family. But it is increasingly apparent that other institutions and bodies, if accessed properly, can mediate this influence. Living in a local area characterised by stability, high levels of collective efficacy and social capital can be a protective factor in enabling disadvantaged young people to 'buck the trend'. Similarly, attendance at high-quality pre-school arrangements, participation in schools characterised by stability, warmth and positive peer influences, and participation in structured or organised extra-curricular activities can all assist in non-cognitive development.

This theoretical and empirical analysis points towards our policy recommendations in the concluding chapter of this report. But it needs to be set in the context of modern Britain – against the most important social, cultural, economic, technological and demographic changes underpinning British society. We cannot expect socialising forces to have the same influence or sway over time; a central theme of this report is that the interdependence between factors is crucial.

Looking at changes over the recent past shows just how important this wider socio-economic context is in determining young people's non-cognitive outcomes. New analysis shows that social and demographic background, particularly the family, became a more important determinant of whether young people in Britain would develop good non-cognitions (such as locus of control, attention, self-esteem, concentration and application) for those born in 1970 than for those born in 1958. While income strongly predicts non-cognitive personal and social skills and attributes for the 1970 cohort (see Table 5.3, chapter 5) (Blanden *et al* 2006; Feinstein and Bynner forthcoming), for the 1958 cohort 'there are no significant relationships between family income and the non-cognitive scales' (Blanden *et al* 2006: 16).

This points to a major inequality in the way young people are socialised in Britain that began to make its impact felt on young people's non-cognitive abilities by the 1970s, with serious implications for social mobility.

Declining social mobility: the importance of personal and social skills

Social mobility studies track the relationship between parental background and children's outcomes later in life, often using people's position in the income distribution at around age 30 as a proxy for wider success. The headline finding of this field of research is that social mobility declined between the 1958 and 1970 cohorts (Ermisch and Nicoletti 2005; Blanden *et al* 2006): parental background became a more important determinant of success. In numerical terms, the correlation between parental background and child earnings aged 30 was 0.291 for children born in 1970 and 0.205 for those born in 1958 (Blanden *et al* 2006). Another way of putting this is that parental background became 42 per cent more important in determining later life chances between these two cohorts. Until very recently, we have

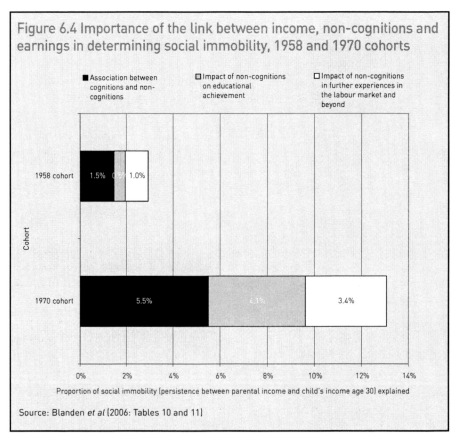

Figure 6.4 Importance of the link between income, non-cognitions and earnings in determining social immobility, 1958 and 1970 cohorts

Source: Blanden *et al* (2006: Tables 10 and 11)

been unable to explain the importance of different factors in this decline.

The analysis presented in the previous three chapters goes some way towards an explanation, by showing that personal and social skills and attributes have become both more important in determining outcomes *and* more strongly related to family background and income. But we need not rely on hypothesis alone: recent research using the cohort studies has now put numbers to exactly how far these shifts have impacted on social mobility (Blanden *et al* 2006).

Comparing the strength of the link between non-cognitions and social mobility for the 1958 and 1970 cohorts reveals that in just 12 years non-cognitions became 33 times more important in determining relative life chances. As Figure 6.4 shows, the rising association between parental income and background, children's personal and social skills and attributes, and subsequent achievement explains 22 per cent of the rise in social immobility between the 1958 and 1970 cohorts (Blanden *et al* 2006), of which nine percentage points occurred at age 16 exams, three percentage points in subsequent educational attainment, two percentage points in protection from unemployment and seven percentage points in further experiences in the labour market and beyond.

This raises a crucial question: what explains the fact that parental income now determines people's non-cognitive development more than ever? The next chapter assesses the evidence, setting youth transitions in the UK in an international and historical context.

References

Note: all web references correct at September 2006

Allen JP, Philliber S, Herrling S and Gabriel KP (1997) 'Preventing teen pregnancy and academic failure: Experimental evaluation of a developmentally based approach' *Child Development* 64: 729-742

Anderson RH and Pavan BN (1992) *Nongradedness: Helping it to happen* Lancaster, PA: Technocratic

Barber BL, Eccles JS and Stone MR (2001) 'Whatever happened to the jock, the brain and the princess? Young adult pathways linked to adolescent activity involvement and social identity' *Journal of Adolescent Research*: Special Issue, 16: 429-455

Bearman P and Brückner H (1999) 'Peer Effects on Adolescent Sexual Debut and Pregnancy: An Analysis of a National Survey of Adolescent Girls.' The National Campaign for the Prevention of Teen Pregnancy, April

Bennett A, Lesch K, Heills A, Long J, Lorenz J, Shoaf S, Champoux M, Suomi S, Linnoila M, and Higley J (2002) 'Early experience and serotonin transporter gene variation interact to influence primate CNS functioning' *Molecular Psychiatry* 7: 118-122

Blanden J, Gregg P and Macmillan L (2006) *Explaining Intergenerational Income Persistence: Non-cognitive Skills, Ability and Education*. Working Paper No. 06/146 Bristol: Centre for Market and Public Organisation, available at www.bris.ac.uk/Depts/CMPO/workingpapers/wp146.pdf

Bowles S and Gintis H (1997) *The Moral Economy of Communities: Structured Populations and the Evolution of Pro-social Norms* University of Massachusetts: Department of Economics, available at www.umass.edu/preferen/gintis/prosocial.pdf

Bronfenbrenner U (1979) *The ecology of human development* Cambridge, MA: Harvard University Press

Brooks-Gunn J, Gross RT, Kraemer HC, Spiker D, and Shapiro S (1992) 'Enhancing the Cognitive Outcomes of Low Birth Weight Premature Infants: For Whom Is Intervention Most Effective?' *Pediatrics* 89 (8): 1209-1215

Buck N and Gordon I (2004) 'Does Spatial Concentration of Disadvantage Contribute to Social Exclusion?' in Boddy M and Parkinson M (eds) *City Matters* Bristol: Policy Press

Carneiro P and Heckman J (2003) 'Human Capital Policy', in Heckman J and Krueger A (eds) *Inequality in America: What Role for Human Capital Policy?* Cambridge: MIT Press

Cote S and Healy T (2001) *The Well-being of Nations. The role of human and social capital* Paris: Organisation for Economic Co-operation and Development

Currie J (2001) 'Early Childhood Intervention Programs: What do we Know?' *Journal of Economic Perspectives* 15: 213-238

Currie J (1995) 'Welfare and the Well-Being of Children' *Fundamentals of Pure and Applied Economics* 59, Chur, Switzerland: Harwood Academic Publishers

Delorenzi S (ed.) (2006) *Going Places: neighbourhood, ethnicity and social mobility* London: Institute for Public Policy Research

Department for Education and Skills (DfES) (2006) *The Social and Emotional Aspects of Learning (SEAL)* London: TSO, available at: www.teachernet.gov.uk/teachingandlearning/socialandpastoral/sebs1/seal/

Dixon M, Rogers B, Reed H and Stone L (2006) *CrimeShare: The unequal impact of crime* London: Institute for Public Policy Research, available at: www.ippr.org.uk/members/download.asp?f=%2Fecomm%2Ffiles%2FCrimeSh are%2Epdf

Ermisch J and Nicoletti C (2005) *Intergenerational earnings mobility: Changes across cohorts in Britain.* ISER Working Paper 2005-19 Essex: ISER, available at: www.iser.essex.ac.uk/pubs/workpaps/pdf/2005-19.pdf

Feinstein L (2003) 'Inequality in the early cognitive development of British Children in the 1970 cohort' *Economica* 70: 277

Feinstein L and Bynner J (forthcoming) *The benefits of assets in childhood as protection against adult social exclusion: the relative effects of financial, human, social and psychological assets.* Unpublished mimeo London: Institute of Education

Feinstein L, Bynner J and Duckworth K (2005) *Leisure contexts in adolescence and their effects on adult outcomes* London: Centre for Research on the Wider Benefits of Learning

Ford BE (1997) 'Multi-Age Grouping in Elementary School and Children's Affective Development' *The Elementary School Journal* 78 (2): 149-159

Furman W, Rahe DF and Hatrup WW (1979) 'Rehabilitation of Socially Withdrawn Preschool Children Through Mixed Age and Same-age Socialisation' *Child Development* 50 (4): 915-922

Gaviria A and Raphael S (1997) *School-Based Peer Effects and Juvenile Behavior,* University of California at San Diego, Economics Working Paper Series 97-21, Department of Economics, UC San Diego

Gibbons S (2006) *School choice, peer groups and segregation.* Unpublished

Glennie S, Treseder G, Williams J and Williams M (2005) *Mini Sure Start Local Programmes: An Overview of their early implementation* Partnership at Work and Associates, available at: www.surestart.gov.uk/_doc/P0001455.pdf

Green G, Grimsley M, Suokas A, Prescott M, Jowitt T and Linacre R (2000) *Social Capital, Health and Economy in South Yorkshire Coalfield Communities* Sheffield: Sheffield Hallam University

Gregg and Machin (2004) 'Mobility and Joblessness' in Card D, Blundell R and Freeman R (eds) *Seeking A premier League Economy* Chicago: University of Chicago Press

Gregg P and Machin S (1999) 'Childhood Disadvantage and Success or Failure in the Labour Market' in Blanchflower D and Freeman R (eds) *Youth Employment and Joblessness in Advanced Countries* Cambridge: NBER

Gregg P and Machin S (2001) 'The Relationship Between Childhood Experiences, Subsequent Educational Attainment and Adult Labour Market Performance', in Vleminckx K and Smeeding T (eds) *Child Well Being in Modern Nations: What do we Know?* Bristol: Policy Press

Grossman JB and Tierney JP (1998) 'Does Mentoring Work? An impact study of the Big Brothers Big Sisters Program' *Evaluation Review* 22: 403-426

Guidestar UK (2006) 'Charities Search' Guidestar UK, available at: www.guidestar.org.uk/index.aspx

Furlong A, Cartmel F, Biggart A, Sweeting H, and West P (2003) *Youth Transitions: Patterns of Vulnerability and Processes of Social Inclusion* Edinburgh: Scottish Executive

Halpern D (1999) *Social capital: the new golden goose* Faculty of Social and Political Sciences, Cambridge University. Unpublished

Halpern D (2001) 'Moral values, social trust and inequality – Can values explain crime?' *British Journal Criminology* 41: 236-251

Heckman J and Wax A (2004) 'Home Alone' *Wall Street Journal*, 23 January

Jones G (2005) *The Thinking and Behaviour of Young Adults, Literature review for the ODPM* London: TSO

Kandel DB (1978) 'Homophily, selection, and socialization in adolescent friendships' *American Journal of Sociology* 84: 427-436

Katz L, Evangelou D and Hartman J (1990) *The case for mixed-age grouping in early education* Washington DC: National Association for the Education of Young Children

Kindermann TA (1996) 'Strategies for the study of individual development within naturally existing peer groups' *Social Development* 5: 158-173

Kindermann TA (1993) 'Natural peer groups as contexts for individual development: The case of children's motivation in school' *Developmental Psychology* 29: 970-977

Kreamer G, Ebert M, Schmidt D and McKinney W (1998) 'A longitudinal study of the effect of different social rearing conditions on cerebrospinal fluid norepinephrine and biogenic amine metabolites in rhesus monkeys' *Neuropsychopharmacology* 2: 175-189

Kutnick P, Sebba S, Blatchford P, Galton M, JT, MacIntyre H and Berdondini L (2005) *The Effects of Pupil Grouping: Literature Review.* DfES Research Report 688 London: TSO

Labour Party, The (2005) *The Labour Party Manifesto 2005: Britain forward not back* London: The Labour Party

Larson RW (2000) 'Toward a psychology of positive youth development' *American Psychologist* 55: 170-183

Lehrer J (2006) 'The Reinvention of the Self: A mind-altering idea reveals how life affects the brain', *Seed Magazine*, February 23, available at: www.seedmagazine. com/news/2006/02/the_reinvention_of_the_self.php?page=all&p=y

MacDonald R and Marsh J (2005) *Disconnected Youth? Growing Up in Poor Britain* Basingstoke: Palgrave

Mahoney JL (2000) 'Participation in school extracurricular activities as a moderator in the development of antisocial patterns' *Child Development* 71: 502-516

Mahoney JL and Cairns R (1997) 'Do extracurricular activities protect against early school dropout?' *Developmental Psychology* 33: 241-253

Mahoney JL, Cairns R and Farmer T (2003) 'Promoting interpersonal competence and educational success through extracurricular activity participation' *Journal of Educational Psychology* 95: 409-418

Mahoney JL, Larson RW and Eccles JS (eds) (2005) *Organized Activities as Contexts for Development* London: Lawrence Elbaum

Magnuson K, Meyers M, Ruhm C and Waldfogel J (2004) 'Inequality in Preschool

Education and School Readiness' *American Educational Research Journal* 41: 115-57

Meyers M, Rosenbaum D, Ruhm C and Waldfogel J (2004) 'Inequality in Early Childhood Care and Education: What do we Know?' in Neckerman K (ed.) *Social Inequality* New York: Russell Sage Foundation

McIntosh H, Metz, E and Youniss J (2005) 'Community Service and identity Formation in Adolescents' in Mahoney JL, Larson RW and Eccles JS (eds) *Organized Activities as Contexts for Development* London: Lawrence Elbaum

Miller B (1990) 'A review of the quantitative research on multi-grade instruction' *Research in Rural Education* 7 (2): 3-12

NICHD Early Child Care Research Network (2003) 'Does amount of time spent in child care predict socioemotional adjustment during the transition to kindergarten?' *Child Development,* 74

OECD (2004) *Learning for tomorrow's world: First Results from PISA 2003* Paris: OECD

Palmer S (2006) *Toxic Childhood: How The Modern World Is Damaging Our Children And What We Can Do About It* London: Orion

Pavan BN (1977) 'The non-graded elementary school: research on academic achievement' *Texas Tech Journal of Education* 4 (2): 91-107

Pavan BN (1992) 'The benefits of non-graded schools' *Educational Leadership* 50(2): 22-25

Pearce N and Paxton W (eds) (2005) *Social Justice: Building a fairer Britain* London: Institute for Public Policy Research/Politico's

Pratt D (1986) 'On the merits of multi-age classrooms' *Research in Rural Education* 3 (3): 111-115

Ramey CT and Ramey SL (2000) 'Early Childhood Experiences and Developmental Competence' Danziger S and Waldfogel J (eds) *Securing the Future: Investing in Children from Birth to College* New York: Russell Sage Foundation Press

Reivich K, Gillham J, Shatté A and Seligman M (2006) *A Resilience Initiative and Depression Prevention Program for Youth and their Parents* University of Pennsylvania: Positive Psychology Center

Robinson MB (2004) *Why Crime? An Integrated Systems Theory of Antisocial Behaviour* Upper Saddle River, NJ: Prentice Hall

Sammons P, Sylva K, Melhuish E, Siraj-Blatchford I, Taggart B and Elliot K (2002) 'Measuring the Impact of Pre-School on Children's Cognitive Progress Over the Pre-School Period', Technical Paper 8A, The Effective Provision of Pre-School Education Project, London: Institute of Education

Sampson RJ (1999) 'What Community Supplies' in Ferguson R and Dickens W (eds) *Urban Problems and Community Development* Washington: Brookings

Sampson RJ and Groves W (1989) 'Community Structure and Crime: Testing

Social-Disorganization Theory' *The American Journal of Sociology* 94 (4)

Sampson RJ and Laub JH (1993) *Crime in the Making: Pathways and Turning Points Through Life* London: Harvard University Press

Sampson R, Raudenbush S and Earls F (1997) 'Neighbourhoods and violent crime: a multilevel study of collective efficacy', quoted in Halpern D (1999) *Social capital: the new golden goose* Faculty of Social and Political sciences, Cambridge University. Unpublished

Simons R, Simons LG, Harbin Burt C, Brody GH and Cutrona C (2005) 'Collective Efficacy, Authoritative Parenting and delinquency: A Longitudinal test of a model of integrating community and family level processes' *Criminology* 43: 989

Skinner EA and Belmont MJ (1993) 'Motivation in the classroom: Reciprocal effects of teacher behavior and student engagement across the school year' *Journal of Educational Psychology* 85: 571-581

Skinner EA, Zimmer-Gembeck MJ and Connell JP (1998) 'Individual differences and the development of perceived control *Monographs of the Society for Research in Child Development* 254 (vol. 63, no. 2-3)

Smith DJ and McVie S (2003) 'Theory and Method in The Edinburgh Study of Youth Transitions and Crime', *British Journal of Criminology* 43: 169-195

Smith M (2006) 'Youth work: an introduction', in Smith M (ed.) *The Encyclopedia of Informal Education* London: Infed, available at: www.infed.org/youthwork/b-yw.htm

Stanley K, Bellamy K and Cooke G (2006) *Equal Access? Appropriate and affordable childcare for every child* London: Institute for Public Policy Research

Stattin H, Kerr M, Mahoney J, Persson A and Magnusson D (2005) 'Explaining why a leisure context is bad for some girls and not for others' in Mahoney JL, Larson RW and Eccles JS (eds) *Organized Activities as Contexts for Development* London: Lawrence Elbaum

Sunstein RC (2003) 'The Law of Group Polarization', in Fishkin JS and Laslett P (eds) *Debating Deliberative Democracy* Oxford: Blackwell

Sweatman R (1867) 'Youths' Clubs and Institutes', in Solly H (ed.) *Working Men's Clubs* (revised ed. 1904) London: Simpkin, Marshall, Hamilton, Kent and Co.

Way JW (1981) 'Achievement and self-concept in multi-age classes reconsidered' *Review of Educational Research* 66 (3): 322-340

Wood M (2005) *Perceptions and experience of antisocial behaviour: findings from the 2003/2004 British Crime Survey.* Home Office Online Report 49/04 London: TSO, available at: www.homeoffice.gov.uk/rds/pdfs04/rdsolr4904.pdf

7: Socialisation in a changing world

This chapter assesses what has gone wrong in the socialisation of modern youth. The evidence so far suggests that family background, social class and affluence became more certain predictors of young people's personal and social development in the period between the 1958 and 1970 cohorts. The research shows that disadvantaged children born in 1958 were only marginally less likely than their more fortunate peers to develop good personal and social skills, but their counterparts born in 1970 faced a very different prospect: their material disadvantages were compounded by a relative lack of opportunity to develop personal and social skills – just as these became more central in determining life chances. Between these two cohorts, social injustice began to play a part, adversely affecting the socialisation of young people and contributing to a decline in social mobility.

We look at why and how these changes to the socialisation of young people occurred – assessing the direction of change in Britain over the past few decades in economic and social terms, and exploring future trends – to identify the prospects for later and future cohorts of children.

We argue that contemporary socio-economic trends, including rising affluence alongside growing inequality, in the UK and in other advanced capitalist societies, which first started to bite in the period between the 1958 and 1970 cohorts, have combined to increase young people's unmediated interactions with the market and consumerism, thereby creating a 'social extension of adolescence'. In many parts of the country, we have failed to replace the shifting, basic building blocks of socialisation into the adult world – the family, religion, more uniform social expectation and rigid employment structures – with any coherent alternative. The result has been young people's increasingly unequal access to the kinds of opportunities that develop personal and social skills, with knock-on effects for life chances. This chapter identifies where gaps in the paths to socialisation for the worst off are becoming most apparent.

We start by outlining the three most important trends that shape people's interaction with consumerism – rising affluence, spending on services and income and wealth inequality – before assessing how structural changes to families and communities have created greater scope for growing consumerism to fundamentally alter the socialisation of young people. This analysis points towards our policy recommendations, outlined in the final chapter.

Unprecedented affluence

It is easy to forget how quickly living standards have improved over the past fifty years. Real GDP per head, a much maligned but still useful measure of prosperity, has increased by more than 283 per cent since 1955 and on average Britons are almost twice as rich today as they were in 1975 (ONS 2006a). Looking ahead, the tide of rising affluence shows no sign of turning.

Current projections estimate that Britons will be 32 per cent richer by 2020: in more tangible terms, the average couple with no children will earn an additional £137 a week in 2006 prices (DWP 2005; HM Treasury 2005). And even these estimates probably understate the scale of change: £137 is likely to go much further by 2020 as more efficient production techniques continue to reduce the cost of manufactured items, bringing more consumer goods within the means of ordinary people.

A look at trends in Britons' ownership of material possessions clearly illustrates the scale of recent rises in affluence. In 1970, around half of households had access to a car and just 30 per cent had central heating. By 2004/05, 75 per cent had access to a car and 95 per cent had central heating (Gibbins and Julian 2006). Figure 7.1 shows that even over the last

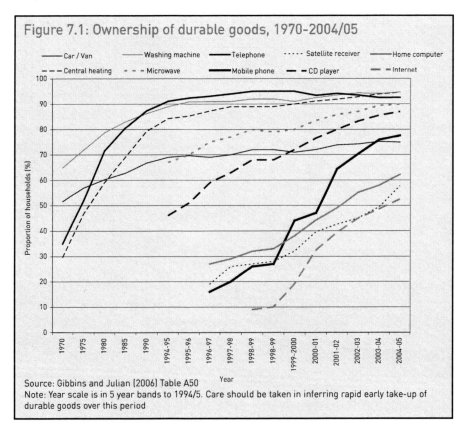

Figure 7.1: Ownership of durable goods, 1970-2004/05

Source: Gibbins and Julian (2006) Table A50
Note: Year scale is in 5 year bands to 1994/5. Care should be taken in inferring rapid early take-up of durable goods over this period

decade, possessions that were once the preserve of the better off have become widespread – and that the spread of new technologies has been particularly rapid in comparison to the earlier spread of basic domestic durables. In 1996/97 just 16 per cent of Britons owned a mobile phone, compared to 78 per cent in 2004/05. Home computers have also become far more common, with 62 per cent of households owning one in 2004/05, compared to 27 per cent in 1996/97.

Perhaps unsurprisingly, looking behind these trends reveals an enduring social class bias. For example, in 2004/05, virtually all of those in the richest decile had a washing machine and central heating, compared to 79 and 90 per cent respectively of those in the poorest decile (ibid). These indicators are compelling signs of enduring social injustice. In terms of the ownership of new technologies, this is even more unequal, probably because these have not yet saturated the market.

In 2004/05, just 25 per cent of the poorest households had a home computer and just 18 per cent an internet connection, compared to 93 per cent and 89 per cent respectively of the richest households (ibid). As people's interaction and capacity to make the best use of new technologies becomes more important in determining life chances, there is substantial cause for concern that children in the poorest social groups have less opportunity to develop these skills in the home through engaging with new technology. And there are other concerns that these traditional ways of measuring income and poverty are becoming less adequate in capturing young people's divergent experiences, as the way that families make use of their income changes.

Spending money: a shift to services

Over the past few decades the way people spend their money has changed. The trends are clear: Britons are consistently spending a smaller proportion of their income on basic necessities, such as fuel, power and food, and a larger proportion on leisure services and household services (and housing); this is shown in Figure 7.2, which tracks the proportion of people's income spent on various categories between 1984 and 2004, with speculative extrapolations to 2020. In 1984 Britons spent seven per cent of their income on leisure services, compared to 14 per cent in 2004. And if current trends continue, by 2020 the average household will spend 19 per cent of its income on leisure services – a radically different picture to that of 20 years ago.

There has been little empirical research into the developmental and social implications of greater leisure and service spending, but commentators and sociologists have been quick to point to plausible hypotheses (see chapter 4). An important result of the analysis in chapter 4 has been that market risk has become increasingly transferred to individuals as firms

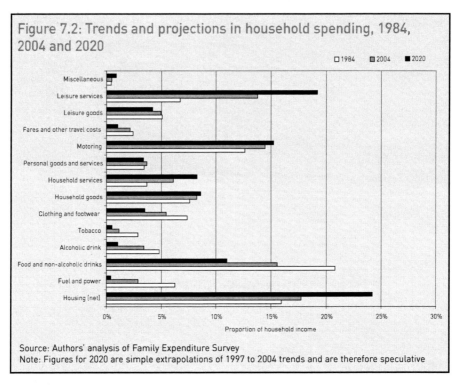

Figure 7.2: Trends and projections in household spending, 1984, 2004 and 2020

Source: Authors' analysis of Family Expenditure Survey
Note: Figures for 2020 are simple extrapolations of 1997 to 2004 trends and are therefore speculative

offer a wider variety of choices and options, and the capacity to choose between service offerings has thereby become more important in determining life chances. For example, those who make poor pensions decisions early in life, or invest with the wrong fund, can see much poorer returns than those who navigate the financial marketplace more cannily (Dixon 2006; Resolution Foundation 2006).

In developmental terms, it seems clear that early experiences in engaging with the market – and parental example – are crucial in setting up norms for young people's interaction with the private sector later in life. And for those young people whose parents have the incomes with which to provide these experiences, the chance of getting it right may be much higher.

Although this shift towards greater leisure spending has been seen across all social groups – in 2004/05, those in the poorest and richest income decile spent 12 and 13 per cent respectively of their gross income on recreation and culture (Gibbins and Julian 2006) – the internationally high level of income inequality in Britain means that the actual *amount* the richest families spend on leisure is much higher than that of the poorest families. As Table 7.1 shows, those in the richest quintile spent £106 a week on recreation and culture, compared to £19.40 for those in the poorest quintile, and £120.90 on transport per week in 2004/05, compared to £15.20 for those in the poorest quintile.

The implications of this are quite straightforward. Richer parents are

Table 7.1: Weekly expenditure on leisure services and various other goods, 2004/05		
	Poorest income quintile	**Richest income quintile**
Transport	£15.20	£120.90
(of which public transport)	*£3.10*	*£17.60*
Recreation and culture	£19.40	£106.00
(of which sports admissions, subscriptions, leisure class fees and equipment hire)	*£0.70*	*£11.90*
(of which cinema, theatre, museums and so on)	*£0.50*	*£4.70*
(of which books, newspapers and magazines)	*£2.60*	*£7.60*
(of which package holidays)	*£2.50*	*£24.40*
Source: Adapted from Gibbins and Julian (2006)		
Note: figures average of bottom two and top two deciles.		

increasingly able to purchase activities and access to institutions that can enhance children's personal and social development, while those in poorer groups are unable to provide similar benefits for their children, meaning they will lose out in relative developmental terms. Looking at young people's travel patterns provides one example. In 2004, the most affluent families made more trips by car, rail and air than poorer families, and travelled further with each trip (DfT 2005) – potentially exposing the former to new experiences and cultures unavailable to their less wealthy contemporaries.

Unfortunately, data restrictions do not allow us to meaningfully compare trends in leisure spending over time between different groups. But while the average parent spends more than £9,300 on their child's hobbies by the time they are 21 and another £6,700 on their other leisure and recreational pursuits (Liverpool Victoria 2005; Maxwell *et al* 2006), it is likely that far less is spent on children from more disadvantaged backgrounds, leaving them further behind – given that the gap in spending power between the richest and poorest groups has increased substantially over recent decades, as inequality rose faster than ever before.

Historically high inequality

Greater affluence has benefited all groups in society. But some groups have fared much better than others over the last three decades as income and wealth inequality rose substantially. During the 1980s and early 1990s those at the top of the income distribution experienced much more rapid income growth than those towards the bottom – the rich got richer faster than the poor (HMRC 2006; Jones 2006).

But since the late 1990s, these trends in inequality seem to have reversed: between 1994 and 2004/05, income growth has been fastest for

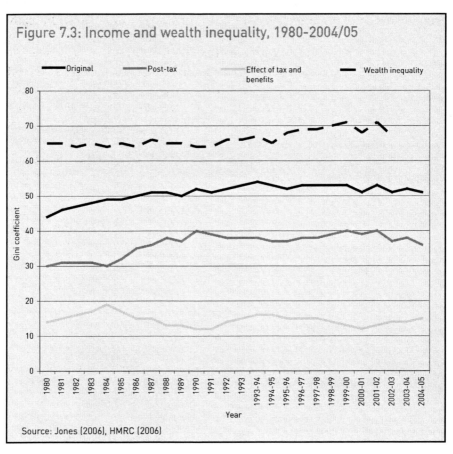

Figure 7.3: Income and wealth inequality, 1980-2004/05

Source: Jones (2006), HMRC (2006)

those towards the bottom of the income distribution (HMRC 2006; Jones 2006). And as Figure 7.3 shows, there are signs that income inequality post tax and transfers – shown by the mid-grey line – is tentatively beginning to decline, although it remains historically and internationally high (Dixon and Paxton 2005). However, figures for wealth inequality, which remains much higher than income inequality, are less encouraging.

Looking in more detail at the chart allows us to trace some of the under-lying factors behind these overall trends. The black line shows original (market) income inequality – what has happened in the labour market before redistribution through tax and transfers. This gives a good idea of trends in market returns (or 'earned' income). It is clear that much of the rise in inequality over the 1980s was due to labour market trends. As we argue in chapter 4, skill-biased technological change has increasingly polarised the labour market into 'lovely' and 'lousy' jobs, with growing dis-parity in pay and little migration between them. The decline of trade union influence may also have contributed to growing wage gaps (Goodman and Oldfield 2004).

These market trends are important. But it is equally apparent that the welfare state became much less redistributive from 1984 until the early 1990s when economic recession and rising unemployment increased dependence on benefits; this is shown by the light grey line, which charts the effect of taxes and benefits in reducing income inequality (Dixon and Paxton 2005). Since 2000/01, the welfare state has begun to work much harder again in reducing income inequality through tax and transfers – but this time against a context of high levels of employment. This is a sure sign that the Tax Credits architecture is working to reduce inequality.

Wider socio-economic factors, including those less suited to direct policy interventions, have also been important. ippr's modelling shows that a fifth of the rise in income inequality between 1979 and 2003/04 was due to demographic change, including the rise in solo living, an ageing population, differential fertility patterns and more complex family types (Dixon and Margo 2006). Increased female participation in the labour market, outlined in detail in chapter 4, has also resulted in a growing disparity between affluent two-earner households and others (Goodman and Oldfield 2004; Dixon and Margo 2006).

Commentators have been quick to point to the pernicious impact of rising inequality, highlighting its various implications for crime rates, health and happiness (Wilkinson 1996; Kahn *et al* 1998; Layard 2005; Pearce and Paxton 2005; Gibbons *et al* 2006). But emerging evidence is beginning to show that another important impact of rising inequality – in combination with rising affluence, service-orientated spending and other socio-economic trends – has been to change the way different groups of young people are socialised: unmediated consumerism has become a quasi-parent for many young people, with differing effects for the most and least advantaged.

Consuming childhood

The impact of capitalism on culture and society has been a matter of great debate ever since its emergence in Europe as an economic system in the late 1700s. Recent decades have seen an emerging strand in the debate around the role of consumption in children's lives, in part driven by a widespread recognition that the children's market has expanded dramatically, in terms of both direct expenditures by children, and their influence on parental purchases (Schor 2004). The nature of the relationship between capitalism and children has changed fundamentally. Today's young people spend increasing amounts of time thinking about, and purchasing, consumer goods and are a large consumer market in their own right – each year they spend an estimated £680 million of their own money on snacks and sweets, £660 million on clothing, £620 million on music and CDs, £400 million on footwear, £350 million on computer software, £250 million on magazines and £83 million on toiletries (Childwise 2005). Add this to 'pester power' and the total net worth of the child-orientated market comes to an estimated £30 billion a year (ibid; Mayo 2005).

These figures are striking. But perhaps the best indicator of young people's growing immersion in unmediated consumerism has been the year-on-year increases in pocket money since records began in the late 1980s, which have consistently outstripped inflation. On average, 12- to 16-year-olds in Britain received £9.76 a week in 2006 – nearly three times as much as their 1987 counterparts (Halifax 2006).

Importantly, pocket money for younger children has risen even faster: seven- to 11-year-olds received £6.30 a week in 2006, more than four-and-a-half times as much as in 1987 (ibid). In pocket money terms alone, this age group is now worth nearly £20 million a year and has become an increasingly lucrative target audience for unscrupulous advertisers eager to harness the 'pester power' of an increasingly brand-aware group of young consumers – 31 per cent of boys and 44 per cent of girls claim that they 'could not go for a whole week without spending any money' (ibid). And looking in more detail at the way children spend their money, it is clear that children's consumer preferences are evolving, becoming more adult as they shift their spending focus away from the traditional core category areas of sweets, food and toys towards mobile phones, cosmetics and clothing products (ibid). With 80 per cent of 13- to 16-year-olds now shopping with their peers, viewing it as a normal leisure activity, they are also taking greater control over making spending decisions.

The crucial difference between the way young people interact with each other today and how they did in previous generations is that it is increasingly unmediated: although parents act as guardians to many consumption practices and control most purchases of goods and services (McKendrick *et al* 2000), young people increasingly act as consumers without adult guidance or supervision (Schor and Holt 2000; Schor 2004). This is a trend that is encouraged by both advertisers and child-orientated corporations but viewed as unwelcome by many parents, 84 per cent of whom stated in 2004 that there was too much marketing directed at children (NFPI 2004).

Unmediated advertising[18]

Although detailed trend data is hard to come by, there is wide consensus among academics, industry analysts and commentators that the advertising industry is becoming increasingly sophisticated and aggressive in its targeting of young people, especially children (NFPI 2004; Schor 2004; Mayo 2005). Advertisers are accused of redefining age-appropriateness by reducing target ages and creating a more adult-like relationship with children

---

18. This section draws heavily on work by Ed Mayo (2005)

earlier. One example of this is the 'tweening' of the six- to 12-year-old market – products previously aimed at teenagers are now also aimed at younger children, encouraging them to care about teenage concerns such as diet and beauty from an earlier age (Schor 2004). More than a century after Coca-Cola's first celebrity spokesperson appeared in an advertisement and 51 years after the first toy was advertised on television[19] (Mayo 2005), public fascination with unscrupulous advertising has led to a plethora of undercover media exposés.

Following are three recent examples. An internal brief from Walker's Crisps explicitly aimed to make children think 'Wotsits are for me. I am going to ... pester mum for them when she next goes shopping'. A job advertisement for a senior researcher in Kellogg's 'kids brands' division asked potential applicants to prove that they could spend 'time understanding kids, finding out what interests them ... and appreciating the realm of pester power'. Perhaps most damningly, an undercover report exposed the agency behind a recent Fruit Winders campaign boasting that their strategy had 'entered the world of kids in a way never done before' and managed to 'not let mum in on the act'. By using a kind of coded language, the ads had set up a conspiratorial relationship between the brand and the child, with the parents on the outside (Freedland 2005).

These pernicious techniques have been accompanied and driven by increasingly creative and intense methods of research into children's consumption habits and interests. Focus groups, consumer panels, market research and advertising firms are now the norm for most marketers (Ogilvy 1995; Earls 2002; Mayo 2005), who are also finding new avenues to promote their products, as standard television advertising has come to comprise a smaller part of total marketing expenditures. Direct advertising is growing and in the US advertisers have even entered into sponsorship agreements with schools (Schor and Holt 2000) – a trend that has fast found its way into British life.

Many British companies now offer incentives to schools for the purchase of products and equipment. Particularly ironic examples include Cadbury's 2003 campaign aimed at encouraging children and parents to buy chocolate bars in exchange for new school sports equipment, which received extensive criticism from health campaigners such as Dr Ian Campbell, Chair of the National Obesity Forum and Kath Dalmeny of the Food Commission for being a 'cynical ploy' (Revill 2003). But this relatively direct approach is just the tip of the marketing iceberg, most of which is hidden from view. For example, the communications agency Boomerang Media, which hit the headlines recently for its promise to give clients access to 'toddlers' play areas, on place mats and lunchboxes ... [and] turn children's parties into a

---

19.   Mr Potato Head made his television debut in 1955 (Mayo 2005)

'communication opportunity' and a 'brand experience for kids" (Freedland 2005), has now extended its remit to the 250 largest indoor children's play areas and boasts of being able to 'create a campaign that's relevant and suitable for the play house environment ... which will engender a feeling of brand generosity ... [with an] average dwell time of 1.5 hours' (Boomerang Media 2006).

The evidence suggests that these techniques are working. Although individual adverts may have limited impact, their combined cultural impact is striking: a recent survey showed that nearly half of 10- to 12-year-olds think that the brand is important when they buy and the average ten-year-old has internalised 300 to 400 brands (Mayo 2005). And famously, while a 2003 report showed that about half of four- and five-year-olds entering school for the first time could not recognise their own names, speak in a way understandable to others or count up to five (Basic Skills Agency 2003), 81 per cent of three- to six-year-olds could recognise the Coca-Cola logo in 2002 and 69 per cent the McDonald's trademark golden arches (Dammler and Middelmann-Motz 2002). And the evidence is growing that advertisements change behaviour and demands, even for this young group.

International research shows that children as young as two years old have established beliefs about specific brands and what the use of them means about lifestyle and personality (for a good overview of the literature

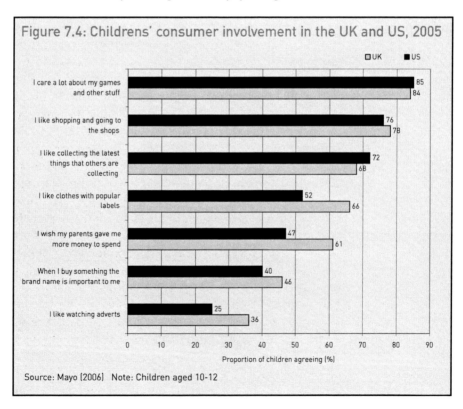

Figure 7.4: Childrens' consumer involvement in the UK and US, 2005

Source: Mayo (2006) Note: Children aged 10-12

see the Kaiser Family Foundation 2001). Children aged three to six who watch a lot of commercial television ask for more items from Father Christmas and demand a higher proportion of branded items than infrequent viewers (Pine and Nash 2001). Heavy viewers of television aged four to ten are more likely to ask for advertised items than infrequent viewers (Adler 1980) and the more frequently children watch television, the more frequently they ask for products advertised on television (Götze and Schlegelmilch 2000).

Worryingly, contemporary British children seem to be more enmeshed in consumerism than even their US counterparts. Last year, children in Britain were more brand aware and less satisfied than American children with what they see as the limited amount of money they have to spend (Mayo 2005). As Figure 7.4 shows, 66 per cent of British children said they 'like clothes with popular labels', compared to 52 per cent of US children, and 46 per cent of British children said the 'brand name is important' compared to 40 per cent of US children.

Perhaps unsurprisingly, British parents consistently say that there is too much marketing aimed at children (NFPI 2004). But there is emerging evidence that children are beginning to agree, demanding curbs on the 'use of inappropriate advertising aimed at young people' (Mayo 2005: 35).

Unmediated (electronic) media

These are contentious issues, with private sector interests heavily stacked in their favour. But governments still have a range of responses, including the example set by Sweden where a 1996 law explicitly states that 'advertising during a TV broadcast may not have as its objective capturing the attention of children under 12 years of age' and advertising is banned immediately 'before or after a programme or a portion of a programme which is oriented primarily to children under 12 years of age' (Swedish Department of Culture 1996: 844). But even these kind of measures do not impinge on children's increasingly unmediated access to (primarily electronic) media.

In 2005, eight in ten children aged five to 16 in the UK had a TV in their room and more than half had a personal video recorder or DVD to go with it (Childwise 2005). And around one in five children – nearly 1.5 million young people (GAD 2005) – have access to the internet in their own room (Livingstone and Bober 2005). This raises familiar concerns around young people's access to inappropriate content, including explicit sexual imagery: 57 per cent of children reported having come into contact with online porn, most of it accidentally such as in the form of pop-ups, and one in four had received pornographic spam. In 2006, although around half of all parents with internet access had some kind of blocking in place to stop their children viewing certain types of websites (Ofcom 2006), just seven per cent of parents in 2005 were aware that their child had received sexual comments through this form of media (Livingstone and Bober 2005).

Technological progress has brought other worries too, particularly in relation to young people's ability to engage in unmediated and unsupervised interaction with other young people (and adults) through interactive websites. A typical and popular example is MySpace.com which purports to be a 'private community ... [where] you can share photos, journals and interests with your growing network of mutual friends' (MySpace.com 2006) and now has more than 65 million members across the world, who make 4.5 million transactions (sending messages, and so on) per minute (E-week.com 2006).

For the vast majority of young people, this presents a welcome learning opportunity, one in which they can interact with peers across the world. But it also heralds new concerns. As young people spend increasing amounts of time online, interacting with peers without adult support and supervision or structure to their interactions, they may be vulnerable to the potentially negative influences that peers often have on each other when they are not subject to the basic building blocks of socialisation that encourage individuals to be emotionally and socially mature. At the most serious level, parents have claimed their children were encouraged to commit suicide by online friends who were simply too young and inexperienced to understand what they were doing (Cobain 2005). On a more common level, it appears that online bullying is increasingly prevalent too.

A report published earlier this year identified seven types of 'cyber-bullying', ranging from abusive text messages, e-mails and phone calls to bullying in internet chatrooms, social networking sites and instant messaging (Smith *et al* 2006). The researchers found that up to one in five pupils in London schools have experienced some form of cyber-bullying and that the psychological impact was similar to or worse than traditional bullying, partly because it allows the bully to target the victim outside of school hours. Worryingly, a third of victims had never told an adult about the problem; in 2005 just four per cent of adults acknowledged that their child had been bullied online (Livingstone and Bober 2005).

The impact of consumed childhood

Tracking the impact of social and cultural change is notoriously difficult. Despite a wealth of theory and hypotheses, there have been few definitive empirical studies assessing links between children's greater involvement in unmediated consumer markets and media, and their mental health and personal and social development. But pulling together existing evidence from disparate research strands enables us to tell a powerful story about the impact of recent changes to children's unmediated interactions with consumerism.

ippr's analysis of cohort study data suggests that media viewing habits, and specifically the watching of violent television programmes, can have a significant impact on personal and social development. Children recorded in the mid 1980s as watching 'a lot' of violent television were likely to develop a less internal locus of control between the ages of 11 and 16, controlling for all other factors. And landmark research has shown that consuming a media diet high in violence is linked to an increase in fear and aggression among children (Donnerstein *et al* 1994; Gentile *et al* 2004; Kaiser Family Foundation 2001). These are relatively well rehearsed concerns, which should remain centre-stage. But changes to the way young people consume such media, particularly the growing tendency to do so alone, may have wider impacts for children's well-being.

Academics have recently criticised the new 'bedroom culture' – a consequence of the rising number of children with access to television in their bedroom – as leading to worsening school performance (Gentile and Walsh 2002). This is supported by research showing that increased amounts of media exposure have been correlated with lower school performance (Kaiser Family Foundation 2001), increased obesity (Livingstone 2006; Gable and Lutz 2000; Robinson 1999) and, perhaps most importantly, a greater incidence of psychological distress (Kraut *et al* 1998; Schor 2004). These effects have not gone unnoticed by parents. As far back as 1999, polls have shown parents are aware of, and critical of, the impacts that advertising and marketing have on children (Schor and Holt 2000; Schor 2004), complaining that the pressure to buy and own products made children depressed and inspired heightened awareness of looks, materialism and sexuality.

Academic research in both the US and UK shows that these concerns have empirical backing. A recent in-depth US study of children's 'involvement' in consumer culture – which asked how much they cared about owning items, how important designer labels and a nice family car were to them, whether they usually were focused on acquiring something new, and how much they wanted to be rich and wanted their parents to be richer – found that the greater the involvement of children in consumerism, the more likely they were to suffer depression, anxiety and stress-related physical discomfort (Schor 2004). A similar study in the UK has replicated these findings, showing that:

> Young people feel pressure to have the latest 'in vogue' items. Girls in particular experience feelings of inadequacy and discomfort as a result of 'images of perfection' promoted by advertising... The more consumerist children were – the ones who were 'brand aware', cared about their possessions and liked collecting – the more likely they were to be dissatisfied more widely.

(Mayo 2005: 3)

What underpins these feelings of dissatisfaction? One persuasive strand of thinking explains the impact of childhood consumerism in terms of its impact on children's perceptions of their identity. The central idea here is that children are becoming more dependent on brands to give them a sense of the aspirations, values and possessions that are important and acceptable – that brands are beginning to powerfully dictate social hierarchies in a way formerly done by communities and parents, effectively making judgements of value about what is appropriate in terms of lifestyle and normative behaviour (Martens *et al* 2004).

By effectively determining which goods and services are considered 'cool', it is no surprise that marketers can predict which toys will sell out next Christmas; this has a powerful socialising effect on young people. Because children are particularly vulnerable to the need to gain acceptance and belong to social groups, buying and owning goods and clothes means that children from relatively affluent backgrounds can find acceptance and belonging within their desired social group and distinguish themselves from other groups of young people (Martens *et al* 2004). But if children and young people are unable to buy and own the desired goods, they may find it harder to gain social acceptance within their peer group: the social con-sequences of not having the 'right' clothes or goods can be severe, such as ostracisation and bullying in the playground (Schor 2004; Mayo 2005). This has obvious negative effects on children's well-being. But it also creates considerable concern for parents, particularly those from poorer back-grounds, who do not want to 'let down' their children and as a result may buy them treats they cannot afford (Martens *et al* 2004); this sometimes leads to serious financial difficulties and a cycle of debt (Dixon 2006).

This impact on young people's social identities is important. But so too is the impact on their sexual and age-related identities. Advertisers are accused of redefining age-appropriateness by reducing target ages and cre-ating a more adult-like relationship with children earlier (Schor 2004). One example of this is the 'tweening' of the six- to 12-year-old market: products previously aimed at teenagers are now also aimed at younger ages, encour-aging them to care about teenage concerns such as diet and beauty from earlier in life. For example, psychologists have found that young children brought up playing with toys like Bratz Dolls (sexy, fashion-conscious, con-sumerist characters marketed to children aged from 4 to 13), or Barbie (with her range of accessories and possessions including houses, cars and boyfriends), are more likely to internalise self-centered consumerist lifestyles, and therefore be 'better consumers' as they grow up, or even while they are young (Schor and Holt 2000).

Exacerbated by poverty

These concerns are worrying. But worse is the fact that the negative impact of increasing childhood consumerism is disproportionately experienced by young people from disadvantaged backgrounds. In the words of one recent

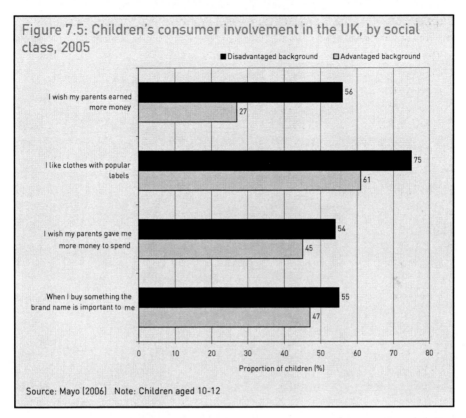

Figure 7.5: Children's consumer involvement in the UK, by social class, 2005

- Disadvantaged background
- Advantaged background

I wish my parents earned more money
- Disadvantaged: 56
- Advantaged: 27

I like clothes with popular labels
- Disadvantaged: 75
- Advantaged: 61

I wish my parents gave me more money to spend
- Disadvantaged: 54
- Advantaged: 45

When I buy something the brand name is important to me
- Disadvantaged: 55
- Advantaged: 47

Proportion of children (%)

Source: Mayo (2006)   Note: Children aged 10-12

report: 'Advertising makes poverty bite' (Mayo 2005: 3). Recent empirical research shows that children from the poorest social groups are the most interested in consumer and materialist concerns. As Figure 7.5 shows, children from disadvantaged backgrounds are more likely than their wealthier peers to say that brand name is important, more likely to favour clothes with popular labels and more likely to wish their parents gave them more money to spend.

The implications of these brand and consumer-orientated concerns are clear. Unmediated interaction with consumerism compounds the disadvantages poorer children face, particularly in altering their relationships with and expectations of their parents. It is striking that the largest gap in attitudes between richer and poorer children in Figure 7.5 is in terms of wishing their parents earned more money. Critics argue that the messages from advertisers often undermine parental and other adult authority, portray parents as 'uncool' or out of touch, or ridicule them, citing research that shows that the more children and young people bought into consumer culture, the more negative they were about their parents, and the more likely they were to fight and disagree with them (Schor and Holt 2000; Schor 2004).

The social extension of adolescence: younger, earlier

Children's ever earlier engagement with consumerism is reflected across their lives, as adolescence extends ever further into childhood. Critics have pointed to computer-literate, fashion-conscious children that are subject to more choice and arguably more pressure to 'grow up quickly' than any recent generation. Contemporary youth live accelerated lives, passing physical, emotional and social milestones at younger ages.

Over the last 50 years, the average age of first sexual intercourse fell from 20 for men and 21 for women in the 1950s to 16 by the mid-1990s, and the proportion of young people who are sexually active before the age of consent has risen from less than one per cent to 25 per cent over the same period (Wellings *et al* 2001). There are also indications of the physical process of puberty happening earlier. Scientists tracking changes in the age of onset of menarche (puberty) in girls over the past 100 years have found it has fallen by about three years (Whincup *et al* 2001; Gluckman and Hanson 2006).

These physical changes have been accompanied by cultural shifts in similar directions. The research outlined above shows how children participate in consumer activities at ever earlier ages, but there is increasing evidence that similar trends can be seen in other adult domains. Pundits point to the

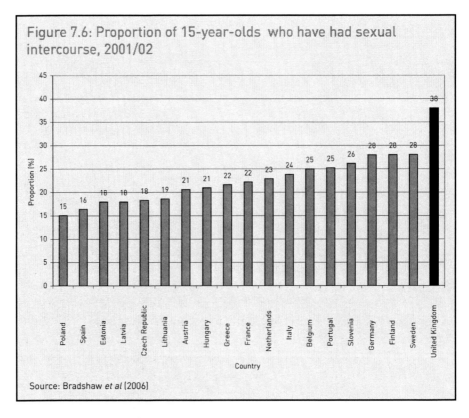

Figure 7.6: Proportion of 15-year-olds who have had sexual intercourse, 2001/02

Source: Bradshaw *et al* (2006)

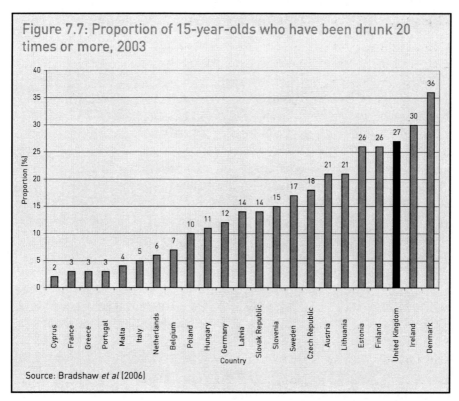

Figure 7.7: Proportion of 15-year-olds who have been drunk 20 times or more, 2003

Source: Bradshaw *et al* (2006)

proliferation of sex tips for teenagers in youth magazines and health and beauty spas for 10-year-old girls as evidence that children are exposed to and expected to navigate adult concerns at younger stages in their development (Schor and Holt 2000; Schor 2004; Mayo 2005). As Figure 7.6 shows, 38 per cent of British 15-year-olds had had sex in 2001/02, a far higher proportion than in any culturally similar European country (Bradshaw *et al* 2006).

Similar patterns can be seen along a range of other 'adult' behaviours. Thirty-eight per cent of British 15-year-olds had tried cannabis in 2003, compared to just seven per cent in Sweden and 27 per cent in Germany. And the international picture for teenage drunkenness is similar: as Figure 7.7 shows, in 2003 British 15-year-olds were more likely than those in any other European country except for Ireland and Denmark to have been drunk 20 times or more in their lives so far (Bradshaw *et al* 2006).

Rising affluence has been an important driver of these trends but tech-nological change has also played an important role. The proliferation of mobile phones – earlier this year 49 per cent of children aged 8 to 11 and 82 per cent of those aged 12 to 15 had their own mobile phone (Ofcom 2006) – in combination with increased internet use has meant that many young people are increasingly able to control their own social lives at younger ages, planning their leisure activities independently of adult supervision.

Delayed adulthood: a middle-class phenomenon?

The counterpoint to the creeping extension of adolescence into childhood is its extension into adulthood, which has attracted a wealth of academic research and theory, including Arnette's idea of 'emerging adulthood' (Arnette 2004). In the media, a plethora of shorthand terms have been mooted for a new generation of 'kidults' and 'boomerang kids' who refuse to grow up and postpone traditional markers of the transition to adulthood. Compared to before, on average, young people in Britain are staying at home for longer, postponing childbirth, cohabiting for longer, living alone for longer, having more relationships, delaying marriage and staying in education for longer.

Although transitions are less extended than in many other European countries (Bynner 2005), the trends over time are indisputable: the average age of first-time mothers increased from 23.7 in 1971 to 27.1 in 2004; the average age of first marriage has increased from 25 for men and 23 for women in 1971 to 31 and 29 respectively in 2003; the proportion of under-60s cohabiting rose from 11 per cent for men and 13 per cent for women in 1986 to 24 per cent and 25 per cent respectively in 2004; the number of men and women aged between 25 and 44 living alone increased nearly six-fold between 1973 and 2004; the numbers participating in higher education rose from 621,000 in 1970/71 to 2,436,000 in 2003/04; and 57 per cent of British men aged 20 to 24 (and 23 per cent of those aged 25 to 29) were still living with their parents in 2005 compared with 38 per cent and 11 per cent respectively of women (Babb *et al* 2006; Dixon and Margo 2006).

But averages can be misleading – we should be wary of drawing broad conclusions from this set of statistics. While some of these trends are universal, affecting all young people, social class cuts strongly across others: 'emerging adulthood' is marked by both stratification and exclusion and by forces that are 'fundamentally social, cultural and structural in nature' (Bynner 2005: 13). Chapter 2 showed the importance of social class in predicting outcomes such as teenage pregnancy and participation in education, employment and training. Looking in more detail at many other indicators of extended adolescence also reveals polarisation. For example, solo living can be a positive lifestyle choice for young affluent urbanites, but is also often the result of misfortune or relationship breakdown (Dixon and Margo 2006).

Taken in the round, the picture is one of deep-rooted inequality: lengthy transitions into adulthood, some characterised by long periods of identity formation (Arnette 2004), tend to be the preserve of the better off, while those less fortunate find themselves entering work and parenthood relatively early, taking on greater responsibility at younger ages. But to fully understand the processes underpinning these differing transition pathways we need to look beyond changes rooted in consumerism, towards the wider social context.

Differing family structures

The last thirty years have seen an ongoing diversification of family types in Britain, as marriage rates have fallen from their 1972 peak, divorce rates have risen, fertility rates have fallen and both unmarried cohabitation and solo living have become more common (Babb *et al* 2006). For the most part these are trends that are expected to continue into the future (Dixon and Pearce 2005; Dixon and Margo 2006). These shifts have brought considerable implications for the familial socialisation experiences of children growing up over the last decades, arguably resulting in increasingly unequal capacity for socialisation and increased importance of micro-level processes within families.

Perhaps the most striking trend is that children are today much less likely to grow up with both natural parents. In the early 1970s, 92 per cent of children lived in a two-parent family and just seven per cent lived in a single-parent family. By early 2005, although two-parent families were still the norm – 76 per cent of children lived with a couple – lone parenting had become much more common, with 24 per cent of children living with one parent, 90 per cent of whom with their mother (Babb *et al* 2006). And for some ethnic groups lone parenting has become more common still: around half of children of Black Caribbean background born in 2000 were living with one parent last year, compared to 13 per cent of children from a White British background and five per cent from Indian or Bangladeshi backgrounds (Babb *et al* 2006).

At the same time, as a result of more complex family formation and partnership patterns, stepfamilies are also far more common than before: around 55 per cent of all divorcing couples had at least one child under 16 in 2003, and in 2004/05, 10 per cent of all families with dependent children in Britain were stepfamilies (ibid). Most children live with their mothers following family break-up and so most stepfamilies tend to include children from the previous relationship of the woman, with around one in ten stepfamilies including children from the father's previous relationship (ibid).

A related shift is that children are less likely to grow up in large families, largely as a result of historically low fertility, due in part to the large 'baby gap' between the number of children Britons want and the number they are able to have (Dixon and Margo 2006). Nine per cent of households in 1971 consisted of families with three or more children, compared to just four per cent of in 2005. Again, an important exception to this rule is that some minority ethnic groups have much larger families than others (Babb *et al* 2006).

In combination, these trends have meant that the impact of traditional familial socialising influences – both natural parents and siblings – has become more differentiated. For the majority of children who still grow up with siblings and both natural parents, their familial experience is relatively similar to that of previous generations. But for the growing numbers of children who have more complex living arrangements or no siblings, their contact with these socialising influences can be more limited: for example, nearly four in ten children born in 2000 who lived with just their mothers had no contact at all with their father in 2003 (Calderwood 2004). And these differences have arguably been amplified by changing employment patterns.

Hard-working families

As highlighted in chapter 4, one of the most fundamental labour market shifts of the past half century has been the increased participation of women in paid work. Working-age women in Britain with dependent children are less likely to be economically active than those without, but this is closely related to the age of their youngest child, with activity increasing with age of the child (ONS 2003). However, working-age men with dependent children are more likely to be economically active than those without, and the age of their children appears to have little impact. In contrast with women, though, those men with the youngest children are most likely to be working (O'Brien and Shemilt 2003; ONS 2003).

Britain also has a distinctively long-hours working culture compared to much of continental Europe. Although this appears to be in decline for men – 30 per cent worked more than 45 hours per week in 2006, down from a peak of 39.6 per cent in November 1997 – trends for women appear much more static. Around 10 per cent of women consistently work more than 45 hours a week and a growing proportion now work more than 35 hours a week (ONS 2006d).

These trends all mean that parents have tended to have less time available to spend with their children, a situation exacerbated by relatively static gender roles within the family. The evidence shows that women's greater labour market participation has not been matched by an increase in men's participation in unpaid household or caring work (Stanley 2005).

In an international context, these trends in work, family life and family structures – in combination with cultural idiosyncrasies – mean that British children spend less time with their parents than in most comparable European countries (Bradshaw *et al* 2006). Recent analysis of the OECD's PISA data shows this clearly: for example, as Figure 7.8 shows, in 2003 just 64 per cent of 15-year-olds in the UK ate with their parents around a table several times a week – a lower proportion than any other country in Europe apart from Finland.

As Figure 7.9 shows, this low level of parental contact is not restricted to

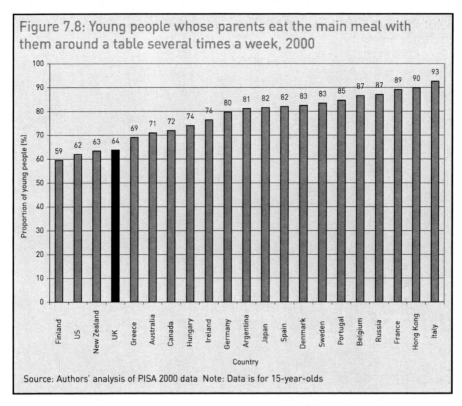

Figure 7.8: Young people whose parents eat the main meal with them around a table several times a week, 2000

Source: Authors' analysis of PISA 2000 data   Note: Data is for 15-year-olds

mealtimes. In 2003, just 62 per cent of 15-year-olds said that their parents spend time 'just talking' to them several times a week, far less than in Italy or Hungary, where nearly 90 per cent of young people spent time with their parents in this way.

This finding resonates strongly with the experiences of both parents and children. Recent MORI polls have shown that while 15 per cent of parents say their main concern is 'not spending enough time with children', 24 per cent of children say their parents are not always there when they need them, 35 per cent say their parents do not make them feel loved and cared for, and 44 per cent say they are unable to talk to their parents about problems (Page and Wallace 2004). When asked in 2002, 49 per cent of parents did not know either exactly where their children are, or whom they are with or what they are doing, after school, at the weekends or during the holidays (Nestlé 2006).

These trends are striking, but we should once again be wary of averages. Many parents feel under increased pressure to ensure their children are equipped with the skills and knowledge necessary for success, for example by scheduling them into a host of after-school activities, taking longer maternity or paternity leave and providing opportunities to travel (Waldfogel 2006). As family sizes have grown smaller and people (particularly professionals) have waited longer to have children, parents place more

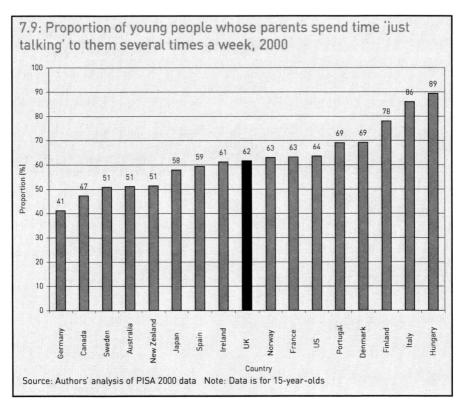

7.9: Proportion of young people whose parents spend time 'just talking' to them several times a week, 2000

Source: Authors' analysis of PISA 2000 data   Note: Data is for 15-year-olds

emotional value on children and are willing to invest more in their development (ibid). But clearly not all parents are equally able or equally willing to provide for their children.

As softer skills – such as motivation, application, self esteem and behaviour – increase in importance, it is the children whose parents are able to invest – financially as well as emotionally – in their children's development who will increasingly succeed. This partly explains why parental background has become a more important determinant of outcomes and why young people's unmediated consumerism has grown over the past few decades. But it has also meant that the role and capacity of the community to socialise young people has become increasingly important: for those young people whose parents play a smaller role in their lives, whether by design or by accident, communities have become more central in determining young people's life chances.

Fragmenting communities?

The previous chapter demonstrated how important collective efficacy is in enabling a community to socialise its young people. Unfortunately, reliable measures tracking this over time are simply not available. Nevertheless, returning to some of the evidence presented in chapter one allows us to draw some initial conclusions.

It seems clear that as crime rates rose through the 1980s and early 1990s, most measures of social trust fell, and as crime rates fell from their mid-1990s apex, social trust appeared to rise. If current trends continue, this bodes well for the ability of communities to effectively socialise young people. But these overall trends do less to inform us about differences between communities over time or the experiences of different groups.

The current picture is one of considerable inequality between areas. In 2005, levels of collective efficacy were strongly related to disadvantage: 92 per cent of those in the most affluent areas said local people would intervene if they saw children spray-painting graffiti, compared to 58 per cent of those in the most deprived areas (Kitchen *et al* 2006). If it is the case that this pattern has held over the last few decades, it seems clear that children from more advantaged communities would have experienced greater levels of intervention from their neighbours and other adults than those from more disadvantaged communities. As the impact of communities became more important, this would have meant a growing divide between the socialisation experiences of the best and worst off. It is not possible to substantiate this hypothesis, given the dearth of good empirical evidence. Nevertheless, there are indicators we can draw on.

Looking at crime rates over time allows us to track at least one form of inequality between local areas. We know that crime rates are currently very unequally distributed: disadvantaged households are more likely to be victims of crime and more likely to suffer severe impacts as the result of being a victim, with knock-on effects for collective efficacy, than more affluent households. For example, nearly 20 per cent of people who are wounded in a violent crime avoid local places following their assault (Dixon *et al* 2006). But research looking at trends shows that while the inequality of the distribution of crime increased during the 1980s (Trickett *et al* 1995), there is growing evidence that it has decreased since 1997: in 2003/04, the poorest households were 1.02 times as likely to be victims of violent crime as the more affluent households, compared to 1.29 times in 1997, and they were 2.3 times as likely to be afraid of physical attack in 2002/03, compared to 2.6 times in 1999 (Dixon *et al* 2006). If crime rates and collective efficacy are linked, which most theorists suggest they are, this would suggest that it is only quite recently that more disadvantaged areas, relative to more affluent areas, have experienced sustained rises in collective efficacy.

These trends suggest that Britain 'pulled apart' during the 1980s and early 1990s, before 'coming together' during the late 1990s and early 2000s. Harder economic measures also appear to confirm this general analysis. Regional trends in Gross Value Added (GVA) per head – a standard measure of output and prosperity – over the past 17 years show that there was growing inequality between regions between 1989 and 1998, which has since stalled: between 1998 and 2004 there was little change in regional inequality on this measure (ONS 2006c).[20]

In addition to these trends, changing patterns of internal and external migration have altered the demographic make-up of many communities. Between 1991 and 2001, the non-white minority ethnic population of the UK rose from 3 million to 4.6 million (8.1 per cent of the British population). Although immigration levels are currently high by historical standards, most of the growth of communities of Caribbean, Indian, Pakistani and Bangladeshi origin has not been from immigration but from a larger number of births than deaths in these populations. On the other hand, the African- and Chinese-origin populations have grown mostly due to immigration. Between 1991 and 2001, some minority ethnic groups grew faster than others – largely related to migration trends. Longer established groups, such as the Black Caribbean-origin population, grew at a much slower rate than more recent immigrant populations, such as the Bangladeshi- and Black African-origin populations.

These trends may have important implications for levels of collective efficacy. In 2005, people from minority ethnic groups were much less likely to say that people in their community would intervene if a child was rude to an adult or if a group of children were spray-painting graffiti than those from a white background. This highlights just how important it is to engage all communities in local issues in a holistic and integrated way, particularly given that younger generations in the UK are much more likely to be from an ethnic minority background than older cohorts.

Unmediated socialisation

Taken together, these trends suggest that while many communities have experienced recent rises in levels of collective efficacy – with positive implications for the socialisation of young people – significant challenges remain, particularly in the most disadvantaged, often minority ethnic communities. So what are the implications for the socialisation of young people?

Throughout this chapter we have argued that many of today's young people are left more open to the unmediated influence of consumerism than previous generations. But this unmediated interaction is likely to play out in other areas – especially in terms of interaction with peers – as the socialising capacity of many parents and communities has waned. A look at the available evidence concerning trends in young people's use of time appears to confirm this hypothesis.

Chapter 2 showed that between 1992 and 2005/06 there was a 60 per cent rise in complaints about 'teenagers hanging around'. This potentially

---

20. This is confirmed by ippr's statistical analysis, which shows that the standard deviation of scores rises between 1989 and 1998 and then remains stable to 2004.

points towards changes in the way young people spend their time, spending more with peers and less with adults and in institutional contexts.

Research is severely hampered in this area by a lack of reliable longitudinal data. But one indicator of rising peer socialisation in contemporary Britain is the estimated number of young people belonging to a gang. This was six per cent of 10- to 19-year-olds in 2006, and 12 per cent of 14- to 16-year-olds (Sharp *et al* 2006). Young people who get on badly with their parents, who spend little or no time with them or who live in areas with high levels of local disorder are much more likely to be members – often citing the fact that there is 'not very much or nothing to do' in their local area as reasons for joining a gang.

Importantly, these gangs are usually centred on a particular location which the group called 'its own', often an open public space: 43 per cent of members said their gang was centred on a park or recreation ground and 39 per cent said it was centred on a street corner or square. Just 25 per cent claimed that their gang was based around a particular property or home (Sharp *et al* 2006). Trends in gang membership are hard to come by, but these figures suggest that a significant proportion of British youth is spending the majority of its time in unmediated, unstructured interaction with peers. International comparisons are revealing here: Figure 7.10 shows that young people in Britain are much more likely to spend time 'with friends' on four or more evenings a week than those in other countries: 45 per cent

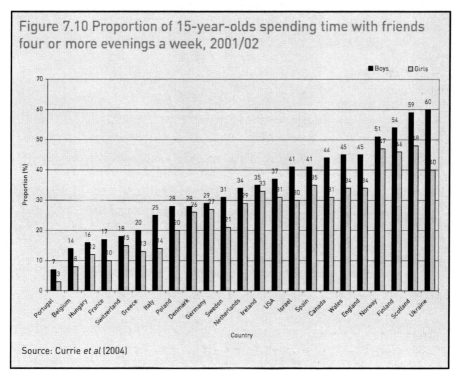

Figure 7.10 Proportion of 15-year-olds spending time with friends four or more evenings a week, 2001/02

Source: Currie *et al* (2004)

of boys and 34 per cent of girls in England said they did this in 2001/02, compared to 37 per cent of boys and 31 per cent of girls in the US, 31 per cent of boys and 21 per cent of girls in Sweden and just 17 per cent of boys and ten per cent of girls in France.

One important cultural shift underpinning these trends in young people's activities has been the widespread decline in religious belief over the past century. In previous decades, religion was a powerful socialising force, shaping the leisure time, attitudes and expectations of young people as well as their behaviour and morality. But it is well known that participation in religious activity has declined markedly in recent decades. Figure 7.11 compares the likelihood of individuals born in different years to hold religious beliefs, attend religious events or be affiliated to religious institutions or organisations. It shows that there has been a rapid decline in religious affiliation, particularly for those born after 1940, that attendance has fallen particularly rapidly for generations born after 1950, and that religious belief has been on a fairly consistent decline since 1900 (Crockett and Voas 2004).

There are countervailing trends. For example, minority ethnic groups of every generation are more religious than the rest of the British population, although religiosity within these groups is declining at a similar rate (ibid). And as certain minority ethnic groups become larger proportions of the population, some religions may become increasingly common: the propor-

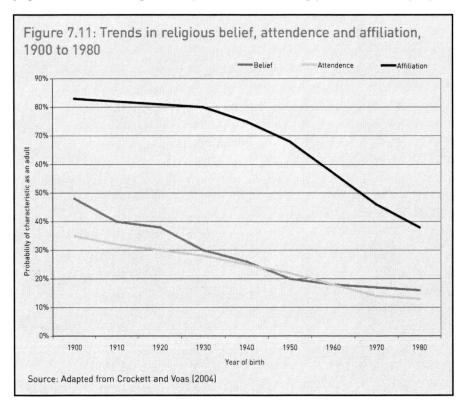

Figure 7.11: Trends in religious belief, attendence and affiliation, 1900 to 1980

Source: Adapted from Crockett and Voas (2004)

tion of people saying they were Muslim doubled from one to two per cent between 1997 and 2001, and it is likely that rates have risen further since. But the implications for the majority of young people are clear: religious institutions play a much smaller role in their lives and in shaping either their values or leisure time than ever before. The original pioneers of dedicated 'youth work' – the Sunday School clubs of the late 18th Century – appear to be facing an inevitable decline. More than 200 years on, it is time to rethink our policy approach to youth once again.

Rethinking youth policy

We have always known that redistributing resources, ensuring access to high quality education and providing opportunities are important to youth policy. But the evidence presented in this and previous chapters shows that we need to think about equality in agency – the actual capacity to take up opportunities – as well. And this means recognising how the world has changed and the implications for the socialisation of young people.

Currently, young people who do not have access to the factors that develop their non-cognitive abilities, who tend to come from disadvantaged backgrounds, have less engaged parents, a less orderly and secure local environment and spend more time with more deviant peers or under the unmediated influence of the media, are increasingly vulnerable to failure, while their better socialised peers will increasingly succeed. The solution is not simply to focus education policy on non-cognitive development but to engineer a more fundamental shift in our thinking. We outline a policy response in the next chapter.

References

Note: web references correct at September 2006

Adler R (1980) *The Effects of Advertising on Children: Review and Recommendations USA* Lexington Books

Arnette G (2004) *Emerging Adulthood: The Winding Road from Late Teens through the Twenties* Oxford: OUP

Babb P, Butcher H, Church J and Zealey L (2006) *Social Trends 36* London: TSO, available at: www.statistics.gov.uk/downloads/theme_social/Social_Trends36/Social_Trends_36.pdf

Basic Skills Agency (2003) *Young Children's Skills on Entry to Education* London: Basic Skills Agency

Boomerang Media (2006) Personal communication to the authors

Bradshaw J, Hoelscher P and Richardson D (2006) 'An Index of Child Well-being in the European Union' *Social Indicators Research* 78(1): 1 – 45

Burgess A (2005) 'Bringing fathers back in: Child support in Australia' *Public Policy Research* March, 12(1)

Bynner J (2005) 'Reconstructing the Youth Phase of the Life Course: the Case of Emerging Adulthood' *Journal of Youth Studies* 8: 367-84

Calderwood L (2004) 'At first the infant: children of the new century', in Stewart I and Vaitilingam R (eds) *Seven Ages of Man and Woman* Swindon: Economic and Social Research Council

Childwise (2005) *ChildWise Monitor Trends Report 2005* Norwich: Childwise

Cobain I (2005) 'Clampdown on chatrooms after two strangers die in first internet death pact' *Guardian*, 11 October, available at: http://technology.guardian.co.uk/online/news/0,12597,1589332,00.html

Crockett A and Voas D (2004) *Religion in Britain: Neither believing nor belonging* (unpublished)

Currie C, Roberts C, Morgan A, Smith R, Settertobulte W, Samdal O, Barnekow Rasmussen V (2004) *Young people's health in context. Health Behaviour in School-aged Children (HBSC) study: international report from the 2001/2002 survey* Copenhagen: World Health Organization Regional Office, available at: www.euro.who.int/Document/e82923.pdf

Dammler A and Middelmann-Motz A (2002) 'I want one with Harry Potter on it' *International Journal of Advertising and Marketing to Children* 3 (2): 3-8

Department for Transport (DfT) (2005) *National Travel Survey 2004* London: TSO

Department of Work and Pensions (DWP) (2005) *Households Below Average Income (HBAI) 1994/95-2004/05* London: TSO, available at: www.dwp.gov.uk/asd/hbai/hbai2005/contents.asp

Dixon M (2006) *Rethinking Financial Capability: Lessons from economic psychology and behavioural finance* London: Institute for Public Policy Research, available at: www.ippr.org.uk/ecomm/files/financial_capabilities.pdf

Dixon M and Margo J (2006) *Population Politics* London: Institute for Public Policy Research, available at: www.ippr.org.uk/publicationsandreports/publication.asp?id=341

Dixon M and Paxton W (2005) 'The State of the Nation: An audit of social injustice', in Pearce N and Paxton W (eds) *Social Justice: Building a fairer Britain* London: Institute for Public Policy Research/Politico's

Dixon M and Pearce N (2005) 'Social Justice in a Changing World', in Pearce N and Paxton W (eds) *Social Justice: Building a fairer Britain* London: Institute for Public Policy Research/Politico's

Dixon M, Rogers B, Reed H and Stone L (2006) *CrimeShare: The unequal impact of crime* London: Institute for Public Policy Research, available at: www.ippr.org.uk/members/download.asp?f=%2Fecomm%2Ffiles%2FCrimeSh

are%2Epdf

Donnerstein E, Slaby RG and Eron LD (1994) 'The mass media and youth aggression' in Eron LD, Gentry JH and Schlegel P (eds.) *Reason to hope: a psychosocial perspective on violence and youth* Washington, DC: American Psychological Association

E-week.com (2006) 'MySpace Makes Room with EMC, Isilon', available at: www.eweek.com/article2/0,1895,1947684,00.asp

Earls M (2002) *Welcome to the Creative Age – Bananas, Business and the Death of Marketing* New York: Wiley

Evans J (2004) speech, July, quoted at www.leaplinx.com/about/quotes.htm

Freedland J (2005) 'The Onslaught' *Guardian* 11 October

Gable S and Lutz S (2000) 'Household, parent, and child contributions to childhood obesity' *Family Relations* 49: 293-300

GAD (2005) *Current national projections (2004-based)* London: TSO, available at: www.gad.gov.uk

Gershuny J, Lader D and Short S (2006) *The Time Use Survey, 2005: How we spend our time. Time use results for 2005 where appropriate compared with the UK 2000 Time Use Survey* London: ONS, available at: www.statistics.gov.uk/articles/nojournal/time_use_2005.pdf

Gentile DA and Walsh DA (2002) 'A Normative Study of Family Media Habits' *Applied Development Psychology* 23: 157-178, available at: www.mediafamily.org/research/report_g_w2002.pdf

Gentile DA, Lynch PJ, Linder JR and Walsh DA (2004) 'The effects of violent video game habits on adolescent hostility, aggressive behaviours, and school performance' *Journal of Adolescence* 27

Gibbins C and Julian G (2006) *Family Spending: A report on the 2004-05 Expenditure and Food Survey* London: TSO, available at: www.statistics.gov.uk/StatBase/Product.asp?vlnk=361

Gibbons S, Green A, Gregg P and Machin S (2006) 'Is Britain Pulling Apart? Area Disparities in Employment, Education and Crime', in Pearce N and Paxton W (eds) *Social Justice: Building a Fairer Britain* London: Institute for Public Policy Research/Politico's

Gluckman PD and Hanson MA (2006) 'Evolution, development and timing of puberty' *Trends in Endocrinology and Metabolism* 17 (1): 7-12

Goodman A and Oldfield Z (2004) *Permanent Differences? Income and Expenditure Inequality in 1990s and 2000s* London: Institute for Fiscal Studies (IFS)

Götze E and Schlegelmilch B (2000) 'Impact of Television Advertising on Purchase Requests of Pre-School Children: An Empirical Analysis,' 29th EMAC Annual Conference Rotterdam: May 23-26

Halifax (2006) *Halifax Pocket Money Survey* London: HBOS

HM Treasury (2005) *Long-term public finance report: an analysis of fiscal sustainability* London: TSO

HM Revenue and Customs (HMRC) (2006) *Distribution among the adult population of marketable wealth (Series C)* (Table 13.5) London: TSO

Jones F (2006) *The effects of taxes and benefits on household income, 2004-05. Analysis of the effects of taxes and benefits on household income* London: TSO

Kahn H, Tatham L, Pamuk E and Heath C (1998) 'Are geographic regions with high income inequality associated with risk of abdominal weight gain?' *Social Science and Medicine* 47: 1-6

Kaiser Family Foundation (2001) *Fact Sheet: Kids and Media* Menlo Park, California: Kaiser Family

Kitchen S, Michaelson J, Wood N and John P (2006) *2005 Citizenship Survey. Active communities topic report* London: DCLG

Kraut R, Patterson M, Lundmark V, Kiesler S, Mukophadhyay T and Scherlis W (1998) 'Internet paradox: a social technology that reduces social involvement and psychological well-being?' *American Psychologist* 53: 1017-1031

Layard R (2005) *Happiness: Lessons from a new science* London: Penguin

Liverpool Victoria (2005) Cost of Raising a Child is £166,000 (Press Release) *Annual Cost of a Child Survey* Liverpool: Liverpool Victoria

Livingstone S (2006) 'Does TV Advertising Make Children Fat: What the evidence tells us', *Public Policy Research* 13 (1): 54-61

Livingstone S and Bober M (2005) *UK Children Go Online: Final report of key project findings* London: LSE

Martens L, Southerton D, Scott S (2004) 'Bringing Children (and Parents) into the Sociology of Consumption' *Journal of Consumer Culture* 4 155-182

Maxwell D, Sodha S and Stanley K (2006) *An asset account for looked after children* London: Institute for Public Policy Research, available at: www.ippr.org.uk/publicationsandreports/publication.asp?id=489

Mayo E (2004) 'Shopping generation' *Young Consumers* 6(4): 43-49, World Advertising Research Centre

Mayo E (2005) *Shopping Generation* London: NCC

McCarthy P, Walker J and Kain J (1998) *Telling It As It Is: the client experience of Relate counselling* Newcastle upon Tyne: Newcastle Centre for Family Studies

McKendrick J, Bradfrod M and Fielder A (2000) 'Kid Customer? Commercialization of Playspace and the Commodification of Childhood' *Childhood* 7 (3): 295-314

MySpace.com (2006) 'About Us' www.myspace.com/Modules/

Common/Pages/AboutUs.aspx

Nestlé (2006) *Make Space for Young People: Nestlé Family Monitor* London: Nestlé UK Ltd, available at: www.4children.org.uk/uploads/information/ NestleFamilyMonitor.pdf

NFPI (2004) *Hard Sell, Soft Targets?* London: NFPI

O'Brien M and Shemilt I (2003) *Working fathers: earning and caring* London: EOC

Ofcom (2006) *Media Literacy Audit: Report on media literacy among children* London: Ofcom

Ogilvy D (1995) *Ogilvy on Advertising* New York: Prion Books

Office of National Statistics (ONS) (2006a) Gross domestic product (Average) per head, CVM market prices (IHXW): SA Not seasonally adjusted Constant 2003 prices Updated on 21/ 7/2006. London: ONS, available at: www.statistics.gov.uk/statbase/TSDdownload2.asp

ONS (2006b) *Lone parents in employment: Rate at 56.5%* London: TSO, available at: www.statistics.gov.uk/cci/nugget.asp?id=409

ONS (2006c) *NUTS1 Regional Gross Value Added (1989-2004)* (data tables) London: ONS

ONS (2006d) *Usual weekly hours of work – First Release dataset* London: ONS, available at: www.statistics.gov.uk/statbase/product.asp?vlnk=8291

ONS (2003) *Labour force survey, spring 2003* London: ONS

Page B and Wallace E (2004) *Families, Children and Young People – Key Issues. Findings from Recent MORI Studies* London: MORI

Pearce N and Paxton W (eds) (2005) *Social Justice: Building a fairer Britain* London: Institute for Public Policy Research/Politico's

Pine K and Nash A (2001) 'Referenced', in Young B (ed.) *The Child's Understanding of Promotional Communication, an update to 2002* London: ITC

Resolution Foundation (2006) *Living in the advice gap: an investigation into the Resolution Foundation's target group.* Report prepared by the Alliance for Health and the Future London: Resolution Foundation

Revill J (2003) 'Cadbury condemned over school sports sweetener' *Observer,* 30 March 2003

Robinson TN (1999) 'Reducing children's television viewing to prevent obesity' *Journal of the American Medical Association* 282: 1561-1567

Schor J (2004) *Born to Buy: The Commercialized Child and the New Consumer Culture* New York: Scribner

Schor J and Holt D (2000) *The Consumer Society: A Reader* New York: New Press

Scott S, O'Connor T, Futh A (2006) *What makes programmes work in disadvantaged areas? The PALS Trial* York: Joseph Rowntree Foundation

Sharp C, Aldridge J and Medina J (2006) *Delinquent youth groups and offending behaviour: findings from the 2004 Offending, Crime and Justice Survey.* Home Office Online Report 14/06 London: TSO, available at: www.homeoffice.gov.uk/rds/pdfs06/rdsolr1406.pdf

Simons J (ed.) (1999) 'High Divorce rates: The State of the Evidence on Reasons and Remedies', Vol. 2 (Papers 4-7) Research Series No. 2/99. London: Lord Chancellor's Department

Smith P, Mahdavi J, Carvalho M and Tippett N (2006) *An investigation into cyberbullying, its forms, awareness and impact, and the relationship between age and gender in cyberbullying. A Report to the Anti-Bullying Alliance* London: Unit for School and Family Studies, Goldsmiths College, University of London

Stanley K (2005) *Daddy Dearest? Active Fatherhood and Public Policy* London: Institute for Public Policy Research

Swedish Department of Culture (1996) *Radio and TV Law* Stockholm: Swedish Department of Culture

Trickett A, Osborn D and Ellingworth D (1995) 'Property Crime Victimisation: The Roles of Individual and Area Influences' *International Review of Victimology* 3: 273-95

Waldfogel J (2006) 'What Children Need', *Public Policy Research* 13 (1): 26-35

Walker A, Kershaw C and Nicholas S (2006) *Crime in England and Wales 2005/06.* HOBS 12/06 London: TSO, available at: www.homeoffice.gov.uk/rds/pdfs06/hosb1206.pdf

Wellings K, Nanchahal KM, McManus S, Erens B, Mercer C, Johnson A, Copas A, Korovessis C, Fenton K and Field J (2001) 'Sexual behaviour in Britain: Early heterosexual experience' *The Lancet* 358: 1843-50

Whincup P, Gilg J, Odoki K, Taylor S and Cook G (2001) 'Age of menarche in contemporary British teenagers: survey of girls born between 1982 and 1986' *British Medical Journal* 322: 1095-96

Wilkinson R (1996) *Unhealthy Societies. The Afflictions of Inequality* London: Routledge

Conclusion

This report has aimed to explain the problems underpinning concerns about the state of modern youth. These concerns, although exaggerated, are at least partly grounded in reality. Certain groups of young people are consistently underperforming across several key areas, and social mobility has stalled.

The aim for policy must be to ensure that all young people are equally able to contribute to society and benefit from the choices and opportunities available to them. Some of the key reasons for lower social mobility and inequalities in youth outcomes are structural: trends in inequality and poverty lie at the root of why some young people do better than others. This is now well understood. But these structural problems are not the whole story. Young people are not simply passive recipients of social forces beyond their control. They make and remake their lives within these social structures.

Having the capacity to meaningfully exercise agency matters more in today's society than it did before, as choices and opportunities have opened up to young people as a result of socio-economic and demographic change. This has affected the disadvantaged in particular, whose life courses were formerly more structured and orderly. But the skill set required to exercise agency is not equally distributed across society, explaining in part why social mobility has stalled and why youth behaviour appears worse than before.

Personal and social skills can predict to an important extent whether a young person will smoke, drink, become a teenage parent, play truant, engage in antisocial behaviour, take up education and training opportunities or benefit to the highest possible degree from compulsory schooling – the issues the public is most concerned about.

Emerging evidence from the behavioural sciences, in combination with our analysis of the British Cohort Studies, shows why some young people are less able to gain personal and social skills than others, revealing the extent of the social justice gap in socialisation facing Britain's youth.

We now consider the appropriate policy response to our findings. Our aim is not to suggest incremental policy improvements. Although many changes to the current system are necessary, reframing the debate is best achieved through bold, clear ideas. We have identified four key challenges: protecting childhood from the forces of consumerism, promoting strong families, gearing youth activities towards positive youth development and supporting communities in developing collective efficacy.

This analysis is still relatively new and we do not claim to have all the answers. But we hope that our analysis and recommendations will enable policy to focus on the areas we highlight, and we also select from earlier work the policy ideas that are most likely to achieve desirable outcomes.

Protecting childhood

The research shows that rising affluence has had a pernicious effect on young people. As society has become richer, the impact on youth society has been to increasingly draw young people into consumerism: increasingly, resources have been invested in products and branded goods for young people, rather than on activities which would be beneficial to them. It is time to rethink how we ensure that children and young people benefit from increasing wealth and are not undermined or damaged by it.

We live in a capitalist society, which means that to an extent consumerism will always remain an important aspect of our children's lives – toys, television and other media, games and activities, pocket money and collectables are a part of childhood. But the evidence cited in this report shows unambiguously that some forms of marketing and advertising to children has pernicious effects on their well-being and relationships with both peers and parents. The last decade has seen a creeping commercialisation of young people's environments, in school as well as outside it, and a growing sophistication of techniques aiming to enter 'the world of kids in a way never done before' without 'let[ting] mum in on the act' (Mayo 2005). The evidence of the impact of brand-awareness on children – encouraging them to care about adult concerns, fashion and materialism from an early age, as well as undermining self-esteem and setting different norms of behaviour – coupled with the finding that in an international context, British children are more brand-conscious and brand-aspirational than even their US contemporaries, should give all of us pause for thought.

We should not be advocating a state of affairs that aims to convert children into consumers as early as possible in their development. A similar approach to that adopted in the mid-1990s in Sweden, which has uncompromisingly banned advertising aiming to capture the attention of children under 12, should be implemented in Britain.

Of course this is a politically contentious issue. But it would be a popular move with the public: research outlined in chapter 7 shows that an overwhelming majority of parents – 84 per cent – consider there to be too much advertising to children. The challenge is to respond to considerable vested interests in the advertising industry, which appears to publicly claim that such advertising does not affect children's development, while simultaneously persuading its clients that it represents a worthwhile investment.

This contentious position has been easier to maintain due to a lack of convincing, holistic evaluations looking at the impact of advertising on young people's development. Previous research has tended to be siloed, looking at the 'effectiveness' of a particular campaign or the impact of advertising on a particular behavioural outcome (such as childhood obesity) (Livingstone and Helsper 2004). Perhaps unsurprisingly, therefore, these studies have leant little support to banning advertising. For example, critics often cite high childhood obesity levels in Sweden as evidence that advertising bans simply do not change behaviour. Yet this is to miss looking at the big picture, and the point that the impact of advertising is cumulative and cultural; we need to look in the round at the psychological and developmental impact of advertising on young people.

The evidence highlighted in this report shows clearly that current practice is having a severely detrimental effect, particularly on the most disadvantaged. Proscribing advertising would have a clear benefit, as well as sending out a positive message about the kind of society we would like Britain to be: one that directs resources towards activities that are good for young people, not towards goods and brands that undermine their psychological well-being.

Recommendations: Preventing childhood consumerism through regulating media and marketing

- Commercial television and print media advertising designed to capture the attention of children of primary school age should be proscribed. This will be a first step, while further consultation should be encouraged to determine the appropriate age limit.
- Commercial advertising through mobile phone and 3G platforms to handsets registered to children of primary school age should be similarly proscribed. Parents should have the option of registering phone numbers with a dedicated body to ensure this happens.
- Commercial advertising in primary schools and other educational institutions for the primary age group must be carefully monitored by Ofsted.

Promoting strong families

The single most important factor in the development and socialisation of young people is their immediate family. In this area policy needs to recognise the importance of hard factors – such as income, poverty and time off work – and softer factors – such as parenting skills and experience, support and advice.

The current government has made welcome improvements in many areas related to these goals and ippr has previously set out recommendations in the areas of childcare provision; parental leave and flexible working; engaging fathers; enabling parents to spend more time with children; supporting better relationships; supporting children who suffer violence and hostility; and supporting families through parental separation (Pearce and Paxton 2005; Stanley 2005; Dixon and Margo 2006). These recommendations should be acted upon and are outlined in Appendix 1. Although these recommendations have been advanced before, the analysis in this report gives additional weight to their importance in the light of new evidence regarding the impact of micro-level processes, such as warmth, interest and time spent with parents, and of family structure on children's development.

The political Left has traditionally been uncomfortable in addressing questions of family structure. But our evidence will be equally difficult for many of those on the political Right who claim modern family structures are the underlying cause of many social problems: parental warmth, consistency and interest remain by far the most important factors in young people's development; family structure makes only an incremental difference. The challenge is to support strong families, help parents to stay together where possible and reduce the number of weak families, without penalising the most disadvantaged.

The political right has often claimed that the tax and benefit system discourages marriage and cohabitation in favour of single-parent families. This is an important claim that needs careful assessment. Its central argument relies on an analysis of the tax credit system, contending that it favours children who live with a lone parent rather than with both parents, resulting in 'the perverse situation in which a child, both of whose parents work full-time at minimum wage, experiences a higher standard of living if he or she lives with one parent rather than both' (O'Neill 2005: 1). This claim is often supported by comparisons with Germany and France, which have welfare systems more geared towards income replacement rather than poverty reduction through means-testing, and lower proportions of single-parent families.

Looking at even the best of this research in detail reveals several important shortcomings. The first is that it does 'not include child care costs or subsidies ... [or] the wide range of regional housing situations, including costs and subsidies' (O'Neill 2005: 3), important parts of the tax credits system, which systematically bias findings. Second, it ignores international counter-examples, historical patterns, political economies and cultural differences. Third and most importantly, it simply assumes that people's decisions about marriage and cohabitation are primarily financial, rather than emotional. Given the dearth of qualitative research in this area, such claims remain conjectural at best; other research looking internationally at different welfare regimes (Simons 1999) has found that financial incentives to marriage appear unlikely to impact on decisions, and the Lord Chancellor's 1999 review of evidence on the causes of marital breakdown found that incentives to promote marriage were unlikely to be successful even if the Government felt able to enter this very private domain of life so overtly (Mansfield *et al* 1999).

Clearly, therefore, we should not attempt to use the tax and benefits system to shape family structures. Such an approach would not only be ineffective but would also divert resources away from those most in need (Dixon and Margo 2006). An appropriate response to the importance of family structure is to promote policies that support strong families, as outlined in Appendix 1, relating to parental working hours and flexible working. This will be vital in enabling parents of older children to spend more time with them. Beyond this, policy should focus more overtly on investing in relationship education and support and in supporting the voluntary sector in delivering such services, also outlined in Appendix 1.

It is vital that policy supports all family types, but in particular it must address the issue of teenage parenthood in order to ensure the next generation benefits from a secure start in life. Research systematically shows that teenage pregnancy is associated with worse outcomes for both mother and child, reduced likelihood of parents staying together and reduced likelihood of sustained, positive paternal engagement (Dixon and Margo 2006; Teenage Pregnancy Unit 2006). Children of younger mothers are more likely than those of older mothers to face all the negative aspects of parenting – disengaged fathers, poverty or low parental income to name just a few.

To this end we support and build on the recommendations from the report *Teenage Pregnancy: Accelerating the Strategy to 2010* (DfES 2006), which aim to provide support for parents to help them improve their confidence and skills in discussing sex and relationships; improve the quality of Personal, Social and Health Education (PSHE); tackle the number of second pregnancies by improving access to support and information for teenage mothers; and provide young people with the aspiration and education that will enable them to recognise the consequences of teenage parenthood.

We further recommend that in order to better reach teenagers, particularly boys, and young men, family-planning clinics should be set up in places such as shops, activity centres and sports halls, where young people can easily go for help and information. And in line with the finding that young people exposed to high quality sex and relationship information early in their education are less likely to become teenage parents or become pregnant as teenagers (DfES 2006), we recommend that rather than merely promote a stronger focus on PSHE in primary schools, statutory sex and relationship education in all schools including primary schools is now essential.

It is worth noting that the high rates of teen pregnancy in Britain are undoubtedly culturally driven. Our research shows that British teenagers tend to engage in sexual activity earlier and more often than their counterparts in the rest of Europe. This is probably because they tend to spend more time with peers and less time with parents than young people in other countries and tend to spend more time with peers in unstructured activities – particularly if they are from disadvantaged backgrounds. British young people also appear more immersed in consumerism than other young people, and tend to spend a lot of unsupervised time online. The research suggests they may therefore be exposed to more messages that promote sex and relationships, from websites, advertisers and other media.

The recommendations outlined elsewhere in this chapter, to protect children from unregulated media and marketing, to help parents to spend more time with children and to introduce an element of structure to young people's leisure time, should in the longer term also impact on rates of teenage sexual activity and conception.

Recommendations: Reducing teen pregnancy

- Teenagers should be offered a full choice of contraception, including long-lasting forms. Condoms should be widely available at low cost, or no cost, to young people in places that they use and are accessible to them, including shops, sports facilities, schools and further education colleges.
- Personal, Social and Health Education (PSHE) including sex and relationship education should become a statutory subject in all primary and secondary schools in England and Wales.
- Parents should be supported in order to help them improve their confidence and skills in discussing sex and relationships. Services for parents, including information on parenting and childcare, access to parenting groups and more specialised support for parents who want and would benefit from it, should be provided through the Extended Schools parenting support core offer.
- Access to support and information for teenage mothers and teenagers who have had abortions should be improved in order to tackle the number of teenagers experiencing second pregnancies.

Gearing youth activities towards positive youth development

While the family is key to improving children's labour market and non-labour market outcomes, for older children, what they do when they are not at home is equally important. Provision of adequate activities and care for children and adolescents should warrant as much attention as that currently given to early years care: we should no more leave our teenagers to wander the streets than we should our toddlers. Moreover, the new evidence outlined here supports the understanding that what happens later in childhood matters just as much as, if not more than, what happens earlier – there is every potential to both dramatically enhance or destroy an individual's life chances between the ages of say six and 16 depending on their experiences.

Every child should be able to enjoy socialising with their peers, and should have the freedom and choice to do so. Putting restrictions and limits on teenagers would be unfair and pointless. But adult society does bear a responsibility to young people to ensure that they are able to socialise in secure and stable environments, even, or perhaps especially, when not with their parent or primary carer.

Both new money and new thinking is required to transform the existing image of youth clubs, which have often been allowed to go into decline. Youth clubs should be vetted for suitability – those that do not offer structure and activity within supportive, safe environments should not be open to use by young people and should urgently be revamped to ensure that they can be. Youth services have already been listed as a priority for spending when departmental budgets are reviewed next year. Funding should be directed towards the development of activity programmes and where possible these should be long-running courses in which young people are working towards achievable and visible goals in, for example, creative fields such as drama and art, and sport and practical activities. Auditing and vetting of training programmes for staff is also essential, although it is likely that most staff will already hold the necessary skills.

The extended schools agenda as set out in the *Youth Matters* Green Paper aims to provide a range of services and activities, beyond the school day, to help meet the needs of children, their families and the wider community. Government wants all schools to offer access to core services by 2010. These will include homework clubs and study support, sport and music tuition.

This approach is to be welcomed. However, our research suggests that a key challenge will be engaging the most disadvantaged young people in structured activities. There are difficult questions around compulsion. The current approach is based on making positive activities attractive to the most disadvantaged, rather than relying on legal or regulatory measures; opening up opportunities has been seen as sufficient. But our analysis, building on the evidence outlined in chapter 6, shows that those young people who would benefit most from structured activities are those least likely to attend – they are caught in an extra-curricular catch 22, where the activities that would give them greater capacity to engage in positive activities are the very activities they lack the capacity to engage in.

As Leon Feinstein and colleagues have convincingly demonstrated, part of the reason young people from disadvantaged backgrounds have been unable to close the gap with their more fortunate peers has been their tendency to gravitate towards less structured activities, while their more affluent contemporaries are encouraged to attend more structured activities by their peers, parents, communities and social norms (Feinstein *et al* 2005).

The challenge for policy here is twofold. First, it needs to promote the provision of those activities that facilitate personal and social development and positive socialisation, without undermining young people's right to choose how they spend their 'free' time; this will require a nuanced approach to voluntary sector funding and the current Extended Schools roll-out. Second, it needs to ensure that all young people have the genuine opportunities to participate. In the current climate, the best evidence shows that this will require elements of compulsion within an overall package of user choice, as we detail below.

Recommendations: Ensuring fair opportunities to participate in extra-curricular activities

- Youth clubs should be vetted for suitability to ensure they offer structure and activity within secure environments. Funding should be directed towards activity programmes that are long running and regular attendance should be promoted.
- An element of compulsion should be introduced to young people's participation in structured, positive extra-curricular activities offered as part of the Extended Schools agenda. But this should be delivered through a framework that emphasises choice.
- Our preferred model would be for young people aged 11 to 14 to be expected to participate in a long-term, positive extra-curricular activity for two hours, one day a week after school, choosing from a range of options, as outlined in the *Youth Matters* Green Paper. This would be mandated through an extension of the school day, creating a legal requirement for parents to ensure participation.
- The proposed 'menu' of activities in the Extended Schools Agenda should be vetted carefully, to ensure the activities on offer will benefit the participants.
- The Children and Young People's Plans, which are currently developed by each local authority in partnership with key stakeholders, should ensure that every child has the genuine opportunity to participate in a choice of structured, positive activities. They should do this by identifying barriers to participation – such as availability, timing and transport – and proposing solutions.

Recommendations: Promoting positive activities through the voluntary sector

- Funding streams should be conditional on activities – such as sport, drama, cadets and some forms of vocational activity – being structured, regular, and constructive with a clear end goal and clearly defined, hierarchical (though malleable) roles.
- Innovation and start-up funding streams should be made available to develop the facilities and provision of positive activities in areas in which they are not available. In order to achieve this, the Department for Communities and Local Government (DCLG) in partnership with the Department for Culture, Media and Sport (DCMS), DfES and the

National Council of Voluntary Organisations (NCVO) should map the provision of local services provided through the voluntary sector, to identify gaps in provision.

These recommendations would go some way to improve the lot of disadvantaged children. But some groups will require further state action, particularly those in care.

Asset-based welfare

Asset-based welfare measures hold enormous potential for developing young people's personal skills, particularly in relation to planning for the future and promoting a sense of agency and control. For example, the original motivation for having the Child Trust Fund – first conceived by ippr in 2000 and rolled out by government in 2005 – was the predicted impact it would have on the life chances of young people in giving them the confidence and ability to take risks or start out on new ventures. The analysis in this report re-emphasises the need for this kind of measure. But it also gives rise to suggestions for new areas in which asset based welfare can improve the life chances of the most disadvantaged, particularly children in care.

An individual asset account that can be accessed before the age of 18 could help children in care to develop a sense of control and some measure of security in their lives, support key transitions post-16, would help overcome some of the barriers to participation in extra-curricular activities and would give greater freedom to access after-school clubs.

Looked-after children – for example, those in care – could use some of the cash in their accounts to pay for after-school clubs such as science or computer clubs; activities like rock-climbing or martial arts; treats that of their peers take for granted, like an mp3 player or a pay-as-you-go mobile phone; and essentials like driving lessons. Access to the accounts would be signed off by a 'gatekeeper' care-worker to stop the money being used for drink and drugs. The rest would accumulate interest and serve as a nest egg for adult life. This is an affordable proposal: indicative costings suggest that the total annual running cost would be in the region of £27.4 million (Maxwell *et al* 2006).

Recommendations: Extending asset-based welfare, particularly for children in care

- Give looked after children their own asset account as a complement to ippr's previous recommendation that local authorities should make annual deposits of £50 into the Child Trust Funds of all children in care.
- This should consist of an initial, modest lump-sum deposit of £200; monthly deposits of £20 plus interest; and a further lump sum of £500 at age 16 to assist with the transition to independent living.
- A proportion each year available to be spent on 'treats', with a 'gatekeeper' worker to countersign all withdrawals.

- Larger amounts should be available for expenditure around age 16, to ensure that the asset supports the transition to independent living. The remaining lump sum should be transferred to a young person's Child Trust Fund at age 18, at which point the full amount may be spent in full, without restriction.
- Larger monthly deposits should be used to support out-of-school-hours structured activities.
- Savings made by the young person into the account could be matched in order to further develop self-efficacy and a propensity to plan.

Within schools

The details of pedagogy and curriculum are increasingly important. The ongoing debate – and ongoing independent review – around the future of teaching, learning and personalisation, and the current consultation around the future of the curriculum, reflect this wider public and policy concern.

A forthcoming report from ippr will investigate these issues in depth, looking in more detail at the structural and pedagogical issues within the education system to make detailed recommendations later this year (Brooks and Tough, forthcoming). In this report we restrict our recommendations to broad system-level changes.

Recommendations: Teaching and learning

- Initial teacher training should be reformed to incorporate specialist teaching strands, based on the current Finnish model, which encourages teachers to specialise in aspects of learning such as child development, conflict resolution and behaviour management, rather in subject areas, as in the UK. This would allow teachers to respond better to individual pupil needs, give better expertise in crucial subject areas, and improve the dissemination of skills through individual schools.
- One of these specialist teaching strands should include a particular focus on pedagogical techniques that improve personal and social skills development and behaviour management. These include metacognitive and behavioural strategies, in-depth and protracted research projects, the appropriate and imaginative use of group work and peer learning, and pupil co-production in learning (Slavin and Madden 1989; Brooks 2002; Dowker 2004).
- Another specialist strand could build on conflict resolution work currently undertaken by voluntary sector organisations such as Leap. This charity offers training in peer mediation and its in-school programmes have been positively evaluated by Ofsted (Ofsted 2004). The in-school programme works to develop a peer mediation/education approach to building young people's responsibility and capacity to take action on conflicts that they are involved in. It provides training for staff and

young people in the design and delivery of such an approach and in the development of curriculum materials.

- Initial teacher training and ongoing professional development for teachers should be reformed to improve skills in the pedagogical techniques above.
- The curriculum at Key Stage 3 should be made increasingly flexible to allow teachers to personalise learning, with a particular focus on the pedagogical techniques above.
- Ofsted's inspection criteria should be broadened to include criteria related to the teaching of personal and social skills.

These pedagogical changes should be accompanied by policies aimed directly at harnessing and shaping peer effects. Much of the influence young people have on each other is formulated within school structures, where social groups form and interact. Despite popular recognition of the importance of peer effects – and advertisers' increasing attempts to harness these for commercial ends – policymakers have remained relatively sanguine about the ability of policy to mediate or shape this influence. Yet evidence from the US, and the analysis presented in this report, shows that in fact, peer effects can be positively influenced and harnessed through in-school strategies, at both classroom and whole-school levels.

At the classroom level, the pedagogical reforms outlined above should impact on peer effects within schools: better in-lesson use of grouping, collaboration and team work, and improved individual personal and social skills would go a long way towards mediating peer influences. Extended schools also offer an opportunity to involve young people in more positive activities than is currently the case. These processes are already well understood and generally well used by teachers. But the broader success of whole-school strategies depends crucially on influencing both the informal and formal structures and cultures of reward within schools. This is not an easy task; it relies heavily on personality and strong leadership within individual schools and what works in one school will not necessarily work in another.

House systems within schools are a good way to harness peer effects in a positive way. There are three main benefits to this approach: it ensures that pupils interact with older and younger peers, that their identity within school is not solely determined by their year or class, and that they are members of structured hierarchies, catalysing informal peer mentoring.

Recommendations: Harnessing and shaping peer effects within schools

- Ofsted inspection criteria should be broadened to include assessment of the provision of positive activities.
- House systems should continue to be introduced or expanded in state schools, in line with current targets (DfES 2005) to encourage students

to work collectively towards achievable goals and to break up traditional peer groups and hierarchies within schools.

Implementing the above would go some way towards positively harnessing peer effects within schools. But this remains a relatively under-researched area in which there are many examples of best practice but limited dissemination channels. Currently, information about in-school intervention programmes is disseminated through the DfES's website TeacherNet or relies on charities' dissemination practices. This could be greatly improved through simple reform.

Recommendations: Improving best practice dissemination
- DfES should provide an annual report for head teachers of best voluntary sector practice in each area.
- DfES should map the provision of local services provided through the voluntary sector, which would also enable policymakers to identify gaps in provision.
- A National Innovation Start-up Fund should be set up to support the development of charities that work to develop young people's personal and social skills as well as those that intervene in schools to set up conflict resolution schemes. In line with comparable schemes, a suitable total funding level for a National Innovation Start-up Fund would be around £5 million, with maximum grants of around £25,000.
- Ofsted's inspection criteria for voluntary sector programmes in schools should be broadened to include criteria related to the teaching of personal and social skills, with greater weight given to whether intervention schemes are based on the best and newest evidence and theory around peer effects.
- DfES could offer to match funding for schools that have employed intervention schemes that have been evaluated to set criteria.

Supporting communities in developing collective efficacy

The recommendations outlined so far draw on a wide evidence base. More can and should be done in each of these areas – we hope that others will build on our ideas in the light of our analysis. But a further key challenge remains in supporting communities to develop collective efficacy. Research consistently shows that the role of the wider community and other adults in socialising young people remains vital. The main focus here should be on strategies to promote collective efficacy, rather than on merely increasing trust and social capital.

The evidence base in this area is patchy and inconsistent, however. It is an indication of the emerging status of this field that no measures reliably track collective efficacy levels in the UK prior to the new Department for

Communities and Local Government (DCLG)'s 2005 Citizenship Survey. While many communities have experienced recent rises in levels of collective efficacy – with positive implications for the socialisation of young people – significant challenges remain, particularly in the most disadvantaged, often minority ethnic communities. ippr has conducted much recent research in this area (Rogers 2005; Dixon *et al* 2006; Keaney 2006; Keaney and Rogers 2006; Khan and Muir 2006).

Recommendations: Creating and protecting public space

There are several ways in which changes could be made to planning and regulation policy that would help to support a richer variety of public spaces and places where people can meet. Among the most important ideas might be:

- Regular audits of 'congregational spaces' in each neighbourhood to be conducted by local authorities to determine how much such space is available and what condition it is in. This information could then be used to inform planning decisions, or public spending decisions.
- An 'Investor in Community' badge to be awarded and monitored by the Commission for Architecture and the Built Environment (CABE). This would be awarded to commercial developers pursuing design policies that fully reflect the principles of sustainable development through the integration of economic, social and environmental factors in design and implementation. Public procurement of new homes and other dwellings should exclude developers not achieving this standard.
- Better strategies for involving local people in planning the development and use of shared space should support the above recommendations.

One of the challenges in supporting communities is the need to find ways of ensuring that different social groups and age groups do not come to lead entirely separate and effectively segregated lives at the local level. Our research suggests this is a real and growing cause for concern. Without integration tensions may arise and it is unlikely that all groups will feel themselves to have an equally secure place in public life. In particular there is good reason to look at activities such as sport, leisure and the arts as ways of encouraging interaction between different social groups. The first action for government should be to map the provision of leisure facilities that encourage young people and adults to socialise together, for example in drama or sport activities, identifying gaps in provision and developing a model of good practice.

Recommendations: Design and liveability of the public realm

Although it is essential that localities provide a wide range of public spaces and amenities where young people can mingle in the public realm with other young people and importantly adults, residents will be unwilling to use these spaces if the area feels threatening or 'overtaken' by young people. In order to support community at the local level, policy must therefore ensure that neighbourhoods are reassuring places in which to move around. The quality of the public environment and its design play an important role in how secure we feel.

Graffiti, vandalism, litter and decay may not directly affect our safety but chapter 5 showed that they do combine to make an area feel insecure. Design is also crucial not just in the obvious sense that certain layouts of buildings, streets and alleyways provide more places to hide, but also in the sense that open, well-overlooked, mixed-use spaces are naturally reassuring.

- More crime prevention money should be directed towards 'constructive' measures that defend public spaces by designing the built environment to encourage constant use, rather than currently dominant 'defensive' strategies such as installing CCTV, which do little to make crime harder to commit. Initiatives targeting design or lighting, for example, in the public realm could actively encourage more use of public space, thereby naturally providing more 'eyes on the street'. CABE should work with local authorities, the crime reduction charity Nacro, and the Home Office to research and develop such a strategy.
- Local authorities are currently charged with drawing up Community Plans to promote the long-term welfare of their areas. We support the recommendations of the Urban Task Force that the process should include the creation, based on genuine consultation with residents, of 'public realm strategies', with plans looking up to 20 years ahead. There should be a focus on the quality of public spaces – the streetscape, parks, green spaces – by Local Strategic Partnerships set up to oversee the process of neighbourhood renewal in disadvantaged localities.

Recommendations: Encouraging civic participation in securing communities

The Respect action plan sets out a range of measures designed to improve local accountability and bring service providers closer to the priorities of people in their local communities. Senior representatives of police and local authorities will hold regular 'face the public' sessions, which we suggest could be open to the media. These sessions should be expanded to mirror the model of Safer Community Councils developed in New Zealand, where local authority representatives, teachers from local schools, representatives of young people's groups, local women's groups, local business and church groups meet regularly with the local police to debate community issues.

New Zealand's Safer Community Councils are not only charged with the responsibility to tackle antisocial behaviour and crime issues in their local areas in partnership with local police, but they are empowered to ask for statistical information on crimes in the local area to be prepared by police and presented at meetings. The Councils do not themselves have any powers to tackle challenging behaviour but are able, through regular meetings, to inform police of concerns and monitor the progress of efforts to tackle them. We recommend that work aimed at empowering communities, which focuses on expanding community justice approaches, currently in its early stages, should be developed further. The idea is that people living in local areas 'take ownership of their police, court, types of crime tackled and unpaid work' (National Community Justice 2006). Recent measures have included a 'community payback' strategy that aims to make unpaid work ordered by courts to be as visible to the community as possible, and to improve communication to local residents about work done to improve local areas as part of this kind of sentencing (Home Office 2005).

But perhaps the most important development so far has been the setting up of a pilot Community Justice Centre in Liverpool, based on experiences from the Red Hook Community Justice Centre in New York. In the Liverpool project, the Judge and his team aim to 'listen and respond to the views of residents to identify and understand the issues that affect their lives' (National Community Justice 2006). They hold regular meetings with two reference groups representing local residents, businesses and young people to help them decide priorities for the work the centre will tackle and the services it provides. They can also make suggestions for tasks to be carried out by offenders doing unpaid work. The pilot is currently being evaluated by PricewaterhouseCoopers, and it is still too early to draw lessons, but the approach appears promising and further investigation and development should be supported.

References

Note: web references correct at September 2006

Adam S and Brewer M (2004) *Supporting families: The financial costs and benefits of children since 1975* Oxford: The Policy Press

Brooks G (2002) *What works for children with literacy difficulties? Effectiveness of intervention schemes* DfES Research Report 380 London: TSO

Department for Education and Skills (DfES) (2005) *Every Child Matters Outcomes Framework* London: TSO

DfES (2006) *Teen Pregnancy: Accelerating the strategy to 2010* London: TSO

Dixon M and Margo J (2006) *Population Politics* London: Institute for Public Policy Research, available at: www.ippr.org.uk/publicationsand reports/publication.asp?id=341

Dixon M, Rogers B, Reed H and Stone L (2006) *CrimeShare: The unequal impact of*

crime London: Institute for Public Policy Research, available at:
www.ippr.org.uk/publicationsandreports/publication.asp?id=454

Dowker A (2004) *What works for children with mathematical difficulties?* DfES
Research Report 554 London: TSO

Equal Opportunities Commission (2006) *Twenty-first Century Dad* London: EOC

Evans J (2004) *Leap Confronting Conflict,* Ofsted Extended Monitoring, London:
Ofsted

Feinstein L, Bynner J and Duckworth K (2005) *Leisure contexts in adolescence and
their effects on adult outcomes* London: Centre for Research on the Wider
Benefits of Learning

Home Office (2005) *Respect Action Plan* London: TSO, available at:
www.homeoffice.gov.uk/documents/respect-action-plan

Keaney E (2006) *From Access to Participation: Cultural policy and civil renewal*
London: Institute for Public Policy Research

Keaney E and Rogers B (2006) *A Citizen's Duty: Voter inequality and the case for
compulsory turnout* London: Institute for Public Policy Research

Khan H and Muir R (eds) (2006) *Sticking Together: Social capital and local
government* London: Institute for Public Policy Research

Livingstone S and Helsper E (2004) *Advertising Foods to Children: Understanding
Promotion in The Context Of Children's Daily Lives. A review of the literature
prepared for the Research Department of the Office of Communications (OFCOM)*
London: Ofcom

Mansfield P, Reynolds J and Arai L (1999) 'What Policy Developments Would be
Most Likely to Secure and Improvement in Marital Stability?' in Simons J (ed.)
High Divorce rates: The State of the Evidence on Reasons and Remedies Vol. 2
(Papers 4-7) Research Series No. 2/99. London: Lord Chancellor's Department

Maxwell D, Sodha S and Stanley K (2006) *An asset account for looked after children*
London: Institute for Public Policy Research

National Community Justice (2006) *What is Community Justice?* London: TSO,
available at: www.communityjustice.gov.uk/whatis.htm

O'Neill R (2005) *Fiscal Policy and the Family: How the family fares in France,
Germany and the UK* London: Civitas

Pearce N and Paxton W (eds) (2005) *Social Justice: Building a fairer Britain*
London: Institute for Public Policy Research/Politico's

Rogers B (2005) *New Directions in Community Justice* London: Institute for Public
Policy Research

Simons J (ed) (1999) *High Divorce rates: The State of the Evidence on Reasons and
Remedies* Vol. 2 (Papers 4-7) Research Series No. 2/99. London: Lord
Chancellor's Department

Slavin R and Madden N (1989) 'Effective classroom programs for students at risk', in Slavin R, Karweit N and Madden N (eds) *Effective Programs for Students At Risk* Boston: Allyn and Bacon

Stanley K (2005) *Daddy Dearest? Active Fatherhood and Public Policy* London: Institute for Public Policy Research

Teenage Pregnancy Unit (2006) *Long-term Consequences of Teenage Births for Parents and their Children* London: TSO

Appendix 1: Families and parenting: additional material

The recommendations outlined in the concluding chapter of this report build on and emphasise the importance of much preceding ippr work. For ease of reference, we reiterate the most salient of these points here.

Promoting strong families

Recent ippr research in this area includes Stanley (2005), Stanley *et al* (2006), Pearce and Paxton (2005) and Dixon and Margo (2006). The key recommendations in light of this report are as follows.

Childcare
The availability of high-quality, affordable childcare is one of the key constraining factors on mothers' and fathers' choices about how they share care and how they balance work and care between them. The Government's 10-year childcare strategy seeks to enhance the state's contribution to shared care, but this is not enough on its own. We set out specific recommendations to improve provision at the end of this section.

Engaging fathers
Maternity services are in the prime position to be the motor for the promotion of active fatherhood. The key to this happening is workforce development. Stanley (2005) showed a need for professional training and development for those working in family services, including information on fathers' roles in child development. This would be boosted by the recruitment of more men in childhood services and ensuring that services are accessible to men.

Stanley also argued that it would be more efficient for maternity services to take the lead in identifying absent or disengaged fathers, rather than Sure Start or the Child Support Agency. The benefits of public investment in paternity leave could be maximised by also equipping fathers who are on leave as carers. This should include specialised work with young fathers in the transition to parenthood. Antenatal classes should include information about infant care and infant and child development, in addition to their role in preparing both mothers and fathers for the social and emotional impact of becoming a parent on each of them as individuals, and on their partnership. Attendance at classes should be actively promoted to prospective fathers.

If they are to properly engage fathers, services will need to provide information in places that men frequent and in forms that men are used to receiving – rather than simply targeting mothers, with whom services are likely to be more familiar with communicating. In light of the gap in support for fathers, particularly for men who are becoming first-time fathers, and post separation, there is a need for a national information service for new fathers that clearly announces society's expectation of active engagement of all fathers in their children's lives.

Relationship support: Helping parents stay together

Evidence of the potential of relationship counselling to help couples stay together is patchy, but there is some indication of which strategies work. Drawing on an enquiry conducted by Relate, the UK's largest provider of relationship counselling, the evidence suggests that relationship therapy including cognitive behavioural therapy and psychodynamic approaches can improve marital relations and help couples come to terms with flaws in a marriage or the breakdown of a marriage, although the results are not spectacular (Simons 1999). Relate found that a year after completing counselling 58 per cent of couples felt that their relationship had improved and 82 per cent were glad that they had gone to counselling (McCarthy *et al* 1998).

There have been signs that the Government wants to see greater support made available for parents with relationships difficulties. The Government's Every Child Matters approach asked how local authorities could develop stress and relationship counselling for couples. The National Service Framework for children, young people and maternity services requires that: 'parents with specific needs such as [those related to] relationship conflict ... have their needs identified early and are provided with effective multi-agency support'. In order to meet this standard there is a clear need for investment in a range of relationship support services. This needs to include new skills for professionals as part of workforce development in the NHS and social services, to enable them to identify and respond to relationship difficulties in couples with whom they come into contact.

There is a clear case for certain interventions that have been shown to be effective in delivering simple and effective early support. Support based on the principles illustrated by the Brief Encounters pilot and discussed in detail in Stanley (2005) should be piloted further.

Considering the lack of evidence, the Government should invest in a UK study similar to the US Fragile Families and Child Well-being study (for details see Stanley 2005). A UK version should focus on the management of change within families rather than the impact of family structures.

The level of funding for relationship support services is extremely low, at £5 million in 2004/05. If the Government is serious about achieving the National Service Framework standards – as well as a wide range of other objectives – then this must be addressed through strategic development, backed by increased resource allocation for research and practice development. And there is already good evidence from existing practice in the voluntary and community sector. The Bristol Community Family Trust, which provides relationship education and support at key life stages, is one such example.

Supporting children who suffer violence and hostility

Another key role for policy is in supporting young people who face violence and hostility in the home. Parental hostility is one of the most damaging factors for children's personal and social development. Where there has been violent behaviour by a father, it is clearly appropriate that children are removed from danger. However, it is unacceptable to simply remove a violent parent – usually a father – from the scene and do nothing to tackle this violence, not least because men can move from one vulnerable family to another without any change in their behaviour. There is an urgent need for a roll-out of perpetrator programmes to tackle the behaviour itself. These programmes need to be integrated into existing projects supporting female victims of violence and their children, as well as into maternity services to tackle violence in pregnancy. Now that health professionals are expected to try to identify violent behaviour, community-based behaviour change programmes are required to deal with it. Probation services should be linked with professionals in children's centres to ensure there is effective local intervention. The fear that violent men create has been a factor in a more general neglect of fathers by practitioners, and has added to the invisibility of men in child protection settings (Stanley 2005).

Supporting parents through separation

A further issue for policy is that we ensure that children are supported in whatever family formation they are born into. Thus we must also consider what policy can do to support children and young people through parental divorce and separation. In circumstances where parents do separate – for whatever reason – there is a need for adequate emotional and practical support for separating families, not least to boost the chances of fathers remaining involved with children, supported by willing mothers. The role of the Child Support Agency, which is currently under review, is critical in this. ippr has published elsewhere a discussion of the lessons that the UK could learn from Australia in the successful operation of child support (Burgess 2005). At present the Child Support Agency frequently perpetuates conflict between parents, whereas it could act to facilitate improved relations if it worked more effectively as it does in Australia. Improvements as recommended in Burgess (2005) would have the added effect of increasing payments received by mothers for the support of their children, which would have an impact on child poverty. To transform the effectiveness of the Agency it will be necessary for the current review to seriously examine the options for radical and fundamental reform. For example, there is a strong case for its functions to be transferred to the Inland Revenue.

Furthermore, the success of the Australian Child Support Agency – based within the Australian Taxation Office – has been in a position to promote exploration of the way in which the benefits system functions in relation to separated families, which could have far-reaching consequences for the ability of non-resident fathers to play an active role in their children's lives. At present the UK tax/benefit system treats non-resident parents as non-parents and this clearly places significant limits on fathers' ability to care for their children.

Finally, we should consider how to better support lone parents. Because of the risk of stigmatising lone parents through targeted classes (which in any case seem unnecessary as lone parents benefit just as much as other parents from parenting classes) and other interventions (Scott *et al* 2006), coupled with legitimate concerns that greater financial support to lone parents may serve to incentivise couples to live apart, we do not consider here special measures for lone parents. Instead, the key issues for lone-parents are covered elsewhere in this section: decent childcare and help to fund suitable and flexible employment are absolutely key.

Recommendations

Childcare

- In the long term, we should move towards free part-time care as an entitlement for all children with means-tested, full-time provision, supplying services through a government-subsidised mixed market, and away from demand-side measures such as tax credits.
- In the short term, the priority should be improved quality of care and more fundamentally improved training for early years staff. Access to childcare support should be simplified, widened, and not dependent on the employment status of the parent.
- Also in the short term, parents need to be empowered with more and better information about local childcare services, child development issues and financial support. This is vital for shaping a responsive childcare market where parents exercise voice and choice over services. Children's Information Services need to be made central to local childcare strategies, with proactive engagement and dissemination to increase the reach and visibility of childcare information.

Parental leave

- There is a need to increase paternity leave pay from £106 per week to 90 per cent of earnings and extending the period of paid leave from two to four weeks.

- Pay for the current unpaid 13 weeks' parental leave should be introduced. This would include a 'daddy month' – at least four weeks specifically allocated to fathers on a use it or lose it basis.

Flexible working
- Better information for parents on the options for requesting flexible working should be provided by the Department for Work and Pensions (DWP) at key transition points, such as during post-natal checkups, through Sure Start and when children start school.
- Better information should be provided through Sure Start on the importance of spending time with children, particularly eating a regular family meal.

Relationship support
- There is a clear need for investment in a range of relationship support services for parents and couples, particularly lone parents. This needs to include new skills for professionals as part of workforce development in the NHS and social services, to enable them to identify and respond to relationship difficulties in couples with whom they come into contact.
- Couple relationship support training and training around working with men and fathers should be included in social worker, health visitor and perinatal training and development, and a pilot scheme to test supportive interventions established.

Engaging fathers
- The development of information and support services for fathers at key transition points, notably in perinatal services and during separation, should be supported.
- A UK cohort study should be established to explore how relationships within families can best be supported by policy.

Supporting children who suffer violence and hostility
- Community-based perpetrator programmes should be rolled out for fathers with violent behaviour is needed.

Supporting families through divorce and separation
- The Child Support Agency should take a critical role in supporting families through divorce and separation. This should be modelled on the Australian Child Support Agency, which takes an active role in facilitating better relations between separating parents.

References

Note: web references correct at September 2006

Burgess, Adrienne (2005) Bringing fathers back in: Child support in Australia. Public Policy Research, March. Volume 12 Issue 1.

Dixon M and Margo J (2006) *Population Politics* London: Institute for Public Policy Research, available at: www.ippr.org.uk/publicationsandreports/ publication.asp?id=341

McCarthy P, Walker J and Kain J (1998) *Telling It As It Is: the client experience of Relate counselling* Newcastle upon Tyne: Newcastle Centre for Family Studies

Pearce N and Paxton W (eds) (2005) *Social Justice: Building a fairer Britain* London: Institute for Public Policy Research/Politico's

Scott S, O'Connor T, Futh A (2006) *What makes programmes work in disadvantaged areas? The PALS Trial* York: Joseph Rowntree Foundation

Simons J (ed.) *1999 High Divorce rates: The State of the Evidence on Reasons and Remedies*, Vol. 2 (Papers 4-7) Research Series No. 2/99. London: Lord Chancellor's Department

Stanley K (2005) *Daddy Dearest? Active Fatherhood and Public Policy* London: Institute for Public Policy Research

Stanley K, Bellamy K and Cooke G (2006) *Equal Access? Appropriate and affordable childcare for every child* London: Institute for Public Policy Research, available at: www.ippr.org.uk/publicationsandreports/publication.asp?id=468

Appendix 2: 1970 cohort analysis

By Howard Reed

The analysis in this report relies heavily on ippr's original analysis of many datasets. This appendix outlines our methodology for the most complex of these analyses, that of the 1970 British Cohort Study, kindly provided by the UK Data Archive. Our results are used for discussion in Chapters 5 and 6 of the report.

Data

The 1970 British Cohort Study (BCS70) began in 1970 when data were collected about the births and families of babies born in England, Scotland and Wales in the week of 5-11 April. Since the 1970 survey there have been six full data collection exercises in order to monitor the cohort members' health, education, social and economic circumstances. These took place in 1975 (age 5), 1980 (age 10), 1986 (age 16), 1996 (age 26), 1999-2000 (age 30), and 2004-05 (age 34 – data not yet available).

The initial birth wave of the British Cohort Study contained 17,200 boys and girls. In subsequent waves there was attrition from the sample as some of the boys and girls could not be traced for subsequent interviews. For our work, which combines information from the 1970, 1980 and 1986 surveys, there are 10,112 boys and girls in the relevant sample.

Methodology

Our empirical analysis of the BCS70 data was designed to analyse factors that were associated with an increase or decrease in 'locus of control' that children experienced between the ages of 10 and 16. The 'locus of control' scores at ages 10 and 16 were constructed from a number of variables in the 1980 and 1986 sweeps of the BCS respectively, and are designed to measure the extent to which a child feels in control of his or her decisions and life course – a key component of youth socialisation (Gammage 1975). The analysis controlled for a range of factors at birth and at ages 10 and 16 (including the child's self-esteem, measured by an 'application score', at age 10.)

This section shows how the locus of control and application scores were constructed and explains the other control variables that were included in the regression specification, before giving details of the main results. A graphical analysis of the main results is presented as Figure 6.4 in the main body of the report.

Table A2.1. Variables contributing to CARALOC 'locus of control' scores at ages 10 and 16

Label – 1980 sweep	Label – 1986 sweep	Variable description	Positive/negative contributor
k075	C5L1	Do you think that most of the time it's not worth trying hard because things never turn out right anyway?	-
k076	C5L2	Do you feel that wishing can make good things happen?	-
k077	C5L3	Are people good to you no matter how you act towards them?	-
k078	C5L4	Do you like taking part in plays or concerts?	+
k079	C5L5	Do you usually feel that it's almost useless to try in school because most of the children are cleverer than you are?	-
k080	C5L7	Are high marks just a matter of 'luck' for you?	-
k081	C5L6	Are you good at spelling?	+
k082	C5L8	Are tests just a lot of guesswork for you?	-
k083	C5L10	Are you blamed for things which just aren't your fault?	-
k084	C5L9	Are you the kind of person who believes that planning ahead makes things turn out better?	+
k085	C5L11	Do you find it easy to get up in the morning?	+
k086	C5L13	When bad things happen to you, is it usually someone else's fault?	-
k087	C5L12	When someone is very angry with you, is it impossible to make him your friend again?	-
k088	C5L14	When nice things happen to you is it only good luck?	-
k089	C5L16	Do you feel sad when it's time to leave school each day?	+
k090	C5L15	When you get into an argument is it usually the other person's fault?	-
k091	C5L17	Are you surprised when your teacher says you've done well?	-
k092	C5L18	Do you usually get low marks even when you study hard?	-
k093	N/A	Do you like to read books?	+
k094	C5L19	Do you think studying for tests is a waste of time?	-
N/A	C5L20	Do you like outdoor games?	+
N/A	C5L21	Do you often feel sad because you have no-one to talk to at school?	-
N/A	C5L22	Do you like writing stories or doing creative writing?	+
N/A	C5L23	Are you good at mathematics?	+
N/A	C5L24	When you have to talk in front of other students, do you usually feel silly?	-
N/A	C5L25	Do you find it difficult to do things like woodwork or knitting?	-

Construction of 'locus of control' scores at ages 10 and 16

Table A2.1 lists the variables used to construct the 'locus of control' scores at ages 10 and 16 from the 1980 and 1986 sweeps of the data. It also shows whether each of the variables was a positive or negative contributor to the score variable. The sets of variables used differ slightly between ages 10 and 16, as recommended by Osborn and Milbank (1986).

Construction of application score, age 10

One of the control variables used in the model is an 'application' or 'self-esteem' score for 10-year-olds, constructed from relevant variables in the 1980 sweep of the BCS according to a previous methodology used by educationalists studying the survey (Lawrence 1978; Osborn and Milbank 1986). Table A2.2 lists the variables used to construct the score and whether each of them was treated as a positive or negative contributor to the score. Each of the variables is a binary variable and for each child, the score was increased by 1 for a 'yes' value if the variable contributes positively to self-esteem, and decreased by 1 for a 'yes' value if the variable contributed negatively to self-esteem.

Table A2.2. Variables contributing to LAWSEQ application score at age 10		
Variable label	Variable description	Positive/negative contributor to score
k010	Do you think that your parents usually like to hear about your ideas?	+
k011	Do you often feel lonely at school?	-
k012	Do other children often break friends or fall out with you?	-
k013	Do you like team games?	+
k014	Do you think that other children often say nasty things about you?	-
k015	When you have to say things in front of teachers, do you usually feel shy?	-
k016	Do you like writing stories or doing other creative writing?	+
k017	Do you often feel sad because you have nobody to play with at school?	-
k018	Are you good at mathematics?	+
k019	Are there lots of things about yourself you would like to change?	-
k020	When you have to say things in front of other children, do you usually feel foolish?	-
k021	Do you find it difficult to do things like woodwork or knitting?	-
k022	When you want to tell a teacher something, do you usually feel foolish?	-
k023	Do you often have to find new friends because your old friends are playing with somebody else?	-
k024	Do you usually feel foolish when you talk to your parents?	-
k025	Do other people often think that you tell lies?	-

An analysis of the correlation between locus of control scores at ages 10 and 16 showed a correlation coefficient between the two scores of 0.0496.

Another 'score variable' which has been constructed by previous researchers in the psychology field working with BCS70 data is the 'internalisation score', which measures the degree of introversion/extroversion (Rutter *et al* 1970). As this variable is not used in the regression results we report here, we do not give details of its construction but Osborn and Milbank (1986) gives full details of the variables involved in the 1980 and 1986 surveys. The correlation between internalisation scores at 10 and 16 is 0.0280.

Other control variables

In addition to the 10-year application score, the following control variables were used in the model:

1970 (birth) sweep
- Sex of child
- Birth weight
- Number of older siblings [dummies for one; two; three or more]
- Mother's age

1980 (ten year) sweep
- Family income per week in 1980 prices [in bands: less than £35; £35-£49; £50-£99 (base category); £100-£149; £150-£199; £200-£249; £250 or more]
- Socio-economic status of head of household [I/II (base category); III manual/III non-manual; IV/V]
- Father's highest qualifications [degree level or equivalent; A level; O level; other qualification; no qualifications (base category)]
- Mother's highest qualifications [categories as for father]
- Child in receipt of free school meals
- Father's attitude towards child is hostile
- Father's attitude towards child is dismissive
- Mother's attitude towards child is hostile
- Mother's attitude towards child is dismissive
- Level of father's interest in child [moderate, low, very low]
- Level of mother's interest in child [moderate, low, very low]
- No father figure in household
- Percentage of children in class from household with low socio-economic status
- Percentage of children in class with low level of academic achievement

1986 (sixteen year) sweep

- Whether child watches violent TV programmes
- Working knowledge of the following skill sets:
    - Filling in a job application form
    - Getting by at an interview
    - Writing an application letter for a job
    - Driving a car
    - Riding a motorbike
    - Information technology
    - Electronics
    - Communications
    - First aid
    - Changing a plug
    - Healthy diet
    - Woodwork/metalwork
    - Washing clothes
    - Sewing/mending
- Instruction in the past 12 months in:
    - Self defence
    - Swimming
    - Dancing
    - Music
    - Drama/speech
    - Dressmaking
    - Shorthand
    - Typing
    - Aerobics/keep fit
- Member of any clubs at school in last 2 years
- Undertaken any charitable activities in last 2 years
- Whether child regularly does any of the following during the school dinner hour:
    - Played an outdoor sport/game
    - Gone to a school club or activity
    - Done a school duty
    - Gone out of school with friends
- Whether child has any hobbies
- Whether child spends more than three hours a week on hobbies
- Whether child shares an interest with mother or father (or both)
- Whether child has been to a sports centre and/or community centre in the past 12 months
- Whether child has been to a sports centre at least once a week in the past 12 months
- Whether child has been to a community centre at least once a week in the past 12 months

- Whether child has been to a youth club in the last 12 months
- Whether child has been to a youth club at least once a week in the past 12 months
- Whether child has been to a uniformed youth organisation (for example, Scouts, Guides) in the past 12 months
- Whether child has been to a uniformed youth organisation at least once a week in the past 12 months
- Whether child has been to 'church' activities (or equivalent activities for other religions/denominations) in the last 12 months
- Whether child has been to 'church' or equivalent at least once a week in the last 12 months

Results

Table A2.3 gives the results from the preferred specification used in Chapter 6 of this report.

Table A2.3. Regression results
Ordinary Least Squares (OLS) regression
Dependent variable: Locus of control score, aged 16
Statistical significance of the results is as follows:
|T-stat| ≥ 1.96 indicates statistical significance at the 5% level.
|T-stat| ≥ 1.963(?) indicates statistical significance at the 10% level.

Explanatory variables	Coefficient	S.E.	|T-stat|
Constructed 'score' variables			
Locus of control score aged 10	.0868	.0096	9.07
Application score aged 10	.0081	.0038	2.15
Aged 16:			
Watches violent TV	-.0799	.0237	3.37
Skills:			
Job application form	-.0325	.0447	0.73
Getting by at an interview	.0266	.0360	0.74
Writing job application letter	.0217	.0424	0.51
Driving car	.0564	.0252	2.24
Riding motorbike	-.0937	.0278	3.33
Information technology	.0482	.0259	1.86
Electronics	-.0546	.0288	1.89
Communications	.0494	.0251	1.97
First aid	.0268	.0239	1.12
Changing plugs etc	-.0455	.0313	1.45
Healthy diet	.0152	.0311	0.49
Woodwork/metalwork	-.0488	.0248	1.96
Washing clothes	.0011	.0338	0.03
Sewing/mending	.0859	.0305	2.82
Received instruction in:			
Self defence	.0357	.0304	1.18
Swimming	-.0827	.0266	3.11
Dancing	-.0308	.0337	0.91
Music	.1067	.0302	3.53

Table A2.3 cont.			
Speech/drama	.1562	.0319	4.89
Dressmaking	-.1122	.0342	3.28
Shorthand	.0062	.0465	0.13
Typing	-.0631	.0292	2.16
Aerobics/keep-fit	-.0114	.0274	0.67
Member of school club(s)	.0774	.0297	2.60
Undertook charitable activities	.0187	.0281	0.67
Does sports/games during dinner hour	-.0182	.0296	0.62
Does school club(s) during dinner hour	.0156	.0371	0.42
Does school duty during dinner hour	.0179	.0339	0.53
With friends during dinner hour	.0309	.0229	1.35
Attended sports centre or community centre at all	.0373	.0259	1.44
Attended sports centre often	-.0412	.0302	1.37
Attended community centre often	.0840	.0563	1.49
Attended youth club	-.1832	.0402	4.56
Attended youth club often	-.1277	.0413	3.09
Attended uniformed activity	.1109	.0791	1.40
Attended uniformed activity often	-.1822	.0858	2.12
Attended church/equivalent	-.0599	.0311	1.92
Attended church/equivalent often	.1365	.0428	3.19
Aged 10:			
Household's socio-economic status – III (medium)	-.0254	.0217	1.17
Household's socio-economic status – IV/V (low)	-.0688	.0290	2.37
Father's highest qualifications – degree	.0040	.0333	0.12
Father's highest qualifications – A level	-.0322	.0306	1.05
Father's highest qualifications – O level	.0141	.0252	0.56
Mother's highest qualifications – degree	.0203	.0561	0.36
Mother's highest qualifications – A level	.0379	.0384	0.99
Mother's highest qualifications – O level	-.0057	.0229	0.25
Child eligible for free school meals	.0302	.0316	0.96
Mother's attitude hostile	-.2533	.1639	1.55
Mother's attitude dismissive	-.1777	.0777	2.28
Father's attitude hostile	-.0721	.1762	0.41
Father's attitude dismissive	.0559	.1060	0.53
Absent father	.0674	.0410	1.64
Father's interest in child moderate	-.0470	.0254	1.85
Father's interest in child low	.0052	.0585	0.09
Father's interest in child very low	-.0205	.0753	0.27
Mother's interest in child moderate	-.0013	.0226	0.06
Mother's interest in child low	.0112	.0532	0.21
Mother's interest in child very low	.1061	.0849	1.25
% of children in class: low SES	-.0001	.0006	0.17
% of children in class: low academic achievement	.0002	.0012	0.19
% of children in class: ethnic minority	-.0004	.0007	0.57
Birth:			
Mother's age	-.0015	.0018	0.80
Birthweight (kilos)	-.0000	.0000	0.69
1 older sibling	-.0444	.0204	2.18
2 older siblings	-.0401	.0270	1.48
3 or more older siblings	-.0438	.0329	1.34
Constant	-.3102	.0993	3.12
Number of observations			10,112
R^2			0.3191

References

Gammage P (1975) *Socialisation, Schooling and Locus of Control* PhD Thesis, Bristol University

Lawrence D (1978) *Counselling Students with Reading Difficulties: A Handbook for Tutors and Organisers* London: Good Reading

Osborn A and Milbank J (1986) *The Effects of Early Education: A Report from the Child Health and Education Study Ward* Lock: Clarendon Press

Rutter M, Tizard J and Whitmore K (1970) *Education, Health and Behaviour* London: Longman